Journeys of the Slave Narrative
in the Early Americas

New World Studies

J. Michael Dash, *Editor*

Frank Moya Pons and
Sandra Pouchet Paquet,
Associate Editors

Journeys of the Slave Narrative in the Early Americas

Edited by Nicole N. Aljoe and Ian Finseth

University of Virginia Press

Charlottesville and London

University of Virginia Press
© 2014 by the Rector and Visitors of the University of Virginia
All rights reserved
Printed in the United States of America on acid-free paper

First published 2014

ISBN 978-0-8139-3637-6 (cloth)
ISBN 978-0-8139-3638-3 (paper)

9 8 7 6 5 4 3 2 1

Library of Congress Cataloging-in-Publication Data
is available from the Library of Congress.

*To the millions of human beings enslaved
during the African Atlantic Slave Trade who
never had the opportunity to provide
written testimonies of their experiences.*

Contents

Acknowledgments

FIRST, WE would like to express our gratitude to our contributors—it has been a very long journey from the 2010 Society of Early Americanists Special Topics conference on Borderlands, from which this collection sprang. Special thanks are owed to Philip Gould (Brown University), Patricia Griffin (Emerita, Florida State University), Jared Hickman (Johns Hopkins University), and Marilyn Miller (Tulane University), who offered crucial contributions during the initial stages of this project. The three anonymous readers who read the manuscript should also be thanked for all their work and for their incisive feedback, which made our collection much better and more significant. We are also grateful to the University of Virginia Press, the editors of the New World Studies series, and Cathie Brettschneider for their support of this project.

Two essays in this collection first appeared elsewhere: Ian Finseth's essay, "Irony and Modernity in the Early Slave Narrative: Bonds of Duty, Contracts of Meaning," appeared in *Early American Literature* 48.1 (February 2013): 29–60. R.J. Boutelle's essay, "'The Most Perfect Picture of Cuban Slavery': The Politics of Authenticity and Transatlantic Bricolage in *Poems by a Slave in the Island of Cuba*," appeared in *Atlantic Studies* 10.4 (2013): 528–49. We are thankful to Johns Hopkins University Press and Taylor and Francis for permission to republish the altered essays.

Journeys of the Slave Narrative
in the Early Americas

Introduction

Remapping the Early American
Slave Narrative

Nicole N. Aljoe

IN *The Black Atlantic: Modernity and Double-Consciousness*, Paul Gilroy offers "the image of ships in motion across the spaces between Europe, America, Africa, and the Caribbean as a central organizing symbol" for his analysis of modernity's roots within the eighteenth- and nineteenth-century African Atlantic slave trade. He explains: "The image of the ship—a living, micro-cultural, micro-political system in motion—is especially important for historical and theoretical reasons. . . . Ships immediately focus attention on the middle passage, on the various projects for redemptive return to an African homeland, on the circulation of ideas and activists as well as the movement of key cultural and political artefacts: tracts, books, gramaphone records, and choirs" (4). As Gilroy suggests, the image of the slave ship provides a compelling chronotope for understanding the transatlantic African slave trade.[1] The chronotope—a figure representing complex cultural systems—emphasizes the circulation, movement, and interaction of ideas, peoples, and artifacts. As an iconic image of a cruel history, the slave ship has become embedded in both scholarly and popular culture, reinforced by the horrifyingly efficient and explicit plans of such notorious vessels as the *Brookes* and the *Henrietta*. Yet as Marcus Rediker, in *The Slave Ship: A Human History*, usefully explains, slave ships could be any type of ship and originally were often built for cargo or smuggling.[2] These ships had to be physically altered with the addition of wooden shelves and chains within the holds to carry slaves. And although a ship might frequently transport slaves, in all likelihood it probably also carried other types of cargo, often simultaneously. Furthermore, on the journeys between Britain, Africa, and the Americas, ships frequently used local resources from the various ports to replace or enhance structural elements of the ship like the mast or decking. Consequently, like many other identities forged in the Creole Atlantic context, the "slave ship" was a new form cobbled together from a variety of elements. The crews themselves were cobbled together, including men (and women) from a variety of places and cultural backgrounds. It is not accidental that the prevailing metaphors for the Black Atlantic are those of movement, transition, and combination.

The fluid, even kaleidoscopic, image of a slave ship resonates with the complex textual testimonies of these vessels' human cargo and of subsequent generations of enslaved persons. These accounts—now understood under the rubric of "slave narrative"—generally aimed to make known, for an overwhelmingly white European readership, the life experiences of Africans, or their descendants in the diaspora, who were held in bondage. They first appeared almost as soon as the European African slave trade began in the sixteenth century and, because the institution of slavery has still not been completely eradicated, continue to be written even today.[3] In circulating both physically and symbolically through the Atlantic world, these "key cultural and political artefacts" of the African diaspora engaged consistently and critically with historical and contemporary notions of liberty and subjectivity.[4] Moreover, beyond contributing in vital ways to the emerging social movement opposed to slavery, they participated in the broader intellectual and social climate of the "Black Atlantic." Yet much critical work remains to be done in understanding the full importance of early slave narratives.

SCHOLARLY INTEREST in the slave narrative dates to at least 1849, when Ephraim Peabody, in an article for the *Christian Examiner,* proclaimed the arrival of this "new department" in world literature: "Without hesitation among the most remarkable productions of the age—remarkable as being pictures of slavery by the slave, remarkable as disclosing under a new light the mixed elements of American civilization, and not less remarkable as a vivid exhibition of the force and working of the native love of freedom in the individual mind."[5] For Peabody, the slave narrative constituted a genre linked to notions of memory and narrative—"pictures of slavery by the slave"—as well as history. It was also a creolized form, in that it communicated the "mixed elements of American civilization." And finally, the slave narrative expressed a distinctly eighteenth-century interest in human interiority, in its emphasis on "the love of freedom in the individual mind." Given the time at which he was writing, Peabody's definition is surprisingly capacious, embracing not only the testimony of particular human beings but larger (inter)national and societal issues as well.

Modern scholarly definitions of the slave narrative have been similarly flexible and inclusive. For example, in 1985 Charles Davis and Henry Louis Gates Jr., drawing upon Marion Wilson Starling's definition, described slave narratives as the "written and dictated testimonies of the enslavement of black human beings."[6] Starling compiled one of the first and most extensive bibliographies of slave narratives in the United States and Great Britain, finding over 6,006 extant texts in the 1940s. After her bibliography was published in 1982, numerous scholars began turning their attention to more intensive study of the rhetorics of the slave narrative. Frances Smith Foster defined slave narratives as "the personal accounts of black slaves and ex-slaves in slavery and their efforts to obtain freedom."[7] More recent critical examinations of the slave narrative have maintained this sense of generic breadth while moving in new theoretical and interpretive directions. Dwight McBride, for example, has emphasized the transnational foundations of the slave narrative grounded in the international abolitionist movement, while historical studies by Stephanie Smallwood and Anne Bailey have endeavored to retrieve the narratives and voices of African slaves located in ships' logs, traveler diaries, and missionary reports.[8]

For some scholars, however, the slave narrative should be defined more narrowly, as the self-written autobiographical accounts of enslaved persons, and approached accordingly. In *To Tell a Free Story* (1986), William L. Andrews asserted the close rhetorical relationship between the genre and autobiographical writing.[9] Similarly, Robert Stepto identified as the "single most impressive feature" of the genre the voice of the slave "recounting, exposing, appealing, apostrophizing, and above all *remembering* his ordeal in bondage."[10] Other scholars, such as Sterling Bland, focus on the quest for liberty and escape from enslavement as foundational aspects of the genre.[11] Moreover, like Gates, Bland also understands the narratives as enabling slaves to discursively construct a sense of their identities—"writing oneself into being."[12] Indeed, the vast majority of current studies of the slave narrative focus on the self-written, separately published, book-length narratives. And although this approach tends to leave out large numbers of texts, the benefits of focused analysis of similar types of texts is certainly invaluable in outlining the contours of a coherent tradition. For example, Gates's discussion of the trope of the "talking book" in several early narratives is significant for revealing the ways in which subsequent fiction and poetry writers have appropriated that motif.[13] Finally, when taken together, the varying, even contradictory ways of defining the slave narrative can actually remind us of the fundamental diversity of the genre.

Still, as Eric Gardner has argued, the field of slave narrative studies has been "radically circumscribed" by emphases on the canonical book-length narratives by William Wells Brown, Frederick Douglass, Harriet Jacobs, and others.[14] Like Gardner, I believe that definitions of the slave narrative will be most useful if they are sufficiently broad to accommodate the wide variety of styles, forms, and contexts in which the testimonies of slaves have historically appeared. In recording not only geographic journeys from country to country, but movements between different emotional states and social situations, the early slave narrative persistently transgresses borders of text, culture, and voice. For all its focus on the seemingly similar experiences of enslavement, what stands out about the genre is its remarkable diversity—of setting, of purpose, of theme. This collection of essays represents an attempt to reconstruct that diversity and to find within the early years of the slave narrative the complexity of individual experience and cultural history, which it embodied.

In his seminal work *Slavery and Social Death,* the sociologist Orlando Patterson traced the diversity of slave cultures in world history, demonstrating that slavery is far from a monolithic and stable institution, even as it follows certain common principles of domination and marginalization.[15] Building on Patterson's research, other sociologists, historians, and anthropologists have found that although there may be similar institutional characteristics among slaveholding cultures, the social practices and individual experiences of slavery are never static, never unitary. Indeed, much historical research has identified various regional distinctions among institutions of enslavement in the United States, the British colonial Caribbean, the Spanish colonial Caribbean, and the French colonial Caribbean, as well as Latin America and South Africa.[16] This diversity is reflected within the early narratives, many of which were written while the African slave trade was still ongoing, and which describe places in Africa as well as the traditions of cultures involved in the trade such as the "Igbo," Fantee, and "Coromontein."[17] Many of the early narratives also include descriptions of slavery across the globe, including the Caribbean, England, South and Latin America, as well as South Africa.

For the purposes of this collection, we understand "early" slave narratives as those that precede the publication of Douglass's *Narrative of the Life of Frederick Douglass, an American Slave, Written by Himself* (1845). As numerous scholars have noted, narratives produced after Douglass's incredibly popular narrative began to imitate the formal structures of his text.[18] The earlier narratives, some written during the height of the international slave trade, which legally ended in Britain and the United States in 1807 and 1808, respectively, are formally and aesthetically less predictable and have received much less scholarly attention than their antebellum and Civil War–era counterparts.

The broad, transnational reach of the institutions of African enslavement and missionary and abolitionist movements, as well as the rapid global expansion of print culture during the seventeenth and eighteenth centuries, facilitated a proliferation of slave narrative forms. Indeed, narratives of slave lives show up in a variety of early texts. They range in length from a couple of paragraphs to books of several volumes.[19] Most frequently, the forms of these early narratives are ephemeral and fragmentary, brief portraits in ship's logs, travel journals, and other colonial documents. They also appear in diaries written by whites, as well as in medical records. As Starling observed, they could be "found in judicial records, broadsides, private printings, abolitionist newspapers and volumes, scholarly journals, as well as preserved in records of the court and church, discovered in the files of periodical publications or massed together in unpublished collections."[20]

Most early slave testimony consisted of dictated texts and interviews written down by a white European auditor/editor. The earliest examples of slave narratives are the interviews conducted in Africa and the Americas by religious missionaries such as Fr. Alonso de Sandoval in Cartegena, Colombia, starting in 1624.[21] These interviews were intended to provide proof for Catholic administrators in Rome that Africans indeed had souls and therefore could and should be converted to Catholicism.[22] As the institution of slavery claimed more victims in the decades and centuries that followed, the variety of texts that we can consider slave narratives expanded steadily, including accounts of slave lives embedded in travelers' diaries and other white-authored texts (such as the narrative of Edward Lewis, embedded in Thomas Gage's seventeenth-century journals about his travels in the Americas, or the narrative of Quashie in James Ramsay's 1784 essay about West Indian slavery); the 1709 overheard "Speech of a Black at a Funeral" (which draws on a sophisticated appropriation of natural rights discourse to challenge slavery); petitions for reparations, such as that by the slave Belinda in Massachusetts in 1783; Abraham Johnstone's 1787 criminal confession; Venture Smith's and Olaudah Equiano's narratives of capitalist disenfranchisement (1798 and 1789, respectively); Jarena Lee's 1830 spiritual autobiography; Nat Turner's "legal confession" of 1831; the Report of the 1822 Vesey Rebellion in Charleston; Boyreau Brinch's 1810 dictated Vermont narrative; Sitiki's narrative of four national systems of enslavement; Mary Prince's intensely gendered 1831 narrative of slavery in the Anglophone Caribbean; Juan Manzano's poetic Cuban narrative (1835/40). What these early texts, like their later counterparts, had in common was that they all aimed to represent, for a European readership, the life experiences of African men, women, and children held in bondage.

As might already be evident, these narratives, most of which were dictated or translated, frequently appeared alongside or within other texts, and their hallmark is a diversity of form and voice. "In their most elementary form," observes Stepto,

> slave narratives are full of other voices, which are frequently just as responsible for articulating a narrative's tale and strategy. These other voices may belong to various "characters" in the "story," but mainly they appear in the appended documents written by slaveholders and abolitionists alike. These documents—and voices—may not always be smoothly integrated with the former slave's tale, but they are nevertheless, parts of the narrative. . . . In literary terms, the documents collectively create something close to a dialogue— of forms as well as voices—which suggests that, in its primal state or first phase, the slave narrative is an eclectic narrative form.[23]

The multiple voices that Stepto highlights in this definition recall the theory of heteroglossia, or overlapping social speech types, that Mikhail Bakhtin described as an inherent characteristic of the novel.[24] Certainly, the early narratives often featured a combination of textual documents, frequently including a portrait, map, or image of some sort, various authenticating documents, prefatory letters, copies of legal documents, and supplementary testimony. In their creative commingling of oral and written forms, the narratives become what Henry Louis Gates Jr. has termed "talking books."[25] Indeed, "[even] in the novels and travelogues written by white visitors survive echoes of the voices of those who, having neither quill nor printing press, left the mark of their exile upon the minds of white observers."[26]

This heterogeneity of form and voice is echoed by a heterogeneity of purpose, in which the narratives were written for a variety of reasons and fulfilled a variety of functions. Although many were associated with the developing antislavery movement, not all were. Narratives of slave lives appeared in everything from legal testimonies and confessions to interviews with and portraits by doctors, to documents offering evidence of spiritual conversions, to name just a few. Slave narratives were read not only for information about slavery but also for sensationally or sentimentally exciting scenes, physical punishments, and picaresque adventures.[27] And most importantly, while some slave narratives came to be read as autobiographies, many were primarily intended to describe the institution and its idiosyncrasies, not necessarily the life of the enslaved individual.

Like the European novel, which arose chronologically alongside the slave narrative, early slave narratives undertook a variety of what could be considered formal experiments that appropriate a variety of discourses and genres—from ethnography and spiritual conversion to the picaresque and the gothic—before the genre cohered into its classic form during the Civil War period in the United States. Indeed, when one begins to look at the roots of the slave narrative tradition, rather than a singular taproot one finds a rhizomatic tangled web.[28] The early narratives both reveal the rhetorical range of stories of slave lives and replicate the varieties of slave experience from the sixteenth through early nineteenth centuries. Moreover, they are linked by the global movement of the slaves themselves (both enforced and voluntary) and are indispensable to our continued mapping of the literary history not only of the African diaspora but of the broader Western world. For, in Starling's words, these "raw accounts of the bitter experience of slavery provided matter and inspiration for all types of literature."[29]

MINDFUL OF that rich and complex history, the essays in this collection explore the rhetorical conditions, thematics, social and cultural contexts, aesthetics, and structural forms of early slave narratives in order to enhance our understandings of this seemingly simple, yet surprisingly complex genre. Focusing on narratives that appeared before 1845, these essays demonstrate that it is well worth our while to look beyond the iconic self-written narratives and those texts connected to nineteenth-century American abolitionism. Moreover, by drawing on narratives from the Caribbean, as well as South and Latin America, this collection illuminates the global nature and circulation of the slave narrative—its inherent transnationality—that challenges traditional views of the genre as specific to the southern United States. Indeed, while not as numerous as those from the United States, a significant number of slave narratives from across the African diaspora have survived to the present day.[30] The importance of notions of diaspora and movement in comprehending the general diversity of the slave narrative is crucial because to focus solely on these texts as a national genre "pre-empts more syncretistic efforts to explore, compare, and contrast wider continental interventions into slave culture and its hardly uniform sites of consciousness and knowledge production."[31]

Consequently, this volume aims to contribute to a fuller, more sophisticated understanding of the slave narrative in its formative decades—an understanding that obliges us to stretch conventional definitions of the genre, to continue the recovery of lesser-known narratives, and to wrestle seriously with the thematic complexities of these vitally important texts.[32]

To do so, we build on the work of a number of scholars who have researched the transnationality of abolitionism and early African Atlantic writing.[33] Recent monographs by Dwight McBride and Christopher Brown, as well as anthologies such as Henry Louis Gates Jr. and William L. Andrews's *Pioneers of the Black Atlantic,* Adam Potkay and Sandra Burr's *Black Atlantic Writers of the Eighteenth Century,* Joanna Brooks and John Saillant's *"Face Zion Forward,"* and Vincent Carretta's *Unchained Voices* have defined the basic territory of the writing of the early African diaspora, emphasizing both the rhetorical sophistication of the early slave narrative and the essential transnationality of life in the Black Atlantic.[34] This current volume seeks to extend and complicate this conversation by embracing the inherent cross-cultural and intertextual synergy of the slave narrative, and by drawing on work from a variety of disciplines, including literary and cultural studies, history, and legal studies, and on insights from such theoretical traditions as poststructuralism, postcolonialism, discourse analysis, and narratology.

Although essay collections such as Michael Drexler and Ed White's *Before Douglass* and Vincent Carretta and Philip Gould's *Genius in Bondage* also focus on early narratives, this volume emphasizes close attention to the materialities and questions of form associated with the genre and gives greater attention to narratives from the Hispanophone Caribbean. Focusing on the variety of early slave narratives is crucial because they helped to establish the narrative and rhetorical paradigms that shaped the development of the genre as it coalesced and matured during the nineteenth century. Close study of these early narratives thus helps to reveal the constituent representational strategies that later narratives would, dialectically, draw upon or react against.

THE COLLECTION opens with two essays that offer new paradigms for understanding the thematic and stylistic innovations of the early slave narratives. In the first essay, Ian Finseth theorizes about the important role played by a heightened concern with principles of and reimagination of the forms of the social contract—both in terms derived from political philosophy and in looser figurations of the moral and emotional bonds linking the human family—in eighteenth-century slave narratives. Finseth argues that contractualism met several critical and related needs in the early slave narrative, namely: "[it] established a psychological ground on which to confront the traumatic fragmentation of African societies and New World black communities [and] . . . helped early slave narrators to imagine a world stitched together through exchange and reciprocity: a world in which the shattering history of the diaspora could be in some measure repaired."[35]

The second essay, by Gretchen Woertendyke, argues for an expansion of the generic parameters of the early slave narrative. In her essay, Woertendyke closely analyses the writing that surrounds two slave rebellions, Denmark Vesey's 1822 rebellion in Charleston, South Carolina, and Nat Turner's 1831 rebellion in Virginia. She argues that although much of the writing generated by the rebellion—such as official reports, and documents such as *An Account of the Late Intended Insurrection among a Portion of the Blacks of this City*, produced in Charleston the year following Vesey's rebellion—are neither self-written nor dictated memoir, but because they are heavily invested in representations of the testimonies of enslaved individuals, they can be productively read as offering a kind of slave narrative. Reading these documents in such a way, Woertendyke argues, can assist scholars endeavoring to re-create the complexity of the lives of the enslaved by tracking their voices, wherever and however they appeared in the archive rather than trying to make the voices fit into more easily recognizable paradigms.

Following these two broad interventions in the genre, the collection offers two engagements with a particular narrative, *The Surprizing Deliverance of Briton Hammon,* in order to highlight the value of closer analysis of these early narratives on their own terms, rather than as the mere precursors to the later narratives. In the first, Jeffrey Gagnon offers compelling new analysis of one of the earliest testimonies by a black man, Briton Hammon. Hammon's narrative has consistently intrigued scholars, not only because he does not explicitly identify himself as a slave, but also because it describes his interactions with a variety of groups across the Americas, as well as his movements over thirteen years between the American colonies and the Spanish and British Caribbean colonies. Gagnon's essay endeavors to fill in some of the gaps regarding Hammon's life and his status as a black man in New England. Gagnon's essay also highlights the importance of cross-cultural encounters in Hammon's narrative such as those narrated by Ibn Said and Juan Antonio, and in so doing offers significantly new interpretations of black-Native alliances that scholars have previously classified as straightforward descriptions of Indian captivity. In addition to drawing on both historical and literary studies showing precedent for black-Native alliances from Florida to Cuba, this chapter offers new contributions to the study of colonial and imperial literature and history in the circum-Atlantic by positioning experiences such as Hammon's within a larger matrix of minority encounters that were fluid, dynamic, and humanizing for subjected men and women.

Offering a compelling literary pendant to the more complex historical understanding of Hammon's text suggested by Gagnon, Keith Green's essay extends Gagnon's analysis in order to articulate a much more expansive definition of the slave narrative genre than has typically been advanced. Among other things, Green's essay seeks to put pressure on static interpretations of Hammon's narrative that tend to overlook the myriad forms of subjection—such as abduction, imprisonment, and indentureship—circulating within Hammon's text. Finally, Green's chapter argues that Hammon's narrative reorients discussions of the genre away from an exclusive focus on the agrarian South and lifelong black bondage toward an exploration of transatlantic exchange and multiple articulations of black identity.

Lynn Johnson focuses on one aspect of these "multiple articulations of black identity" by illuminating the intriguing ways in which Boyreau Brinch employs as "alimentary grammar" in his 1820 dictated narrative. She argues that Brinch's narrative extensively draws upon the language and metaphors associated with food in order to describe his experiences of enslavement. In so doing, she reveals the manner in which this grammar "effectively assists him in vocalizing the impact that the politics of hunger and water deprivation has—specifically on African children who endured the transatlantic voyage."[36] Her reading allows us to understand narrative agency—here exemplified by a sign system focused on food—in more flexible ways.

The next two essays in the collection contribute to this reconsideration of early slave narratives by offering readings of two narratives from the Hispanophone Caribbean. Although Spain was one of the earliest participants in the African Atlantic slave trade, scholarly analysis of narratives of slave lives from the various Spanish colonies in the New World is relatively rare. What scholarly attention there is tends to focus on the

Cuban narratives of Juan Francisco Manzano from 1834 or the 1963 "testimonio" of Esteban Montejo by Miguel Barnet. In this collection, R. J. Boutelle enhances our understanding of Juan Manzano's narrative by offering an analysis of the rhetorical conditions that facilitated its creation. This fascinating but infrequently discussed narrative illuminates the very different conditions that facilitated the production of slave narratives on the Spanish colony of Cuba. By detailing the multiple hands through which the narrative passed during production, Boutelle productively illuminates the intriguing polyphony of this Cuban slave text, which echoes the multiple voices at work in most early slave narratives.

The second essay in this section by José Guadalupe Ortega introduces us to a "new" slave narrative, while similarly and simultaneously complicating questions about what constitutes the formal parameters of a slave narrative. Utilizing judicial documents culled from the Cuban National Archives (ANC), Ortega details the journey of Juan Antonio ("el inglés"), an English runaway slave who escaped the Bahamas and traveled to Cuba to seek his freedom. Ortega excavates Antonio's slave narrative from testimonies he provided to Spanish colonial officials, public defenders, and notaries. These statements, depositions, and witness testimonies "reveal the hopes and aspirations for emancipation and freedom of enslaved peoples as they encountered burdensome institutions across Atlantic legal slave regimes during the turbulent 1790s."[37] Moreover, Ortega's analysis reveals the ways in which Juan's narrative of his travels to Cuba "outlines the existence of a complex of social networks linking peoples of African descent with larger political and economic developments during the eras of the French and Haitian Revolutions."[38]

This more complex understanding of the social networks linking the various members of the African diaspora is manifested in an essay by Basima Kamel Shaheen, which closely analyses *The Life of Omar Ibn Said,* one of several narratives produced by Islamic Africans.[39] Initially published in 1831, the narrative was originally written in Arabic and then translated into English. Most importantly, as Shaheen's essay illuminates, in constructing his narrative of enslavement, Ibn Said drew very heavily upon Qur'anic Arabic idiom. Consequently, Shaheen reveals another crucial transnational constituent element necessary for understanding the development of the rhetorics that the early slave narrative incorporated.

The collection concludes with a coda/meditation by Kristina Bross, which endeavors to answer the general question raised by this collection: Given their generic indeterminacy and ambiguity, how are we to read and thoughtfully engage with the early texts of the African Atlantic slave era? Bross's essay offers wonderfully insightful commentary on and lucid engagement with the intellectual ramifications of the essays in this collection. As a coda in keeping with the overall tenor of the collection, it does not offer a ringing, singular conclusion but rather highlights the intriguing possibilities of rethinking the absent-presence of voices of the enslaved within the archives of global systems of slavery.

One immediately apparent avenue for extending the conversation we have begun with this collection concerns the role of gender. Although none of the essays in the collection are focused on the narratives of enslaved female individuals, in calling for an expanded understanding of the genre of the slave narrative, this collection of essays builds upon the foundational work by scholars of female narratives such as Frances Smith Foster, Joycelyn Moody, and Valerie Smith.

THESE EARLY narratives highlight the important intersections between the "roots and routes" traveled by generic forms and rhetorical strategies. The hybridity and polyvocality of the testimonies of slaves illuminates the fluid parameters and heterogeneous origins of the slave narrative form. Far from a rigid or unchanging genre, it incorporates numerous rhetorical and narrative strategies that develop out of each narrative's particular cultural context. Because slavery—whether on a plantation, in a domestic setting, aboard ship, or in the city—was an incredibly complex and varied system of power relationships, so too must we consider the various ways in which slaves communicated their stories. Attention to the fluid and diasporic features among the various testimonies of slave lives highlights the eclecticism of the slave narrative form and makes it impossible to view the slave narrative as static genre. Drawing on the global nature and effects of slavery embraces the intrinsic movement and multiplicity inherent to the process of the African slave diaspora that has been written into the slave narrative genre.

Notes

1. Gilroy, *Black Atlantic*, 225n2. Gilroy is using M. M. Bakhtin's definition of the "chronotope" as "A unit of analysis for studying texts according to the ratio and nature of the temporal and spatial categories represented. . . . The chronotope is an optic for reading texts as x-rays of the forces at work in the culture system from which they spring." Bakhtin, *Dialogic Imagination*, 426.

2. Rediker, *Slave Ship*.

3. For example, the pope sent missionaries to interview Africans to establish whether or not they had souls. See Von Germeten, *Treatise*. Nazer's twenty-first-

century slave narrative *Slave* recounts her experience as an enslaved household servant to a Sudanese diplomat living in London.

4. Gilroy, *Black Atlantic*, 4.

5. Peabody, "Narratives of Fugitive Slaves," 61–92.

6. C. Davis and Gates, *Slave's Narrative*, iv.

7. Foster, *Witnessing Slavery*, 3.

8. McBride, *Impossible Witnesses*; Smallwood, *Saltwater Slavery*; Bailey, *African Voices*.

9. Andrews, *To Tell a Free Story*; James Olney suggests there are important distinctions between slave narratives and autobiographies that make conflation of the two genres problematic. Olney, "'I Was Born,'" 148–74.

10. Stepto, *From behind the Veil*, 3.

11. Bland, *Voices of the Fugitives*, 4.

12. Ibid., 6.

13. See Gates, *Figures in Black* and *Signifying Monkey*.

14. Gardner, *Unexpected Places*, 10.

15. Patterson, *Slavery and Social Death*.

16. D. B. Davis, "Looking at Slavery," 452–66; Drescher, *From Slavery to Freedom*.

17. Many of the historical names of West African nations are of European designation. So, for example, "Igbo" was the name given to related (yet importantly distinct) social groups that were not necessarily of the same "nation," according our contemporary understanding of the term.

18. See Stepto, *From behind the Veil*, for example.

19. Starling, *Slave Narrative*.

20. Ibid., 311.

21. Von Germeten, *Treatise on Slavery*.

22. Ibid., "Introduction," ix–xxx.

23. Stepto, *From behind the Veil*, 256.

24. See Bakhtin, *Dialogic Imagination*.

25. Gates, *Signifying Monkey*, 127–40.

26. D'Costa and Lalla, *Voices in Exile*, 8.

27. See Gould, "Rise, Development, and Circulation," 11–27.

28. DeLeuze and Guattari, *Thousand Plateaus*, 21.

29. Starling, *Slave Narrative*, 3.

30. See Kang, "'As If I Had Entered a Paradise'"; Aljoe, *Creole Testimonies*.

31. Kang, "'As If I Had Entered Paradise,'" 434.

32. I am thankful to Ian Finseth for helping me clarify my articulation of the stakes at hand here.

33. McBride, *Impossible Witnesses*; Brown, *Moral Capital*.

34. Gates and Andrews, *Pioneers of the Black Atlantic*; Carretta, *Unchained Voices*; Brooks and Saillant, *"Face Zion Forward"*; Potkay and Burr, *Black Atlantic Writers*.

35. Ian Finseth, this volume, 19.

36. Lynn Johnson, this volume, 128.

37. José Guadalupe Ortega, this volume, 171.

38. Ibid.
39. Bluett, *Some Memoirs;* "The Narrative of Abu-Bakr al-Sadiqa" (1834) in Madden, *Twelvemonth's Residence.*

Bibliography

Aljoe, Nicole N. *Creole Testimonies: Slave Narratives from the British West Indies, 1709–1836.* New York: Palgrave Macmillan, 2012.
Bailey, Anne. *African Voices of the Atlantic Slave Trade: Beyond the Silence and the Shame.* Boston: Beacon Press, 2006.
Bakhtin, Mikhail. *The Dialogic Imagination.* Ed. and trans. Michael Holquist. Austin: University of Texas Press, 1981.
Bland, Sterling L. *Voices of the Fugitives: Runaway Slave Stories and Their Fictions of Self-Creation.* Westport, CT: Greenwood, 2000.
Bluett, Thomas. *Some Memoirs of the Life of Job, the Son of Solomon, the High Priest of Boonda in Africa.* London: Richard Ford, 1734.
Brooks, Joanna, and John Saillant, eds. *"Face Zion Forward": First Writers of the Black Atlantic, 1785–1798.* Boston: Northeastern University Press, 2002.
Brown, Christopher Leslie. *Moral Capital: Foundations of British Abolitionism.* Chapel Hill: University of North Carolina Press, 2006.
Carretta, Vincent, ed. *Unchained Voices: An Anthology of Black Authors in the English-Speaking World of the Eighteenth Century.* Lexington: University Press of Kentucky, 2003.
Carretta, Vincent, and Philip Gould, eds. *Genius in Bondage: Literature of the Early Black Atlantic.* Lexington: University Press of Kentucky, 2001.
Davis, Charles, and Henry Louis Gates Jr., eds. *The Slave's Narrative.* New York: Oxford University Press, 1986.
Davis, David Brion. "Looking at Slavery from Broader Perspectives." *American Historical Review* 105.2 (April 2000): 452–66.
D'Costa, Jean, and Barbara Lalla, eds. *Voices in Exile: Jamaican Texts of the 18th and 19th Centuries.* Tuscaloosa: University of Alabama Press, 2009.
DeLeuze, Gilles, and Felix Guattari. *A Thousand Plateaus: Capitalism and Schizophrenia.* Minneapolis: University of Minnesota Press, 1987.
Drescher, Seymour. *From Slavery to Freedom: Comparative Studies in the Rise and Fall of Atlantic Slavery.* New York: New York University Press, 1999.
Drexler, Michael, and Ed White, eds. *Beyond Douglass: New Perspectives on Early African-American Literature.* Lewisburg, PA: Bucknell University Press, 2008.
Foster, Frances Smith. *Witnessing Slavery: The Development of Ante-Bellum Slave Narratives.* Madison: University of Wisconsin Press, 1994.
Gardner, Eric. *Unexpected Places: Relocating Nineteenth Century African American Literature.* Jackson: University of Mississippi Press, 2009.
Gates, Henry Louis, Jr. *Figures in Black: Words, Signs, and the "Racial" Self.* New York: Oxford University Press, 1989.
———. *The Signifying Monkey: A Theory of African-American Literary Criticism.* New York: Oxford University Press, 1989.
Gates, Henry Louis, Jr., and William L. Andrews, eds. *Pioneers of the Black Atlantic: Five Slave Narratives, 1772–1815.* New York: Basic Civitas Books, 1998.

Gilroy, Paul. *The Black Atlantic: Modernity and Double Consciousness.* Cambridge, MA: Harvard University Press, 1993.

Gould, Philip, "The Rise, Development, and Circulation of the Slave Narrative." In *The Cambridge Companion to the African American Slave Narrative.* Ed. Audrey Fisch. New York: Cambridge University Press, 2007. 11–27.

Kang, Nancy. "'As If I Had Entered a Paradise': Fugitive Slave Narratives and Cross-Border Literary History." *African American Review* 39.3 (Fall 2005): 431–57.

Madden, Richard Robert. *A Twelvemonth's Residence in the West Indies, during the transition from slavery to apprenticeship.* Philadelphia: Carey, Lea and Blanchard, 1835.

McBride, Dwight. *Impossible Witnesses: Truth, Abolitionism, and Slave Testimony.* New York: New York University Press, 2001.

Moody, Joycelyn. *Sentimental Confessions: Spiritual Narratives of Nineteenth-Century African American Women.* Athens: University of Georgia Press, 2003.

Nazer, Mende. *Slave: My True Story.* With Damien Lewis. London: Public Affairs Press, 2005.

Olney, James. "'I Was Born': Slave Narratives and Their Status as Autobiography." In *The Slave's Narrative.* Ed. Charles Davis and Henry Louis Gates Jr. New York: Oxford University Press, 1991. 148–74.

Patterson, Orlando. *Slavery and Social Death.* Cambridge, MA: Harvard University Press, 1982.

Peabody, Ephraim. "Narratives of Fugitive Slaves." *Christian Examiner* (Boston), July 1849, 61–92.

Potkay, Adam, and Sandra Burr, eds. *Black Atlantic Writers of the Eighteenth Century: Living the New Exodus in England and the Americas.* London: Palgrave Macmillan, 1995.

Rediker, Marcus. *The Slave Ship: A Human History.* New York: Penguin, 2008.

Smallwood, Stephanie E. *Saltwater Slavery: A Middle Passage from Africa to American Diaspora.* Cambridge, MA: Harvard University Press, 2008.

Smith, Valeris. *Self-Discovery and Authority in Afro-American Narrative.* Cambridge, MA: Harvard University Press, 1991.

Starling, Marian W. *The Slave Narrative: Its Place in American History.* Washington, DC: Howard University Press, 1988.

Stepto, Robert. *From behind the Veil: A Study of Afro-American Narrative.* 2nd ed. Chicago: University of Chicago Press, 1991.

von Germeten, Nicole, ed. and trans. *Treatise on Slavery: Selections from "De instauranda Aethiopum salute" by Alonso De Sandoval, S.J.* 1627. Indianapolis: Hackett, 2008.

Irony and Modernity in the Early Slave Narrative
Bonds of Duty, Contracts of Meaning

Ian Finseth

IN HIS 1810 narrative, the African American Methodist deacon George White recounts a particularly terrifying dream he experienced following a camp-meeting in 1804. Some time after awaking, White tells his wife about the dream and its visions of hell: "I related the whole to my bosom companion; who, having heard it with astonishment, and much affection, was desirous to know what I thought would be the result; concerning which, I gave her my opinion in full; and we covenanted together from that time, to be more faithful to God than ever, and to escape, if possible, the torments I had seen" (White 11). A similar moment of mutual "covenanting" occurs in the 1810 narrative of Boyrereau Brinch, which extends from Brinch's childhood in Africa, through the Middle Passage, to his service in the American Revolution and his struggle for economic independence in Vermont. In Barbados, where he and the other slaves are put up for sale, Brinch meets an African brother and sister who "had pledged themselves never to part but by death" (Brinch and Prentiss 101). Yet the brother, Bangoo, is soon sold to a man "who had doubtless been devoted to the covenants of our Lord and Saviour, perhaps had crossed himself before the image of Christ, suspended upon the cross" (101).

What these passages, among many others in the literature of the Black Atlantic, help to illuminate is the power of "covenanting together" in the early slave narrative. That phrase aptly captures both the religious and the personal dimensions of a whole pattern of meaning that runs throughout the genre, one in which the Christian doctrine of duty to God is mirrored and supplemented by, and at times even secondary to, an ethic of interpersonal obligation. For many writers of the Black Atlantic, the ancient notion of a covenant with God, rooted in biblical theology, provided a means of understanding suffering within a providential framework and promised that the faithful would be rewarded and the unfaithful punished. Yet an evolving intellectual and ideological environment rendered traditional covenantalism, in and of itself, insufficient as a strategy of either survival or literary rhetoric. "Man is accountable to God and his fellow creatures," wrote Adam Smith in 1759. "But tho' he is, no doubt, principally accountable to God, in the order of time, he must necessarily conceive himself as accountable to his fellow creatures, before he can form any idea of the Deity, or of the rules by which that Divine Being will judge of his conduct" (A. Smith 130n2). Not all of his contemporaries would have agreed, but Smith's observation, offered during his exegesis of moral judgment, reflects a subtle epistemic shift, toward a kind of ethical pragmatism whereby responsible conduct in this world becomes, "necessarily," a prerequisite to religious understanding. Here was a more secular form of thinking about duty, one less reliant on scriptural doctrine and more embedded in the evolving social currents of the eighteenth-century world. What I argue in this essay is that this expanded concept of human duty, especially as captured in the notion of a "social contract," functioned as a complex, unpredictable, and energizing force in the slave narrative during its formative decades.

This perspective provides leverage on a key issue that has intrigued, even bedeviled, scholarship on the eighteenth-century Atlantic world, namely the relation—philosophical, social, and material—between the emergence of Western "modernity" during this period and the African or "black" persons who found themselves caught up in the international system of commerce managed by European imperial powers. In any analysis of that relation, difficult questions press forward: How did Enlightenment liberalism—with its image of the rational, accountable, and essentially "free" human subject—interact with intensifying political debates surrounding slavery, abolition, and race? How were those debates influenced, and their participants imagined, by the testimony of African-descended persons; and conversely, how was this testimony itself shaped and constrained by the discursive protocols that they observed? How are we to understand the published writings of Black Atlantic narrators as they (and often their white editors) triangulated their experiences between different value systems and worldviews? What were the gains and tradeoffs of achieving or articulating a subjectivity recognizable by a white literate audience? And what bearing might such a subjectivity, with its "specific forms of double consciousness" (Gilroy 1), have had on the historical and cultural formations of modernity that arose in the nineteenth century?

I propose that the scholarly and critical response to such questions should take into account, more fully than it has done so far, the ways in

which Black Atlantic literature imagines and reimagines the social contract, by which I refer both to the philosophical tradition associated with
Hobbes, Locke, Rousseau, and others,[1] and to a more expansive, more
fluid conception of the role of interpersonal duty in human life. While
Philip Gould, Helen Thomas, Gene Jarrett, and others have begun to
map out the early slave narrative's complex engagement with the economic and political claims of natural rights theory and Western liberalism,[2] we are in need of further investigation into how contractualism,
in its psychological as well as political and economic aspects, operated
within the genre. Early slave narratives are rife with the language of contract; they frequently make mention of "promises" made, kept, or broken; of "agreements" struck; of "conditions" imposed; of quid-pro-quo
arrangements; of various "obligations" and "pledges" that knit together
the fabric of social life. They also treat personal or legal duty themati-
cally and narratively; it becomes a factor in character formation, in the
causal sequence of events, and even in the course of an individual life.
The dynamics of such contractualism, as I term it, operate both functionally, as the narrators enter into social agreements or arrangements in the
first place, and rhetorically, as they narrate those original events for an
imagined readership.

My broad argument—based on the autobiographical narratives of
Olaudah Equiano, Boyrereau Brinch, Abraham Johnstone, Venture Smith,
James Albert Ukawsaw Gronniosaw, Ottabah Cuguano, and John
Marrant—holds that contractualism deeply informed these writers' efforts
both to conceive and to project a diasporic black subjectivity.[3] If we understand the relationship between black cultural expression and political
agency in the more expansive terms that Jarrett has recently called for, we
can regard the early slave narrative's contractual language as a symbolic
field wherein the abstractions of Western philosophy are adapted to the
exigencies of individual survival and racial solidarity.[4] Predicated not only
on the autonomy and capacity of the individual human being, but on the
moral and emotional bonds linking the human family, contractualism
established a psychological ground on which to confront the traumatic
fragmentation of African societies and New World black communities. It
helped early slave narrators to imagine a world stitched together through
exchange and reciprocity: a world in which the shattering history of
the diaspora could be in some measure repaired. *In some measure:* For
although the basic performance of contractual relations—making agreements, keeping promises, working within systems—enabled Black Atlantic narrators to demonstrate their fitness for a newly competitive social

and economic order (and thus, implicitly, their importance to human history), this came at the cost of acquiescing, to some degree, to the universalizing, rationalizing, and financializing logic of the very modernity of which the African diaspora was both sign and symptom.

That dilemma has been the subject of intensive critical commentary, from Paul Gilroy's seminal work through more recent studies by Ian Baucom, Laura Doyle, Saidiya Hartman, and others. A potent line of critique that has emerged from this work focuses on the connections between liberalism, race, and modernity and traces out the continuities, not just symbolic but causal, between Enlightenment philosophy, a logic of slaveholding, and the development of a modern globalized world whose economic and racial injustices are in a real sense outgrowths of the eighteenth century.[5] In this critique, the classical notion of the social contract is held as deeply complicit or at least highly problematic. Doyle, in her wide-ranging analysis of the "racialization of liberty" (Doyle 13) in Anglo-Atlantic culture, suggests that the contract, even as it points toward the principle of free participation in society, presupposes a logic of social contingency. Calling attention to "the alienations and elisions entailed in the contractual republic," she argues that "a contractual society positions everyone as a lone outsider who *must join a race* if he or she wants security" (12) and that hereby "we begin to see how race, that backward myth, came to drive modern revolutions and bind modern communities" (12). Similarly, Hartman sees the supposed "liberty of contract" in the postbellum period as a convenient fiction that white society employed "to enforce black subordination and legitimize a range of coercive measures, from the contract system [of employment] to the regulation of domestic affairs" (Hartman 146). For Baucom, these abuses transcend their original history; he finds in the *Zong* slave-ship massacre of 1781, in which 133 slaves were thrown overboard so that the ship's owners could collect the insurance money they were contractually owed, the symbolic and literal prefiguration of an entire modern ontology of quantification and depersonalization. "This fatal Atlantic 'beginning' of the modern," he writes, "is more properly understood as an ending without end," (Baucom 333) for in the "speculative epistemology, mode of subjectivity, and value form" that the *Zong*'s insurance contract embodied, "modernity (our long contemporaneity) finds itself demonstrated, anticipated and recollected" (117).[6]

In face of such critiques of liberalism, modernity, and the contract, what warrants the rather more optimistic view of contractualism in the early slave narrative put forward here? My answer to that question leads into the more specific argument this essay advances. In reimagining the social contract as a constitutive element of black subject formation and political agency, the early slave narrative works on building a "contract of meaning" between the narrator and the reader or, more broadly, between the narrator and an imagined transatlantic audience. Not only does the genre employ a variety of rhetorical strategies intended to secure the reader's trust in the narrator and, in turn, to signal that that trust will be repaid, but it also displays a serious interest in the nature of language itself, which in the eighteenth century was increasingly theorized as a culturally saturated domain of social convention. In many of these narratives, language's role in mediating human relations and embodying the social contract is carefully thematized; the common aim is to ground black subjectivity in a secure domain of shared meaning that could counteract the pernicious claims of slave economics and race theory. At the same time, there is a great deal of anxiety about the ambiguity and corruptibility of language, about the abuses to which it can be put. This skepticism toward language was a common theme in the eighteenth century, but in the slave narrative the meanings of words are a matter of life and death, not simply of philosophical dispute. Language represented literal survival and a vital opportunity to project an identity into the public sphere and into history, but it was also shaky ground on which to build, given the referential slipperiness and mutability of words themselves. Identities projected in words are therefore fragile, and a "diasporic black subjectivity" as reflected in text becomes layered, complex, and to a high degree indeterminate. What we find, in consequence, is a pattern of rhetorical irony emerging in the early slave narrative, irony that derives from a recognition of the manipulability of language and that depends on an artful control of subtext and on the reader's implicit participation in meaning making. This development in the genre, I suggest, by no means neutralized the problematics of liberalism these narratives encode, but it did point the way toward the more critical engagement with the discursive formations and dynamics of modernity that would characterize the politics of later African American and African Atlantic literature.

IN ONE OF the earliest known slave narratives, Thomas Bluett's *Life of Job* (1734), Job's social identity is expressed not simply by his slave status or his race but by such qualities as his temper, his graces, his "natural Parts," and the "Acuteness of his Genius," (Bluett 46, 47). It has almost nothing to do, in Bluett's telling, with his economic aspirations, struggles, or achievements, and this is a useful point of comparison. While a narrator's good character would always be important to the genre, by the 1780s the emphasis had discernibly shifted, and a narrator's social identity now took on a more overtly economic dimension, usually manifest in whatever money-making arrangements he could enter into. Olaudah Equiano, for example, agrees to oversee a slave plantation on the Mosquito Coast because "the harvest was fully ripe in those parts" (Equiano 172) for converting the native Indians, but the experience also allows him to harvest the good will of the plantation's founder, Dr. Charles Irving. Irving, who had "said that he would trust me with his estate in preference to any one" (172), later writes a letter of reference attesting that Equiano "has served me several years with strict honesty, sobriety, and fidelity" (193). The advantages that Equiano subsequently derives from his good reputation are, in a direct and tangible sense, economic, and they trace directly to his effectiveness, shown on the Mosquito Coast and elsewhere, at holding up his end of the bargain, even if that bargain involves the servitude of other people. Boyrereau Brinch also, over the course of the narrative, forges a social identity out of his labors, his deals, and his property: he cultivates, as it were, his economic personhood. After being emancipated in recognition of his service on the American side in the Revolutionary War, he travels to Lennox, Massachusetts, where, he proudly recalls, "for the first time I made a bargain as a freeman for labor" (Brinch and Prentiss 169). Here, at last, is an economic sign, indeed function, of the citizenship for which Brinch was already fighting physically. Having fulfilled this "contract" (170), he then pursues a broader fulfillment of his economic citizenship through all the reciprocal agreements into which he enters over the years, whether fruitful or not, even descending for a period into a veritable farrago of disputes, claims, counterclaims, suits, and legal settlements with a couple of neighbors who, he says, keep cheating him.

We can see the dynamics of economic contractualism—striking a deal, repaying a debt, claiming one's due—operating throughout early Black Atlantic literature, but this pattern leads us into an interpretive quandary. On one hand, we can readily argue that slave narrators (or recently freed narrators) are able to achieve a measure of independence by undertaking a variety of everyday economic agreements. In classical contract theory, entering into social compacts was one of the prerequisites for political citizenship, and although slaves or freedmen enjoyed precious few, if any, of the privileges of formal citizenship, we can still see them asserting themselves as members of a legal and political order. The ability to rent a cabin, or hire out one's labor, or simply to buy and sell goods, was easy for whites to take for granted; for early slave narrators, these actions provided a foothold, however tenuous, in their struggle for membership in a largely hostile polity. Those who succeeded could find themselves taking greater control of their lives, becoming economic agents, even businessmen. To push the argument further: by counteracting the relentless monetization of the black body, economic contractualism can be seen as preserving the slave narrator against both the logic and the system of commodification. In self-possession, at once expressed and reinforced by the social contract, inheres an essential quality of freedom.

But by the very same token, goes the counterargument, the notion that economic contractualism promotes freedom implies a capitulation to the values and practices of an exclusionary political and economic order—Euro-American capitalism—and overlooks the role of the contract in the whole system of property rights, bureaucratic depersonalization, and rationalized "modernity" upon which the international oppression of blacks depended.[7] During the mid- to late-eighteenth century, British capitalism secured itself as the dominant Atlantic economic system, a system that saw the interconnected rise of both international commodity trade and speculative trade, and that was highly dependent on an interlocking system of contracts. From this perspective, economic contractualism in the slave narrative appears as an important thread in the historical narrative of what Baucom, following Giovanni Arrighi, has called the "long twentieth century": a narrative of the rise and triumph of finance capitalism.[8] Baucom writes that this period represented one of "the highest moments of finance capital, moments in which capital seems to turn its back entirely on the thingly world, sets itself free from the material constraints of production and distribution, and revels in its pure capacity to breed money from money" (Baucom 27). Within this economic system, then, black economic agency conferred a measure of autonomy—a degree of distance from the "thingly world"—but it also circumscribed that autonomy reactively, within the psychic and cultural frameworks of the financial system. To put it more strongly, the human subject predicated by classical contract theory manifested most powerfully or most recognizably as human only within a system that was capable of reducing people to the status of things. Economic contractualism of course reared itself on a material base, but it also formed a domain of abstraction, of interchangeability, of linguistic and numerical representation, and at some level it implied that in order to demonstrate their non-thingness, people had to *make* things, or to make other people *into* things.

The 1798 narrative of Venture Smith has become something like Exhibit A for critics inclined to this view, with Smith himself standing as an exemplar of the steep costs of entering the domain of the "human" or the "modern" on terms established by white, European, or Western society.[9] Certainly, the narrative suggests that the willed transmutation of slave narrator from object to agent of the capitalist system—from *homo Africanus* to *homo economicus*—depends upon his successful navigation of the day-to-day contractual arrangements by which white society regulated itself. The pattern is set early. At the age of eight, having been taken to Rhode Island as the property of one Robertson Mumford, Smith is entrusted with the keys to his master's trunk, and "to his directions I promised faithfully to conform" (Smith 14). Even when Mumford's father demands the keys, he refuses: "I told him that my master intrusted me with the care of them until he should return, and that I had given him my word to be faithful to the trust, and could not therefore give him or any other person the keys without my master's directions" (14). This episode arguably has less to do with Smith's being loyal to his master than with positioning himself effectively, in the manner of Benjamin Franklin, to take advantage of opportunities that arise within his social environment. Indeed, it is by earning a reputation as an "honest negro" that Smith is able to earn his living and ultimately to purchase his own freedom and that of most of his family. As the years go by, what the narrative focuses on is not Smith's interiority or intellectual or spiritual growth, but his savviness at bargaining with his masters to hire out his time; at holding up his end of the deal; at leveraging resources and opportunities such that he "ma[kes] considerable money with seemingly nothing to derive it from" (24), hinting at, in Baucom's phrase, a "pure capacity to breed money from money."

As Smith's successive contractual arrangements enable him to reap some of the profits from his own labors, and to save up enough money to buy himself and then most of his family, the narrative invites us to regard him as asserting his identity as a human subject in an economic system increasingly based on the exchange of objects—as practicing what Houston A. Baker Jr. has called the "brilliant economic expressive strategies designed by Africans in the New World and the Old to negotiate the dwarfing spaces and paternally aberrant arrangements of western slavery" (Baker 31). A recent biography goes so far as to declare that he "lived the American dream" (Saint and Krimsky 98) and that he "embarked on a journey to build a new country with no less a role than that of the founding fathers" (106). There is certainly much to admire about

Smith's perseverance, cleverness, and force of will. Yet we have to reckon with several passages where he seems to succumb to the logic of commodification, presenting human beings, even his family, in terms of their monetary value. After noting that his son Solomon died on a whaling voyage, Smith laments that "Church has never yet paid me the least of his wages. In my son, besides the loss of his life, I lost equal to seventy-five pounds" (Smith 26). Somewhat later, "being in my forty-fourth year, I purchased my wife Meg, and thereby prevented having another child to buy, as she was then pregnant. I gave forty pounds for her" (27). Then, recalling the mortal illness that claims his daughter Hannah, Smith blandly notes that "the physician's bills for attending her during her illness amounted to forty pounds" (28). For a number of critics, these passages convey the moral costs incurred by one who has been forced to think in terms of the commercial value of human beings.[10] Indeed, they suggest that Saint and Krimsky's comparison of Smith to the founding fathers might be unintentionally apt—a kind of parable in which black and white join together in building the modern nation state ("a new country") by surmounting traditional economic and political hierarchies ("the American dream").

Smith's narrative thus suggests that the recurring interpretive predicament I have described—the role of economic contractualism in the early slave narrative—derives from the paradoxes of "double consciousness" as a psychosocial phenomenon of the African diaspora, and that it cannot be disentangled from the larger problem of understanding the relation between economic liberalism, national modernity, and black subjectivity. In the remainder of this essay, I would like to both complicate this problem further and offer avenues of fruitful analysis by considering how the genre reimagines and thus revises the social contract and, in particular, by exploring how contractualism informs the early slave narrative's treatment of language and literary authority.

To see how the genre reimagines or adapt the social compact, we should begin with how it supplements the traditional language of the covenant with a more modern vocabulary of the contract. I noted earlier that Black Atlantic literature is often deeply invested in the doctrine of a divine covenant, whereby human salvation depends on the fulfillment of our duties to God. This is particularly true in the case of those texts arising from or intersecting with the tradition of Protestant spiritual autobiography. The narrative of the black Methodist preacher John Jea, for instance, is virtually a case study in the psychological, cultural, and rhetorical power of covenantal theology. To cite just one moment among many, Jea writes that his travails in the West Indies, and then in Virginia and Baltimore, "were very severe but God delivered me by his grace, for he has promised to be with us in six troubles, and in the seventh he will not leave us nor forsake us; and that there shall be nothing to harm or hurt us, if we are followers of that which is good. By these promises I was encouraged not to repine at the losses and crosses I had met with" (Jea 80–81). If less insistently, covenantal theology is also a central concern in the narratives of James Gronniosaw, George White, and Olaudah Equiano, all of whom recount their conversion to Christianity and their efforts to lead faithful Christian lives; "I made a promise in my mind to God," writes Equiano, "that I would be good if ever I should recover" from a life-threatening "fever and ague" (Equiano 265, 264).

In these and other narratives, however, the characteristic pattern involves two overlapping registers of contractual language: the level of the divine covenant, where man has binding obligations to God, and the level of the earthly contract, arrangement, or deal, whereby the covenant with God gets translated—or not—into daily actions and relationships. Boyrereau Brinch's narrative, for example, begins by describing the inhabitants of the "kingdom of Bow-woo" in West Africa, who though originally heathen are intrinsically worthy of "that blessing promised to those who have faith in God, and continue to the end in ways of well doing" (Brinch and Prentiss 57). Citing several verses from the Old Testament, Brinch seeks to rescue African society from the popular image of heathenish chaos and to incorporate Africans into a recognizable history of Judeo-Christian civilization, one socially and theologically structured by the covenant, not by the law of the jungle. But the narrative soon shifts its thematic focus toward, even gives priority to, the dynamics of interpersonal duty in daily social life rather than (or as a reflection of) the imperative of human duty to God. This narrative turn comes shortly after the appearance of Europeans in the text, and shortly after the text switches to the first person, a suggestive mark of its increasingly personal dimension.[11] Moreover, in place of earlier passages from the Old Testament that emphasized duty to God, Brinch's narrative now includes passages from the New Testament—excerpts from Matthew 7:7 (on doing unto others) and Luke 10:25 (on the good Samaritan)—whose exhortation concerns the treatment of our fellow human beings.[12] The narrative context for this shift involves the arrival of slave traders on the West African coast and the subsequent journey across the Middle Passage, and Brinch's account is suffused with the language of the social contract. After recounting his kidnapping at the hands of the "white Vultures" (71), and then their prosecution of the slave trade in African villages,

Brinch describes how one of the traders, an Englishman, "pledge[d]" (86) to give his African bride an education and then return with her in two years; he later breaks that promise by selling her handmaidens into slavery, and she rebukes him for violating the "conditions" of the "treaty" allowing her to go with him in the first place (108).

These passages are doubly paradigmatic. One, by gauging personal experience against scripture they also measure religious discourse by its applicability to individual history; more on this below. Two, Brinch's opposition of white perfidy and black fidelity is more than merely rhetorical. Slave narrators routinely contrast the sustaining bonds of familial emotion to all the false dealings and broken promises that are signs or symptoms of a broken covenant with God. They express a vision of human community grounded in those defining qualities of late eighteenth-century social theory: sensibility, empathy, and moral feeling.[13] "Such is the force of natural pity, which the most depraved morals still have difficulty destroying" (152), Rousseau had written in the *Discourse on the Origin and Foundations of Inequality,* and that appeal to sympathy as the essential social adhesive can be heard to echo throughout the early slave narrative—each time family members are torn from each other, each time a slave finds comfort in the words of a friend or protector, each time he keeps faith with another sufferer or another fugitive. "When about nineteen," recalls George White, "the sympathy of nature, awakened in my mind, such a sense of filial affection" that he manages to get permission "to return to the place of my nativity, to see my mother" (White 5). In *The Theory of Moral Sentiments* (1759), Adam Smith, though from a very different angle, had joined Rousseau in regarding human society as held together by the force of sympathy or compassion, enabled by the ethical imagination, and standing as a counterbalance to the ceaseless pressure of self-interest. This understanding of human emotion underlay both Smith's and Rousseau's political philosophies, historical views, and understanding of the social contract—and for slave narrators these were not abstractions but matters of life and death, survival and sanity.

What stands forth in the early slave narrative, accordingly, is less the scriptural basis of covenantal theology than the narrator's day-to-day negotiations of a social world of enormous uncertainty, danger, and violence, where, in Brinch's words, "it still seemed to me as it ever had done, that I was fortunes [sic] football, and must depend upon her gentle kicks" (Brinch and Prentiss 170). It is a world wherein words, actions, and intentions must be constantly assessed for their value as predictors of the future or markers of fate—a world wherein the entire philosophical tradition of the social compact plays out on the moral and emotional planes of an individual life. For narrators such as Brinch, White, Equiano and others, interpersonal duty, or the contract of feelings and words that weave together the social fabric, provides a measure of stability amidst the vicissitudes of slave life. When James Gronniosaw, for example, is counseled by his English employer not to marry the woman he fancies, Betty, because she is a poor widow with a child, he falls back on first principles: "I had promised and was resolved to have her," and in the end "I have found her a blessed partner, and we have never repented, tho' we have gone through many great troubles and difficulties" (Gronniosaw 30). Here and elsewhere, the basic social contract—a promise between emotionally linked individuals—is not some abstract concept or rhetorical device, but a way of stitching together black communities and forging a new black subjectivity in the Atlantic crucible.

Indeed, the slave narratives remind us that philosophical "universals" such as the state of nature or the liberal subject must be derived from individual experience and should be held accountable to it; hereby could black subjectivity and black history be brought into the putatively abstract precincts of Western philosophy. The genre arose not spontaneously, but as a cultural form actively and critically engaged with the "discursive terrain," to borrow Dwight McBride's term, of transatlantic culture, and while it adapted to the social and intellectual currents of its historical moment, it also helped to shape those currents. The extent to which Black Atlantic literature critically engaged Western philosophical traditions should not be underestimated,[14] and one its key accomplishments was to reveal the human dimensions, real-life costs, and real-life importance of the social contract. Doing so went a good distance toward addressing one of the perennial challenges of African American and African Atlantic literature, that of fusing experiential testimony, political rhetoric, and intellectual independence in the construction of autobiographical black identity.

Yet here we are confronted with the problem that such an "identity" could only be projected into the public sphere, and into history, through the medium of language; and this problem is one that slave narrators themselves thematized in their work. It is a "problem" because language, by the late eighteenth century, was increasingly understood as a murky domain of social convention, saturated with cultural history and dependent for its meanings on the particular situation obtaining between speakers and listeners, or writers and readers.[15] In that context, an "identity" manifest in language was necessarily unstable, necessarily distributed; it was something to be built and maintained against the forces of linguistic entropy, through what might be called a "contract of meaning."

That this larger intellectual context had a bearing on the development of the early slave narrative is suggested by the anxiety these texts manifest regarding language—particularly in relation to how to forge and communicate a coherent identity, both in a skeptical publishing environment and in the very struggle to survive, adapt, and form relationships in the diaspora in the first place. More specifically, we can regard the problem of language in the slave narrative as a central dimension of how the social contract was imagined and negotiated. To put it more forcefully, language is the essential material of the contract; whether printed or spoken, a contract can only come into being through language. Underlying that contract will be some amalgam of uncommunicated emotions, understandings, and interests, but none of this in itself constitutes an articulated contract; words themselves are the indispensable material by which social obligations are made explicit. Such words, whether written or spoken, constitute speech acts, and if we take an expansive view of these linguistic performatives as extending from the most fleeting verbal exchange to the textual self-fashioning of a narrator, the importance of the social contract to the slave narrative comes into sharper focus.[16] For this perspective allows us to organize a whole range of textual evidence, from a slave owner's promise to a freeman's labor agreement to the entire narrative structure of an autobiography, from moments where characters either lie or keep faith, to the conversion narrative, confession, or spiritual autobiography, all of which can be seen as extended verbal performances premised on a contractualist understanding of the nature of language. They are not merely "representation" but action. The brother and sister in Brinch's narrative who "pledge[] themselves never to part but by death" thereby enact a social bond of profound psychological significance; the narrator who assures his reader of the veracity of his testimony thereby not only enacts a promise but projects an identity, one that is capable in the first place of making such a promise. These are contracts of meaning, built from a shared language, yet like all contracts they are susceptible to revision, to breaking, to misunderstanding, and to the inevitable ambiguities of language. What is remarkable is that the early slave narrative, far from approaching language uncritically, consistently thematizes how the social fabric is imperfectly woven from such contracts of meaning.[17]

The 1797 narrative of Abraham Johnstone vividly illustrates what is at stake; its anxiety about the potential abuse of language is not only palpable but narratively motive. This fascinating text is presented as the final testament of a condemned man, transcribed by an unidentified editor. Johnstone, we learn, faces execution for the murder of one Thomas Read, a "Guinea Negro" (Johnstone 40), who had brought a lawsuit against Johnstone after a spate of local property crimes. Interestingly, rather than getting into the details of his guilt or innocence right away, Johnstone frames his narrative as "counsel" (6) to his colored brethren "to be upright, and circumspect in your conduct" (6), especially since his case "might be made a handle of" (8) to "cast a general reflection on all those of our colour" (7) or to denigrate the antislavery movement. Johnstone shows a clear awareness, that is, of how he will function as a type, of how his individuality threatens to be submerged in a larger political and cultural struggle. So the narrative becomes a form of self-authorized character testimony, a defense and recuperation of his individuality that is ultimately meant to vindicate himself for history as well as for his immediate audience.

After exhorting his readers to good conduct, Johnstone launches into his real polemic, one directed toward the problem of false verbal testimony (i.e., perjury), which he says corrupted his own trial and led to his unjust conviction. What stands out is not only the passion of Johnstone's diatribe but the generality of his argument: "There is no sin whatever, not even murder itself, that so surely, and in so particular a manner, calls down it's [sic] own punishment in this life as perjury—and the reason for it is very plain and evident; because that abominable crime must in many cases, be hidden from, and escape the judgement of mankind, and be known only to the heart of the criminal and to God whose holy name he has prostituted and made subservient to injustice" (24). Johnstone in fact spends several pages railing against "this most execrable and horrid crime" (26), and he attributes its ostensible frequency to "the administ[e]ring an oath on every slight occasion, and the indecent irreverent manner in which it is administ[e]red by some Justices" (26). Johnstone's anger is not simply the resentment of the falsely accused, for he mounts the argument in broad legal and religious terms, suggesting that the real issue for him extends to the ways in which guilt or innocence is determined socially.

And it is determined, of course, largely through verbal declaration. In this sense, the oath constitutes a formal speech act, or legal performative, that serves as a crucial hinge between the divine covenant and the social contract.[18] Its religious dimension is expressed through the ritual of swearing upon a Bible (the regular practice in eighteenth-century American courts), and its legal dimension reflected in the codification of the crime of perjury: a kind of second-order speech act that is determinable only by reference to the first speech act, the oath. Both of these speech acts are public, and both are performative, although in different ways; the oath is a performance of fidelity to the laws of man and God, while perjury hides behind the performance of sincerity. Moreover, along with other performatives such as a confession or victim's statement, both the oath and the testified statement (whether perjurious or not) are central gears in the story-making machinery of a criminal trial, the former serving to heighten the authority and authenticity of the latter. Yet, no surprise, the stories that emerge are not always consistent, and those that prevail not always true. In a trial, "'reality' is always disassembled into multiple, conflicting, and partly overlapping versions, each version presented as true, each fighting to be declared 'what really happened'—with very high stakes riding on that ultimate declaration" (Gewirtz 8).

Johnstone makes it abundantly clear that he regards the narrative that prevailed at trial to be false, and the strongest impression he leaves is a profound distrust of the truth value of words themselves, a fear that the social compact as manifest in language is corruptible, uncertain, suspect. Again, the paradigmatic contrast is between white duplicity and black authenticity, but now it is more vivid, extended, and explicit. In the third segment of his memoir, subtitled "The Dying Words of Abraham Johnstone," he renarrates the events that led up to his conviction, rearguing the evidence and naming names. The details of the case are too intricate to merit rehearsal here, but it appears (at least in Johnstone's telling, for we have no corroboration) that a number of local people simply had it out for Johnstone, whose growing prosperity made him "an object of envy and hatred" (39), and that they lied about him at trial. Johnstone's surprising magnanimity ("I most freely and heartily forgive them, and desire my love and blessing to themselves and family" [40]) might strike us as implausible, but it serves Johnstone's larger effort to repair, even regenerate, his social identity. He is in effect entering himself—his words, his thoughts, his actions, his feelings, his experiences—into the permanent historical record, with the help of those who edited and published his work (listed simply as "The Purchasers"). Acutely aware of the wreckage of language, he seeks to rebuild an identity in language, and to do so he must rely on his audience. His authority and authenticity are, in a kind of trick of logic, self-authorized—for he is writing, after all, as a condemned man—and so Johnstone needs us to hold up our end of the bargain.

But what "bargain" would that be? At the most general level, it is the implied contract that obtains between all writers and readers: the tacit agreement that if one invests time, energy, and cognitive resources into the task of working through a text, he or she will be repaid with pleasure, wisdom, cognitive enrichment, broadened horizons, important truths.[19] In the more specific case of autobiography, the terms of the contract are somewhat narrowed: the reader opens to the possibility of learning something valuable or at least interesting from the recounted experience of another human being, and the writer, while free to stylize that experience, remains faithful to the essential facts. (Hence the sense of betrayal that can arise on either side when this contract is broken, as with autobiographical hoaxes or readerly dismissals of true testimony.) This sense of mutual obligation is particularly charged in testimonies of trauma: we expect the narrator to report the truth, even if a highly wrought truth, and in turn we withhold our skepticism, submitting in some degree to the narrator's authority and granting the text's authenticity. Not surprisingly, this dynamic was highly vexed in Black Atlantic literature, which had to assert itself against the pressures of a racialized literary marketplace in which the "authority" of black narrators and the "authenticity" of their stories were not easily, if at all, granted. It is for that reason, as we know, that these texts repeatedly, even anxiously, gesture toward their own truth value, and a significant amount of recent scholarship has focused on the rhetorical strategies that they employed to gain a foothold in the literal and symbolic economies of the Atlantic world. Particularly relevant are those critical perspectives that highlight the canniness and agency of Black Atlantic writers in managing their relationship with an imagined audience; these include Joanna Brooks's analysis of how early African American writers formed "their own distinctive traditions of using print to advance the political status of their community" (Brooks, "Early American" 88); Brooks's reconstruction of Phillis Wheatley's participation in a "transactional, sentimental culture of mourning" (Brooks, "Our Phillis" 8); and Joseph Rezek's discussion of the ways in which African American print culture could construct a "counterpublic imagined as limitless and unending" (Rezek 655).

The "transactional" strategies of the slave narrative as it calls into being an imagined "counterpublic" provide a useful frame for understanding a more specifically rhetorical development: the emergent phenomenon of irony in the early slave narrative, which operates precisely at the place where literary contractualism, the slipperiness of language, and the problems of identity formation intersect. Notwithstanding their great seriousness of purpose and their often earnest religiosity, early slave narrators begin to express, here and there, with greater or lesser force, a distinctly ironic sensibility. This phenomenon prefigures the motifs of disguise, subversion, double-talking, and misdirection that are well-known features of nineteenth-century African American literature, and in some ways my perspective aligns with work that has been done on the relation between irony and slavery in the work of such later writers as Frederick Douglass, Herman Melville, and Mark Twain.[20] By pushing the horizon of analysis back into the context of eighteenth-century contract theory, however, and by focusing on irony as a linguistic performance, we arrive at a richer account of the early years of the slave narrative. Moments of irony are important, I suggest, for several reasons: they recruit the reader into a subtle alliance with the narrator; they articulate between the narrative problems of artfulness and sincerity; and they reflect an essential indeterminacy in language, thus seriously complicating the narrated relation between "black" identity and "white" philosophical or ideological discourse. Fundamentally, it disrupts what McBride has described as a kind of preknowing that a reader might bring to the text: "The slave is the 'real' body, the 'real' evidence, the 'real' fulfillment of what has been told before. Before the slave ever speaks, we know the slave; we know what his or her experience is, and we know how to read that experience" (McBride 5).

Irony in the early slave narrative is usually rhetorical and tonal, rather than situational or dramatic, and it often takes the form of sarcasm. The sarcasm can be angry and unmistakable, and at these times the target is usually white hypocrisy, as when Brinch describes a slaveholder "who had doubtless been devoted to the covenants of our Lord and Saviour, perhaps had crossed himself before the image of Christ, suspended upon the cross" (Brinch and Prentiss 101) or when he parodically ventriloquizes the proslavery rejection of scriptural enjoinments to kindness: "Not so, my Lord, you did not mean that the African negroes should be included in this, thy Law, because they bear a different complexion from us thy chosen people" (102–3). Likewise Venture Smith, after being egregiously cheated: "Captain Hart was a *white gentleman,* and I *a poor African,* therefore it was *all right, and good enough for the black dog*" (Smith 30, original emphasis). The irony can be more playful, even when making a serious point. "We did not wait for pigs and geese to die of old age, when we could get a chance to steal them," remembers William Grimes. "Steal? Yes, steal them. Why, I have been so hungry for meat that I could have eat my mother" (Grimes 114). Ordinarily, the audience for such ironic comment is the reader, and the sarcasm is a matter of narrational style. On occasion, however, irony appears in a narrator's direct address to other figures or persons in the narrative, in which case it usually runs to archness rather than anger. After Smith, for example, is arrested for fighting and then returned home, he relates his reaction: "I presented myself before my mistress, shewed her my hand-cuffs, and gave her thanks for my gold rings" (V. Smith 20).

In *The Critical Mythology of Irony,* Joseph A. Dane, tracing the evolving history of the concept in Western critical discourse dating back to the Greeks, offers this warning: "There is no correct understanding of the word irony, [and] no historically valid reading of irony." He also suggests that the "element of contempt [toward irony] found in the earliest definitions has never been eliminated; it has been suppressed and modified, to emerge finally in the privileged stance of critics and metacritics over their materials" (Dane 191). Bearing this warning and this suggestion in mind, we can pursue a line of argument about irony in the slave narrative that recognizes its positive potentialities without reducing it to some fixed or predictable function. Starting with the relatively noncontroversial claim that irony derives from a difference between what is literally said and what is actually meant, I would propose that it thereby implies a certain attitude toward communication, one in which the "cloudy medium" of language (Madison 183) presents opportunities for creative manipulation. Ironic language operates as a field of freedom more than of constraint, a space wherein the intentions of the speaker/writer and the disposition of the listener/reader interact to enable meanings that are not immediately manifest in words.

In the case of Black Atlantic literature, this claim has several implications. At one level, rhetorical irony demonstrates not only the narrator's artfulness, his or her ability to manipulate language in creative ways, but also, in the context of the eighteenth century's association of language and reason, the narrator's capacity for "civilization" and his or her very humanness.[21] In this respect, irony joined earnestness in allowing a slave narrator to project, through the medium of text, an identity that was recognizably human—long before the techniques of rhetorical subtlety were raised to an art form in the antebellum American slave narrative.

Moreover, if irony communicated that one possessed civilization's all-important criterion of reason, it did so in part by providing a rhetorical method for managing the supposedly disruptive influence of intense feeling. The case of Ignatius Sancho is instructive. "It is the most puzzling affair in nature," wrote Sancho in an early letter, "to a mind that labours under obligations, to know how to express its feelings" (Sancho 50). In his remarkable correspondence produced over the coming years—a kind of running epistolary autobiography—Sancho developed a creative solution to that "puzzling affair," a literary style that mingled sincerity and irony in such a way as both to invite and to regulate intimacy. There is great feeling in his letters but also gentle raillery, pungent wit, and racial self-deprecation, and the cumulative effect is to present black experience, both painful and pleasurable, in the guise of "sensibility" and rhetorical fashion. If less consistently than Sancho, other African Atlantic narrators, in expressing grief, pain, and resentment, also wanted to suggest that these emotions have been processed and kept in check; Venture Smith's sarcastic gratitude for his "gold-rings," for example, conveys both anger and self-control. Rousseau's notion that a primordial "cry of Nature" (Rousseau 146) represented a kind of standard for authentic linguistic utterance was not, for obvious reasons, the view espoused by slave narrators struggling for recognition and inclusion in the domain of Culture. Closer to the mark was Wordsworth's famous claim that poetry "takes its origin from emotion recollected in tranquillity"—that the "spontaneous overflow of powerful feelings" caused by some experience must, to endure, be subsequently reconstructed in language (Wordsworth and Coleridge 407). Irony thus represents a seemingly paradoxical form of authenticity (implying that some feelings are too strong or too transgressive for direct expression) and an unusual form of narratorial authority (drawing the reader almost irresistibly into the narrator's purposes).

Clearly these potentialities of irony all depend on the participation of the reader—and here we are brought around to its more profound significance and its subtle relation to contractual thought. In encountering irony, we as readers are asked to interpret in the spirit of the text, not to take it literally, and to recognize the difference between reality and appearance as that difference manifests in language. To do so requires, in Wayne Booth's terms, a "reconstruction" of the underlying meaning of an ironic statement, in which the critical interpretive step involves our judgment about an author's intentions and beliefs; only that step allows a distinction between irony and its alternatives. This dynamic resembles a social contract, for "the whole thing cannot work at all unless both parties to the exchange have confidence that they are moving together in identical patterns" (Booth 13). Holding up our end of that contract, even though it often happens below the level of conscious awareness, is like paying our debt to the author, discharging our obligations as sensitive readers—that very sensitivity being proleptically imagined and constructed by the text that recruits us.

This dynamic has profound ethical significance in the way it conditions the relation between narrator and reader: "Even the most simpleminded irony, when it succeeds, reveals in both participants a kind of meeting with other minds that contradicts a great deal that gets said about who we are and whether we can know each other" (Booth 13). If irony generates "mutual knowledge of how other minds work" (14), then irony in the slave narrative represents a subtle yet powerful method for eroding the barrier of race separating a black narrator from a white audience. This represents a crucial and historically specific response to a general philosophical problem described by Richard Rorty, that of bridging "private irony" and "liberal hope," or the ironist's awareness of the "contingency and fragility" (Rorty 74) of language and identity and liberalism's metaphysical faith in freedom as part of a determinable "relation between human beings and 'reality'" (75). A liberal form of irony does not foreclose on solidarity or a basic human substrate, but it offers no assurance that the "right redescription [of experience] can make us free" (90). Rorty's analysis of where the liberal ironist parts ways with the liberal metaphysician is particularly relevant:

> She thinks that what unites her with the rest of the species is not a common language but *just* susceptibility to pain and in particular to that special sort of pain which the brutes do not share with the humans—humiliation. On her conception, human solidarity is not a matter of sharing a common truth or a common goal but of sharing a common selfish hope, the hope that one's world—the little things around which one has woven into one's final vocabulary—will not be destroyed. (92, original emphasis)

From this perspective, expressions of irony in the slave narrative constitute a method of turning the humiliations routinely suffered by slaves toward the goal of establishing a sense of human solidarity with the reader (as the very act of writing an autobiography for publication implies), even if there is a divergence in "final vocabularies." Equiano, for example, after relating several "cruel punishments" (Equiano 171) he witnessed in Jamaica, demurs at describing more: "I pass over numerous instances, in order to relieve the reader by a milder scene of roguery" (172), an episode in which he is cheated (humiliated) by a white man who breaks a contract for payment. "Relieving" the reader is clearly what Equiano does *not* want to do, and this ironic comment, a sudden twist in the rhetoric, not only invokes the reader's ability to recognize suffering in fellow human beings but mischievously augments Equiano's authority by suggesting that the reader needs to be "relieved"—for the very word presupposes that the reader has suffered by the descriptions just read!—while calling attention to the discrepancy between the pains of reading and the pains of slavery.

Taking the long view, moments such as this grow more common in the slave narrative, and in Black Atlantic literature generally, as we enter the nineteenth century and as narrators continue to expand their horizon of rhetorical possibilities. To be sure, emotional sincerity and polemical certitude retained their rhetorical primacy in the slave narrative, for they underlay and gave expression to a genuine belief in the universal validity of the value of freedom and in a common human nature that narrator and reader share and can mutually discover. At the same time, archness, sarcasm, and other forms of irony become increasingly salient over time because they call attention to the contingency of language and thus both undermine the doctrine of essential racial identity and enable, in Rorty's phrase, a "redescription" of the vocabularies of power. In other words, to the extent that slavery's entire ideological framework depended on particular uses of language, ironic gestures that highlighted the flexible relationship between words and meanings worked, however subtly, to call into question the philosophical basis of the system. When Equiano, for instance, after managing to purchase himself, writes that he has regained his "original free African state," and when, three pages later, following a dispute with his ship's captain about labor, he writes that "I consented to slave on as before" (Equiano 138, 141), the meanings of such critical words as *consent, freedom, slavery,* and even *African* grow blurrier. This is not to suggest that slave narrators were on their way to becoming deconstructionists, but that there is a growing recognition in their writings that the instability of language is vitally and directly important to real people's real lives. Abraham Johnstone's denunciation of perjury represents a non-ironic expression of this; Brinch's parody of proslavery scriptural exegesis, suggesting that even the meaning of the words of the Bible is up for grabs, represents its ironic counterpart.

If the referential malleability of words, however, represents an opportunity for ironic critique, it also complicates the representation of a coherent identity. More specifically: the two "levels" of irony—surface and depth, denotative and connotative meaning—are structurally analogous to the psychological dualism of "double-consciousness," and in both cases the "contradiction of double aims" (Du Bois 4) can be difficult to determine or interpret. Pertinent here is Booth's distinction between *stable* irony, in which an underlying meaning is determinable and "is intended to reinforce a rhetoric" (Booth 228), and *unstable* irony, "in which the truth asserted or implied is that no stable reconstruction can be made out of the ruins revealed through the irony" (240). Similarly, when confronted with something that seems like an expression of "double-consciousness," some intersection or overlapping of "white" and "black" perceptions or values, we can never be entirely sure where the one begins and the other leaves off. Who are we dealing with, exactly, behind the veil of words? The answer to that question might be that we never arrive at some "true" identity, discovering rather, like Nabokov reading Gogol's "The Overcoat," that "amid the whirling masks, one mask [might] turn out to be a real face, or at least the place where that face ought to be" (Nabokov 141).

This interpretive problem might help to account for the recent rise of critical interest in Venture Smith's narrative, which stands out for its sly tone and the concomitant difficulty of knowing where our narrator's "real face" is, or in John Sekora's terms, of distinguishing between a "black message" and a "white envelope."[22] An early episode in the auto-biography gives a sense of the slipperiness of Smith's rhetoric. He recounts a fight that breaks out between his mistress and his wife, over a "mere trifle[,] such a small affair that I forbear to put my mistress to the shame of having it known" (V. Smith 18–19). It is a passing reference, but the effect, here as elsewhere, is to present himself as the rational actor and arbiter of representation, in the position of protecting the reputation of a white person yet making it clear that such protection could be withdrawn. He shows here an artful control of language, as in one gesture he both withholds information (what "trifle"?) and imparts vivid meaning (his mistress could be "shamed"), and it is in that space between a paucity of information and a plenitude of meaning that Smith's irony comes to life. In the process, Smith also exerts a subtle form of mastery over the reader, who is drawn into the narrator's purposes and made inevitably complicit in the determination of a deeper meaning.

In other instances, however, it is possible but not self-evident that Smith is being ironic and, accordingly, tempting but impossible to determine where his real investments lie, what his real identity is. His references to the monetary value of his wife and children, discussed above, are a case in point. At a minimum, certainly, attaching dollar figures to his son's life, his daughter's fatal illness, and his pregnant wife's freedom represents virtually the antithesis of an ethics grounded in common human feeling and the capacity of the moral imagination to circumscribe self-interest. Yet these passages, when read from a slightly different perspective, can seem *too* cold, *too* callously mercantilist. Smith may express coldness, but is he really experiencing it, either in the first place or at the time of writing? Can we not read between the lines, or underneath the surface of the text, at such jarring moments? Perhaps we are meant to grow uncomfortable when we read that Smith has saved money on his unborn child, and in that discomfort to recognize anew the human feelings that are affronted by the commercialism Smith seems to embrace. We might even admit the possibility that these passages represent a deliberate attempt on Smith's part to bring home to his readership the obscenity of capitalistic values when applied to human beings. This is the position of Ginerva Geraci, who argues that here "the equation between slave and money is being subtly challenged" and that "from a wider point of view, the whole narrative is an ironic statement aiming not simply at conveying a meaning that is opposite to the literal meaning, but at disrupting a hierarchy of values" (Geraci 218).[23] This is entirely possible—and yet that "wider point of view" proves quite elusive, for like Archimedes, we have no firm place to stand, nor lever long enough, to move the text into fixed position, to resolve its unstable ironies or its problems of identity. Indeed, its ultimate meanings, especially as regards Smith's apparent commodification of human beings, are richly indeterminate: either we have a tragic case of double consciousness or we have a savage form of irony, or, most likely, we have some of both yet no means to disentangle them. The reader thus occupies the unenviable position of entering into a contract of meaning whose terms are uncertain, riddled with illegibilities and blanks. How those terms are rewritten depends largely on the disposition and interests of the reader, both in Smith's era and today, and his narrative's unpredictable energies and effects—its "modernity"—goes far toward explaining its ongoing canonization in Black Atlantic scholarship.

WHAT I have argued is that closely attending to the phenomenon of irony in the early slave narrative allows us to better understand how linguistic contractualism, and the broader philosophy of the social compact, gave Black Atlantic writers special tools for projecting a particular kind of identity into the world and for constructing a particular kind of relationship with the reader, indeed for building a readership in the first place. That argument helps us address the questions about modernity and the Black Atlantic raised at the outset of this essay. In adapting the philosophy of the social compact to its own purposes, and in exploring the possibilities of a distinctly modern sense of the necessary but shaky relationship between language and identity, Black Atlantic literature participated in modernity in ways more fruitful and less debilitating than usually allowed for by the pessimistic narrative of an unholy alliance between liberalism, capitalism, and racial oppression. African American and Afro-British narrators, much earlier than commonly recognized, were creatively and critically engaged with contemporary intellectual currents, and the rhetorical patterns derived from a language of contract—of "covenanting together," of securing and fulfilling commitments, of relying on the reader's good sense to read between the lines—all represent ways of salvaging individual and communal meaning from the systematic and tyrannical abuse of meaning that the slave system entailed. The principle of the social compact, and the language for expressing it, were imperfect resources but resources nonetheless, and they portended a tradition of critical protest that would gain strength and sophistication throughout the nineteenth century.

Notes

1. As it had evolved by the mid-eighteenth century, Western contract theory formed a loosely defined branch of political philosophy that emphasized both the existence of certain "natural" rights and the voluntary relinquishment of those rights in order to achieve a smoothly functioning social state. These concepts reflected a tidal (if gradual) philosophical shift away from the patriarchal monarchicalism by which political and religious elites had traditionally grounded their authority in a supernatural Christian framework. What the idea of the contract, or commonly "social compact," offered was a conceptual mechanism for defining and regulating the relation between the individual and the state, and between individuals. (This necessarily abbreviated discussion of classical contract theory draws on Hampton; Kavka; Boucher and Kelly; Morris; Button, esp. chs. 1–4.)

2. See also Carey; Aravamudan; Drescher.

3. Here I have in mind Michelle M. Wright's warning that "seeking to determine Black subjectivity in the African diaspora means constantly negotiating" between a "hypercollective, essentialist identity" and a "hyperindividual identity." "Any truly accurate definition of an African diasporic identity," she writes, "must somehow simultaneously incorporate the diversity of Black identities in the diaspora yet also link all those identities to show that they indeed constitute a diaspora rather than an unconnected aggregate of different peoples linked only in name" (2). The social contract, I maintain, represented an unexpectedly vital way of bridging the individual and the collective and is thus a key hermeneutic for Black Atlantic studies.

4. Jarrett argues for a historiography and a methodology that, rather than separating knowledge from power, and literary art from political action, see them as forming an organic if complex whole in African American literary history: "Texts of intellectual culture from the era of Jefferson to that of Obama supply the evidence of how African Americans came to understand and demonstrate their own agency for social change against racial injustice, or of how they and their critics came to articulate African American political subjectivity, action, and representation" (16).

5. Gilroy, for instance, critiquing Jurgen Habermas's "deep faith in the democratic potential of modernity," argued that "the universality and rationality of enlightened Europe and America were used to sustain and relocate rather than eradicate an order of racial difference inherited from the premodern era" (49). See also Riss, who critically examines the concept of "personhood" in liberal theory; Levecq, who traces the rise of a liberal form of abolitionism more invested in self-interest than its earlier republican counterpart; Hensley; Mills; Scott.

6. Faced with fatal overcrowding and disease during its crossing from Africa to Jamaiac, the *Zong*'s captain and officers threw the slaves overboard in the reasonable belief that they would be compensated for this insured "cargo." The ship's owners' insurance claim, adjudicated in court, was ultimately denied, but not before the case became a cause célèbre for the antislavery movement. For an excellent recent account of the episode, which also finds in it some of the seeds of the modern world, see Walvin. Webster and Oldham focus on the legal issues involved in the *Zong* case.

7. It is this objection that underlies, for example, Doyle's argument that "Atlantic freedom functions as a tar baby because it is offered on terms that are not free and not universally shared, terms whose conception and institutionalization reflect a long, compromised, and greedy history" (22–23).

8. See Baucom, esp. part 1, and Arrighi.

9. Kazanjian, for example, has argued that we can identify in black mariner narratives such as Smith's the emergence of "a mutually constitutive relationship . . . among hierarchically codified racial and national identities, and a formal, abstract equality characteristic of modern capitalism" (151).

10. The most forceful critique is that of Gould, who argues that Smith "commodifies even the most intimate of familial relations" ("Free" 676) and therefore himself "commits the sin of slavery" (677).

11. The role of Prentiss in editing or embellishing Brinch's account is impossible to determine, but at the beginning of chapter 3, the narrative switches to the first person, with the comment that "here the writer takes the language of the narrator" (50). For purposes of simplicity, I refer to the primary narrator/author as "Brinch," even though his agency is thus obscured.

12. Brinch invokes the relatively recent theory that Africans had descended from the ancient Jews and provides three extracts from the Old Testament: Ezekiel 2:1 on Israel's rebelliousness; Deuteronomy 28:62 on the scattering of the Israelites and their enslavement; and Exodus 22:20 on God's promised vengeance against transgressors.

13. This point resonates with Christine Levecq's interesting distinction between republican and liberal forms of sympathy, which structures her argument that the latter, over time, came to dominate abolitionist rhetoric. Liberal sympathy, she writes, focused on innate individual rights and thus "fostered a movement toward interiority, an (often unsuccessful) attempt to turn a blind eye to the politics of the body" (191). Republican sympathy, by contrast, "acknowledges the separateness of identity and need" (24) and seeks to imagine human solidarity beyond those differences; it "is open to radicalization through an extension of the notion of common good" (25). Both forms are co-present in the early slave narrative, but in complex ways, and at those moments when black familial or personal

obligations are honored, they seem fused; then the texts appeal to the interior capacities, rights, and feelings of the individual, yet in the interest of building community through mutual recognition.

14. McGary and Lawson observe that "in the writings of slaves and former slaves, we find discussion and speculation on such concepts as oppression, paternalism, resistance, political obligation, citizenship, and forgiveness" and argue that "attention to these voices can be useful in gaining philosophical insight" (xvii).

15. Taking up Locke's contention, in the *Essay Concerning Human Understanding,* that words have no "natural connexion" to things, a variety of writers in the eighteenth century began to challenge the traditional belief in a "correspondence between the taxonomy of linguistic elements and the natural order of things in the world" (Cohen 20–21). This new emphasis on the artificiality or arbitrariness of words enabled a number of critical ideas to take root: language reflects subjective and objective reality aslant, not transparently; meaning depends on both the essential quiddity of words and their reception; and various kinds of language have evolved in conjunction with different human needs. (This summary of developments in eighteenth-century linguistic theory draws on Aarsleff; Formigari; Howell; Land; Kramer; Montgomery.)

16. My use of the term *speech act* follows the classic discussions given in Austin and Searle, esp. ch. 2.

17. Susanna Egan, though concerned with contemporary literature, defines the issue well. The "autobiographer of diaspora," she writes, "discriminates among a plurality of possible [subject] positions, all incomplete and in continuous process, in order to recognize who speaks, who is spoken, and just who might be listening." Readers, therefore, "are closely implicated in the interactions that constitute even temporary meaning, and are accordingly required to be conscious of their own positions in relation to the autobiographer. Many texts invite this self-consciousness, explicitly constructing an ideal or desired reader" (121).

18. For technical discussions of legal performatives, see Hancher; Visconti.

19. This idea draws on Boyd, esp. part 3.

20. See, for example, Jones; Van Leer; Sweeney.

21. See Hudson.

22. This problem is taken up in detail and depth by Vincent Carretta, who focuses on the tension between the rhetorical, narrational, and paratextual aspects of Smith's narrative and concludes that "the Venture Smith we hear in the Narrative successfully resists the attempt to reappropriate his identity" as a faithful servant (180). Carretta's essay appears in James Brewer Stewart's recent collection of essays on Smith, a volume that marks the extent to which Smith has been taken up as an object of serious critical inquiry.

23. Anna Mae Duane offers a highly nuanced reading of Smith's complex, ambivalent relationship to money, arguing that it conditions his narrative's treatment of loss and grief. "When read against the expectations of the emerging sentimentalist genre," Duane writes, "Smith's focus on money instead of love emerges as a different form of resistance. In other words, Smith's doggedly unemotional prose refuses to tell us where the real treasure lies" (196). Money may have "served Smith faithfully as he secured it to gain his family's freedom,"

but when his daughter is dying, it "loses its regenerative power—power that for Smith was intimately connected to his homeland" (200).

Bibliography

Aarsleff, Hans. *The Study of Language in England, 1780–1860*. Princeton: Princeton UP, 1967.

Aravamudan, Srinivas. *Tropicopolitans: Colonialism and Agency, 1688–1804*. Durham: Duke UP, 1999.

Arrighi, Giovanni. *The Long Twentieth Century: Money, Power, and the Origins of Our Times*. London: Verso, 1994.

Austin, John L. *How to Do Things with Words: The William James Lectures Delivered at Harvard University in 1955*. Oxford: Clarendon P, 1962.

Baker, Houston A., Jr. *Blues, Ideology, and Afro-American Literature*. Chicago: U of Chicago P, 1984.

Baucom, Ian. *Specters of the Atlantic: Finance Capital, Slavery, and the Philosophy of History*. Durham: Duke UP, 2005.

Bluett, Thomas. *Some Memoirs of the Life of Job, the Son of Solomon, the High Priest of Boonda in Africa . . .* London, 1734.

Booth, Wayne. *A Rhetoric of Irony*. Chicago: U of Chicago P, 1974.

Boucher, David, and Paul Kelly, eds. *The Social Contract from Hobbes to Rawls*. New York: Routledge, 1994.

Boyd, Brian. *On the Origin of Stories: Evolution, Cognition, and Fiction*. Cambridge: Belknap P of Harvard UP, 2009.

Brinch, Boyrereau, and Benjamin F. Prentiss. *The Blind African Slave, or Memoirs of Boyrereau Brinch, Nick-named Jeffrey Brace. Containing an Account of the Kingdom of Bow-Woo, in the Interior of Africa; with the Climate and Natural Productions, Laws, and Customs Peculiar to That Place. . . .* St. Albans, VT: Harry Whitney, 1810.

Brooks, Joanna. "The Early American Public Sphere and the Emergence of a Black Print Counterpublic." *William and Mary Quarterly* 62.1 (2005): 67–92.

———. "Our Phillis, Ourselves." *American Literature* 82.1 (2010): 1–28.

Button, Mark E. *Contract, Culture, and Citizenship: Transformative Liberalism from Hobbes to Rawls*. University Park: Pennsylvania State UP, 2008.

Campbell, Kofi Omoniyi Sylvanus. *Literature and Culture in the Black Atlantic: From Pre- to Postcolonial*. New York: Palgrave Macmillan, 2006.

Carey, Brycchan. *British Abolitionism and the Rhetoric of Sensibility: Writing, Sentiment, and Slavery, 1760–1807*. New York: Palgrave Macmillan, 2005.

Carretta, Vincent. "Venture Smith, One of a Kind." In Stewart, ed., *Venture Smith and the Business of Slavery and Freedom*, 163–83.

Cohen, Murray. *Sensible Words: Linguistic Practice in England, 1640–1785*. Baltimore: Johns Hopkins UP, 1977.

Cugoano, Ottobah. *Narrative of the Enslavement of Ottobah Cugoano, a Native of Africa; Published by Himself in the Year 1787*. In *The Negro's Memorial; or, Abolitionist's Catechism*. Ed. Thomas Fisher. London, 1825. 120–27.

Dane, Joseph A. *The Critical Mythology of Irony*. Athens: U of Georgia P, 1991.

Doyle, Laura. *Freedom's Empire: Race and the Rise of the Novel in Atlantic Modernity, 1640–1940*. Durham: Duke UP, 2008.

Drescher, Seymour. *The Mighty Experiment: Free Labor versus Slavery in British Emancipation*. Oxford: Oxford UP, 2002.

Duane, Anna Mae. "Keeping His Word: Money, Love, and Privacy in the Narrative of Venture Smith." *Venture Smith and the Business of Slavery and Freedom*. Ed. James Brewer Stewart. Amherst: U of Massachusetts P, 2010.

Du Bois, W. E. B. *The Souls of Black Folk: Essays and Sketches*. Chicago: A. C. McClurg, 1903.

Egan, Susanna. *Mirror Talk: Genres of Crisis in Contemporary Autobiography*. Chapel Hill: U of North Carolina P, 1999.

Equiano, Olaudah. *The Interesting Narrative of the Life of Olaudah Equiano, or Gustavus Vassa, the African. Written by Himself*. London, 1789.

Formigari, Lia. *Signs, Science and Politics: Philosophies of Language in Europe, 1700–1830*. Trans. William Dodd. Amsterdam: John Benjamins, 1993.

Geraci, Ginevra. "Venture Smith and James Baldwin: Two Strangers in the Village." *Recharting the Black Atlantic: Modern Cultures, Local Communities, Global Connections*. Ed. Annalisa Oboe and Anna Scacchi. New York: Routledge, 2008. 212–24.

Gewirtz, Paul. "Narrative and Rhetoric in the Law." *Law's Stories: Narrative and Rhetoric in the Law*. Ed. Peter Brooks and Paul Gewirtz. New Haven: Yale UP, 1996. 2–13.

Gilroy, Paul. *The Black Atlantic: Modernity and Double Consciousness*. Cambridge: Harvard UP, 1993.

Gould, Philip. *Barbaric Traffic: Commerce and Antislavery in the Eighteenth-Century Atlantic World*. Cambridge: Harvard UP, 2003.

———. "The Economies of the Slave Narrative." *A Companion to African American Literature*. Ed. Gene Andrew Jarrett. Malden, MA: Wiley-Blackwell, 2010.

———. "Free Carpenter, Venture Capitalist: Reading the Lives of the Early Black Atlantic." *American Literary History* 12.4 (2000): 659–84.

Grimes, William. *Life of William Grimes, the Runaway Slave. Written by Himself*. New York, 1825.

Gronniosaw, James Albert Ukawsaw. *A Narrative of the Most Remarkable Particulars in the Life of James Albert Ukawsaw Gronniosaw, an African Prince, as Related by Himself*. Bath, England, 1772.

Hampton, Jean. *Hobbes and the Social Contract Tradition*. Cambridge: Cambridge UP, 1986.

Hancher, Michael. "Speech Acts and the Law." *Language Use and the Uses of Language*. Ed. Roger W. Shuy and Anna Shnukal. Washington: Georgetown UP, 1976. 245–56.

Hartman, Saidiya V. *Scenes of Subjection: Terror, Slavery, and Self-Making in Nineteenth-Century America*. New York: Oxford UP, 1997.

Hawthorne, Walter. *From Africa to Brazil: Culture, Identity, and an Atlantic Slave Trade, 1600–1830*. Cambridge: Cambridge UP, 2010.

Hensley, Nathan K. "*Armadale* and the Logic of Liberalism." *Victorian Studies* 51.4 (2009): 607–32.

Howell, Wilbur Samuel. *Eighteenth-Century British Logic and Rhetoric.* Princeton: Princeton UP, 1971.

Hudson, Nicholas. "Eighteenth-Century Language Theory." *Eighteenth-Century Life* 20.3 (1996): 81–91.

Jarrett, Gene. *Representing the Race: A New Political History of African American Literature.* New York: New York UP, 2011.

Jea, John. *The Life, History, and Unparalleled Sufferings of John Jea, the African Preacher. Compiled and Written by Himself.* Portsea, England, c. 1811.

Johnstone, Abraham. *The Address of Abraham Johnstone, a Black Man, Who Was Hanged at Woodbury, in the County of Glocester, and State of New Jersey, on Saturday the the [sic] 8th Day of July Last; to the People of Colour. . . .* Philadelphia, 1797.

Jones, Anne Goodwyn. "Engendered in the South: Blood and Irony in Douglass and Jacobs." *Haunted Bodies: Gender and Southern Texts.* Ed. Anne Goodwyn Jones and Susan V. Donaldson. Charlottesville: UP of Virginia, 1997.

Kavka, Gregory S. *Hobbesian Moral and Political Theory.* Princeton: Princeton UP, 1986.

Kazanjian, David. "Mercantile Exchanges, Mercantilist Enclosures: Racial Capitalism in the Black Mariner Narratives of Venture Smith and John Jea." *CR: The New Centennial Review* 3.1 (2003): 147–78.

Kramer, Michael. *Imagining Language in America: From the Revolution to the Civil War.* Princeton: Princeton UP, 1992.

Land, Stephen K. *From Signs to Propositions: The Concept of Form in Eighteenth-Century Semantic Theory.* London: Longman, 1974.

Levecq, Christine. *Slavery and Sentiment: The Politics of Feeling in Black Atlantic Antislavery Writing, 1770–1850.* Durham: U of New Hampshire P, 2008.

Madison, James. "The Federalist No. 37." *The Federalist Papers.* Ed. Ian Shapiro. New Haven: Yale UP, 2009. 173–85.

Marrant, John. *A Narrative of the Lord's Wonderful Dealings with John Marrant, A Black.* London, 1785.

McBride, Dwight. *Impossible Witnesses: Truth, Abolitionism, and Slave Testimony.* New York: New York UP, 2001.

McGary, Howard, Jr., and Bill E. Lawson. *Between Slavery and Freedom: Philosophy and American Slavery.* Bloomington: Indiana UP, 1992.

Mills, Charles W. *The Racial Contract.* Ithaca: Cornell UP, 1997.

Montgomery, Robert. *Terms of Response: Language and Audience in Seventeenth- and Eighteenth-Century Theory.* University Park: Pennsylvania State UP, 1992.

Morris, Christopher W., ed. *The Social Contract Theorists: Critical Essays on Hobbes, Locke, and Rousseau.* Lanham: Rowman & Littlefield, 1999.

Nabokov, Vladimir. *Nikolai Gogol.* New York: New Directions Books, 1961.

Oldham, James. "Insurance Litigation Involving the Zong and Other British Slave Ships, 1780–1807." *Journal of Legal History* 28.3 (2007): 299–318.

Rezek, Joseph. "The Orations on the Abolition of the Slave Trade and the Uses of Print in the Early Black Atlantic." *Early American Literature* 45.3 (2010): 655–82.

Riss, Arthur. *Race, Slavery, and Liberalism in Nineteenth-Century American Literature.* Cambridge: Cambridge UP, 2006.

Rorty, Richard. *Contingency, Irony, and Solidarity.* Cambridge: Cambridge UP, 1989.

Rousseau, Jean-Jacques. "Discourse on the Origin and the Foundations of Inequality." *The Discourses and Other Early Political Writings.* Ed. and trans. Victor Gourevitch. Cambridge: Cambridge UP, 1997.

Saint, Chandler, and George Krimsky. *Making Freedom: The Extraordinary Life of Venture Smith.* Middletown: Wesleyan UP, 2009.

Sancho, Ignatius. *Letters of the Late Ignatius Sancho, an African.* Ed. Vincent Carretta. New York: Penguin Books, 1998.

Scott, Helen. "Was There a Time before Race? Capitalist Modernity and the Origins of Racism." *Marxism, Modernity, and Postcolonial Studies.* Ed. Crystal Bartolovich and Neil Lazarus. Cambridge: Cambridge UP, 2002. 167–82.

Searle, John R. *Speech Acts: An Essay in the Philosophy of Language.* Cambridge: Cambridge UP, 1969.

Sekora, John. "Black Message/White Envelope: Genre, Authenticity, and Authority in the Antebellum Slave Narrative." *Callaloo* 32 (Summer 1987): 482–515.

Smith, Adam. *The Theory of Moral Sentiments.* Ed. Knud Haakonssen. Cambridge: Cambridge UP, 2002.

Smith, Venture. *A Narrative of the Life and Adventures of Venture, a Native of Africa: But Resident above Sixty Years in the United States of America. Related by Himself.* New London, Conn., 1798.

Stevenson, Brenda E. *Life in Black and White: Family and Community in the Slave South.* New York: Oxford UP, 1996.

Stewart, James Brewer, ed. *Venture Smith and the Business of Slavery and Freedom.* Amherst: U of Massachusetts P, 2010.

Sweeney, Fionnghuala. "'Mask in Motion': Dialect Spaces and Class Representations in Frederick Douglass' Atlantic Rhetoric." *Monuments of the Black Atlantic: Slavery and Memory.* Ed. Joanne M. Braxton and Maria I. Diedrich. Münster, Germany: LIT, 2004. 29–43.

Thomas, Helen. *Romanticism and Slave Narratives: Transatlantic Testimonies.* Cambridge: Cambridge UP, 2000.

Van Leer, David. "Reading Slavery: The Anxiety of Ethnicity in Douglass's Narrative." *Frederick Douglass: New Literary and Historical Essays.* Ed. Eric J. Sundquist. Cambridge: Cambridge UP, 1991. 118–40.

Visconti, Jacqueline. "Speech Acts in Legal Language." *Journal of Pragmatics* 41.3 (2009): 393–400.

Walvin, James. *The Zong: A Massacre, the Law and the End of Slavery.* New Haven: Yale UP, 2011.

Webster, Jane. "The Zong in the Context of the Eighteenth-Century Slave Trade." *Journal of Legal History* 28.3 (2007): 285–98.

White, George. *A Brief Account of the Life, Experience, Travels, and Gospel Labours of George White, an African; Written by Himself, and Revised by a Friend.* New York, 1810.

Wordsworth, William, and Samuel Coleridge. *Lyrical Ballads and Related Writings.* Ed. William Richey and Daniel Robinson. Boston: Houghton Mifflin, 2002.

Wright, Michelle M. *Becoming Black: Creating Identity in the African Diaspora.* Durham: Duke UP, 2004.

Trials and Confessions of Fugitive Slave Narratives

Gretchen J. Woertendyke

FEW SLAVE conspiracies rattled nineteenth-century Americans as much as those of Denmark Vesey (1822) and Nat Turner (1831). Taking place less than a decade apart, both events saturated newspaper accounts, trial transcripts, and quasi-literary narratives, in addition to resulting in large-scale executions, deportations, and imprisonments. Yet despite their infamous status in the annals of slave historiography and local lore, the hypothetical conspiracy of Denmark Vesey in Charleston, South Carolina, and actual insurrection of Nat Turner in Southampton, Virginia, have not been considered slave narratives. Why?

Neither self-written memoirs nor dictated biographies, the writing produced in the wake of these spectacular events does not quite fit the traditional forms, tropes, and pathos of slave narratives like those of Olaudah Equiano, Frederick Douglass, or Harriet Jacobs. And yet to dismiss the major accounts of these events—Kennedy and Parker's *An Official Report of the Trials of Sundry Negroes* (1822), Hamilton's *An Account of the Late Intended Insurrection among a Portion of the Blacks of this City* (1823), and Gray's *The Confessions of Nat Turner* (1831; reprinted in Greenberg, *Confessions*), among others that resist neat generic placement—inadvertently reinforces one of the most troubling outcomes of slave narratives: the silence of the slave. That is, unlike the traditional slave narrative, fugitive slave narratives foreground mediation by white amanuenses, transcribers, officials, and readers—the voices of Denmark Vesey and Nat Turner are almost entirely silenced.

In this essay I look at the two trial "reports" of Denmark Vesey and Thomas Gray's widely distributed "confessions" of Nat Turner, in order to explore the various forms of mediation that forestall sympathy and identification with Vesey and Turner. I want to consider how generic markers of the "report" and "confession" recast the slave narrative for quite different rhetorical purposes. Unlike those of Douglass and Jacobs, the rhetorical aims of these narratives are redemptive and liberating for the white slaveholding communities rather than for black slaves.

Scholars have defined traditional slave narratives, most simply, as the "written and dictated testimonies of enslaved black human beings."[1] In their earliest instantiations, as Nicole Aljoe has shown, they were meant to reveal the life experiences of Africans for a predominantly white European readership. Bound up with abolitionist discourses circulating throughout the Atlantic world, these narratives navigate a complex range of historical, political, and affective registers. Moreover, the slave narrative could both testify to the interiority of slaves and make it possible for a slave to write oneself into being.[2] Fugitive slave narratives, however, labor to contain such agency and either minimize—or distort—the interior lives of slaves. Still a "new form cobbled together," like the slave ship, the fugitive slave narrative is most invested in the performance of white power over the black body.[3] In such narratives, what little interiority available to the reader is visible only by the degree to which racial domination is enacted and the slave is silenced. As such, fugitive slave narratives elicit sympathy for all past, and possible future, white victims of slave violence while frustrating readers' inclination to sympathize with the slave.

In part, fugitive slave narratives are able to achieve sympathy from white readers by relocating slave violence from southern plantations to the broader Atlantic world. The displaced origins of insurrection at once policed the lone renegade slave and shored up U.S. boundaries. I want to imagine the narratives of Vesey and Turner not as *failed* slave narratives, then, but as fugitive—occasional, fleeting, and ultimately banished from the region. It is in the genre's fugitive state that the nation and the hemisphere are relational; as such, slaves become inseparable from Atlantic trafficking, circum-Atlantic revolutions, and the blurred boundaries produced by Haitian refugees, miscegenation, and an increasing free-black population.

Fugitive Archives

A rich history of associations with desertion, banishment, exile, and wandering helps to account for the ways in which *fugitive* is an apt description for many forms of slave narrative. Literary references from the nineteenth century include Byron's 1820 *Blues* and an 1864 *Spectator* editorial that claimed "the greater part of periodical literature is meant to be, and ought to remain, fugitive."[4] Archives of slavery, like that of

Ian Baucom's *Zong* in *Specters of the Atlantic*, are especially fugitive—
exiled, fleeting, outside of the law—so much so, in fact, that traditional
slave narratives come to seem more exceptional than the norm against
which the fragmentary narratives of diaspora are frequently overlooked.

In their "The Constitution of Toussaint: Another Origin of African
American Literature," Michael J. Drexler and Ed White argue for a "re-
conceptualization of textual and authorial classification" when considering African American writing. Claiming for Toussaint L'Ouverture's 1801
Haitian Constitution the status of "fugitive slave narrative," Drexler
and White complicate the nation- and period-specific categories that too
often occlude the most provocative and influential "black" writing of the
diaspora.[5] Opening up the archive to include transcribed, anonymous,
multiauthored, and otherwise mediated writing invested in either suppressing or liberating black people—free and enslaved—reconfigures literary form and literary history. Neither traditional slave narrative nor
autobiography, free Vesey's and enslaved Turner's *fugitive* slave narratives provide a prehistory of a vital nineteenth-century American literary form, one that cannot be understood apart from a broader Atlantic
world.[6]

In the wake of another slave conspiracy, that of Gabriel Prosser's 1800
planned rebellion in Richmond, Virginia, the *New England Palladium*
printed the following poetic fragment by Timothy Dwight:

> Proceed great state—thy arts renew,
> With double zeal thy course pursue,
> Call on thy sister states t'obey,
> And boldly grasp at sovereign sway—
> Then pause—Remember ere too late,
> The tale of St. Domingo's fate.
> Though Gabriel dies, a host remain
> Oppress'd with slavery's galling chain,
> And soon or late the hour will come,
> Mark'd with Virginia's dreadful doom.[7]

Dwight, an early antislavery advocate, Evangelical theologian, and
former Yale University president, warned of the evils of slavery, but
such warnings, as the *New England Palladium* makes visible, could be
brought to bear on proslavery and antislavery positions alike. By refer-
encing "St. Domingo," the newspaper makes explicit the connection between the slave revolution in the Caribbean and slave revolts in the U.S.
South. At that time, the governor of Virginia, James Monroe, managed

the crisis that quickly became known as Gabriel's Rebellion. At a loss to account for the "unexampled enterprise" of the slaves, Monroe describes events with far less commentary in a letter to *The Speaker of the General Assembly* (December 5, 1800): "Strange that the slaves should embark in this novel and unexampled enterprise of their own accord. Their treatment has been more favorable since the revolution, and as the importation was prohibited among the first acts of our independence, their number has not increased in proportion with that of the Whites. It was natural to suspect they were prompted to it by others who were invisible, but whose agency might be powerful." He concludes by claiming that this "invisible" force made it "more difficult to estimate the extent of the combination and the consequent real importance of the crisis."[8] The limited documentation of Gabriel Prosser's suspected slave conspiracy establishes a few important features taken up by the later slave narratives treated here: first, the inability to comprehend any motivation for slave insurrection and, second, the belief that the origins of slave violence remain invisible and somewhere else, across the Americas. That Gabriel's Rebellion is narrated by a government official and does not publicly circulate nevertheless prefigures the more recognizable genre; it also fails to fully suppress Prosser's embedded tale. As Jeffrey Gagnon understands Briton Hammon's narrative silences as active omissions—resistance to white domination—we might read the relationship between Prosser's absence and Monroe's presence as constitutive strands of the fugitive slave narrative.[9] In Gabriel Prosser's fugitive narrative, the more formal features and thematic concerns that become standard in its later more literary form are visible even while its exclusive readership delimits its capacity to either stir or placate Virginians.

Monroe's document first registers disbelief and then performs a disavowal of southern slavery by rendering it legible only away from its local context. In *Modernity Disavowed: Haiti and the Cultures of Slavery in the Age of Revolution* (2004), Sibylle Fischer describes hemispheric reactions to the monumental events in Saint-Domingue where slavery persisted—in Cuba, Brazil, and the United States—as a process of disavowal, even amidst the more fraught debates over the future of slavery across southern states by midcentury. "While radical antislavery was a formation that did not consolidate itself territorially beyond the confines of Haiti," explains Fischer, "it certainly did leave a deep imprint on the psyches of those most involved in the slave trade and plantation economy. Fantasy, paranoia, identificatory desires, and disavowal were always a part of this formation."[10]

When read against the newspaper reports of the Prosser conspiracy, Monroe's official narrative performs both simultaneously: an explicit linkage to the events in Haiti and its implicit disavowal. For example, the *Virginia Gazette* blames the conspiracy on "the French principle of Liberty and Equality," and of contaminating "the minds of the negroes." An anonymous comment asserts that it originated with "some vile French Jacobins, [and was] aided and abetted by some of our own profligate and abandoned democrats."[11] Such dislocation means that systemic slavery— or what Elizabeth Fox-Genovese and Eugene D. Genovese have defined as "Slavery in the Abstract"—escapes scrutiny and ensures that the slave is silenced or effaced. Instead, we find images of Haitian slaves, their heads filled with French revolutionary principles, willing to kill and die for their freedom.[12] The urgent need to disassociate U.S. slavery from the southern states and project it onto the landscape of the broader hemisphere helps to account for the warped and partial portraits of Prosser, Vesey, and Turner we inherit from their nineteenth-century chroniclers. It is precisely because of their translation of history, effacement of slaves, and what we might think of as the novelization of slave violence that we are reluctant to identify these fugitive histories as slave narratives.[13]

There are, of course, legitimate reasons why the writings about Denmark Vesey and Nat Turner have not been considered a part of the slave narrative tradition. However, what if we consider the copious amounts of print surrounding these slave conspiracies a *fugitive archive,* made up of narratives out of which later slave narratives become formally coherent and against which they are most legible?[14] Such a gesture requires reading the trial transcripts of Denmark Vesey and "Confessions" of Nat Turner, and responses found in newspapers and official documents, not only for how slave conspiracies participate in both proslavery and abolitionist discourses in the antebellum period, but also for how slave narratives can complicate readers' ability to sympathize with the slave. While ostensibly produced for competing aims—to justify the executions of Vesey and Turner on the one hand and to illustrate the humanity of the slave on the other—both fugitive and traditional slave narratives depend upon collective beliefs about freedom and imprisonment and locate meaning not in slavery in the abstract, but in one slave in particular.

Sympathy, Silence, and Mediation

We have come to expect certain tropes, scenes, plots, and narrative sequences from slave narratives, the result in part from reading those of Frederick Douglass and Harriet Jacobs back onto previous forms. One of these, Philip Gould identifies, is the assertion of economic value through slave exchange in public, particularly as such scenes allow for sympathetic identification with the family, especially by northern white women. Gould highlights a very "particular narrative sequence: first, the capitalist exchange of money for human beings, and then the sentimental exchange of feelings among family members experiencing loss, one to which the reader's feelings succumb as well."[15] A similar exercise in analysis of the economic and exchange value of the Vesey and Turner cases suggest the danger in inflating a slave's worth, especially when that worth is, in some measure, the result of his intellectual capacity. Both Vesey and Turner were thought of as exceptionally intelligent and charismatic leaders who had, in many regards, earned the respect of their communities, including its white citizens.

When we compare traditionally understood slave narratives and fugitive slave narratives, it becomes clear that Vesey and Turner are the precondition for *white* redemption, rather than the objects of recovery, growth, or emancipation. While in the "experience narrative" of Juan Antonio a slave's identity is figured from "contestation, negotiation, and collaboration," the fugitive slave narrative's performance of white domination is nearly exclusive.[16] Even if we understand Turner's confession as collaborative, the negotiation of his story and Thomas Gray's remains a product of white mediation and white reception.

The Vesey archive is rich and deep, yielding two widely circulated narratives of the Denmark Vesey conspiracy in 1822—*An Account* and *An Official Report*—along with newspaper articles, editorials, personal correspondence, separate and confidential witness testimony, and internal government documents.[17] In addition to controversies found in the historical archive, the Vesey conspiracy has generated heated debate in contemporary scholarship.[18] Although the precise date and place of his birth is not known, Denmark Vesey was thought to have been born around 1767 in the place where Captain Joseph Vesey purchased him—in either Saint Thomas or Saint-Domingue—part of Denmark's West Indian empire.[19] Denmark Vesey's purchase entered the historical record when Charleston-based Vesey came over looking for slaves to buy and sell in 1781. Before returning to Charleston, Vesey sold Denmark along with his cargo of slaves to planters in Le Cap, a city of about fifty thousand people, in Saint-Domingue. Shortly after Vesey was sold, however, his new owner diagnosed him as "unsound, and subject to epileptic fits."[20] When Joseph Vesey returned to Saint-Domingue later that year, he repossessed Denmark, not wanting to taint his name with the reputation of selling "damaged goods." After a period of sailing for many years, a time when, as Edward A. Pearson argues, Denmark's radical political consciousness was probably fostered, Joseph Vesey returned to Charleston in 1790. Here, Denmark hired himself out as a carpenter, making $1.50 per day and establishing a reputation as a man of "great strength and activity."[21] This allowed him an uncommon degree of mobility and independence, so much so that he bought a $6 lottery ticket in 1799. Denmark Vesey won $1,500 on November 9 of that year, affording him the opportunity to purchase his own freedom, which he did for $600—"much less than his real value"—on the last day of December 1799.[22]

The trial record of Denmark Vesey, and the ninety-one other free and enslaved black men who stood trial in the summer of 1822, provides interesting glimpses into how the white community perceived the character, plans, and faith of the "blood-thirsty" man accused of planning the insurrection. The absence of Vesey's own words (he is always only interpolated through witnesses) provides the most obvious departure from traditional slave narratives; but there is almost no resemblance to neo-slave narratives either (unless we read Vesey's silence as eloquent, much like Babo's head defiantly staring from its stake in Herman Melville's *Benito Cereno*). The first narrative is *An Account of the Late Intended Insurrection Among A Portion of the Blacks of This City*, written by James Hamilton Jr., who "served as an officer during the War of 1812 before purchasing several cotton plantations on the Sea Islands."[23] Hamilton was charged with municipal safety in Charleston, commanding a small force of about one hundred men aided by a number of constables from each ward to keep the peace. Hamilton was the first person on the scene of the investigation into the insurrection conspiracy and entered national politics in the wake of the Vesey trials, completing the term of low-country politician William Lowndes in the U.S. House of Representatives, and after which he became governor of the state in 1830.

Hamilton was also the first to construct a highly complex narrative of the conspiracy, so complicated in fact, that Governor Bennett nearly laughed at its implausibility. Hamilton's portrait of Vesey, however, fits an emerging composite of black communities across southern states, particularly those in which free black men existed. Vesey's access to the white community as a free black man and his role as class leader in the African Methodist Episcopal Church convinced Hamilton of his powerful oratorical skills. The AME Church—established in 1816 by disaffected black Charlestonians who had found their funds and freedom restricted by their parent affiliation with the white-dominated Methodist

Church—became "the most important institution" for the black community. Vesey's role in the already oppositional church provided Hamilton with a prehistory, one in which Vesey's conspiratorial plans would be perceived as inevitable.

Both narratives attribute the seeds of resistance to Vesey's time at the AME, but the solidarity between Vesey and his co-conspirators as described in *An Account* and *An Official Report* was not primarily religious. Instead, Hamilton framed the conspiracy by political, social, and, ultimately, transnational concerns. Vesey's experience in Le Cap just prior to and at the onset of slave uprisings in Saint-Domingue and his sea travels where he learned to read, write, and speak other languages seemed to set him apart from other insurrectionary leaders. As a result, Hamilton presents Vesey as a powerful, articulate, and intelligent man capable of galvanizing hundreds of people. But it was his connection to Haiti, real and imaginary, that proved the most threatening element of his conspiracy and helps to explain the narrative gaps in both written accounts that were feverishly consumed across South Carolina.

Hamilton's preface shares qualities with Thomas Gray's preface to *The Confessions of Nat Turner:*

> To The Public.
> In complying with the objects of the above Resolution, I have not been insensible to the difficulties and embarrassments necessarily incident to the subject, as to what it might be politic either to publish or suppress. With the advice, however, of the Corporation, I have deemed a full publication of the prominent circumstances of the late commotion, as the most judicious course, as suppression might assume the appearance of timidity or injustice. Whilst such a statement is due to the character of our community, and justification of our laws, there can be no harm in the salutary inculcation of one lesson, among a certain portion of our population, that there is nothing they are bad enough to do, that we are not powerful enough to punish.[24]

Hamilton is keenly aware of how "politic" his narrative is. While recognizing public fear he never succumbs to it, instead emphasizing the collective white community and character as signs of legitimate domination. As a symbolic gesture of power, Hamilton, like Monroe before him, stages authority through narration, writing an a priori account of the conspiracy's future failure. Vesey's insurrection never happened but remains one of the most controversial and enduring images of slave violence in American historiography.

While Hamilton's account of the conspiracy is shaped by the religious sermon and popular tale, Kennedy and Parker's *Official Report* is framed as a transcription. Adorning itself in the legal language of a courtroom, the much more widely circulated "report" is openly didactic in its attempt to justify the death and expulsion of a large portion of Charleston's black community. In late October of 1822, they submitted to the public, "at the request of the court," what was meant as a corrective to James Hamilton's account of the insurrection—billed as "more authentic."[25] It is, they claim, presented to the public in order to comply with an act of Congress: "for the encouragement of learning, by securing the copies of maps, charts, and books, to the authors and proprietors of such copies, during the times therein mentioned"; and the supplementary act, "extending the benefits thereof to the arts of designing, engraving, and etching historical and other prints."[26] If we understand Hamilton's twenty-five-cent *Account* as popular, sensational fiction, Kennedy and Parker's *Official Report* more closely corresponds to formal realism: framed as an "authentic report of human experience," its referential language and sequential plotting of events provide an alternative to sensationalism.[27] Compelled by cartographic design, the *Official Report* counterbalances the emotionalism of the *Account* and maps the management of slaves onto the borders and possibilities of U.S territory.

Kennedy and Parker take great pains to illustrate fairness in sentencing by listing the fundamental rights of the defendants, but two important procedural facts remain conspicuously absent in their preamble: first, that 96 percent of all testimony in the trials was given in secret, and second, that the court used three "superstar" witnesses who provided 75 percent of testimony while three other men provided 20 percent—and all were arrested slaves with their lives at stake. Kennedy and Parker cite a case in Antigua, 1736, and in New York, 1741, where slaves had been indicted for conspiracy to insurrection entirely in private, a precedent provided as evidence of the objectivity and formality of legal proceedings against Denmark Vesey and his co-conspirators. That these slave insurrections occurred almost a century earlier, in distant locations, is not factored into their assessment.

Vesey's knowledge and manipulation of "the Scriptures," which he could "readily quote to [slaves] to prove that slavery was contrary to the laws of God," is meant to substantiate his ability to read, interpret, and communicate his message over and beyond the comprehension of the white community. Finally, they argue that such facility with biblical, political, and idiosyncratic regional discourses gave Vesey "incredible influence among persons of color" and conclude that "many feared him more than their owners, and one of them declared, even more than his God."[28]

All those accused are silent in the *Official Report:* "of the thirty-five men eventually hanged, twenty-four remained mute" while the rest were exiled from the United States.[29] Like the report itself, which was burned or hidden from slaves, Vesey's words were thought influential enough to create revolutionary impulses upon reading. And his absence allows the justices to construct Vesey to fit their own narrative designs: the plot Parker and Kennedy create is not that of Vesey and his conspirators but is the counternarrative of the white community. Its importance rests in its ability to reassure the white community of its dominance, and it is only one of the countless ways in which domination is performed and reenacted. The spectacle of a courtroom drama, which culminated in the executions and deportations of Vesey and his peers, terrorized the black population as well.

Two notable instances of dissent from the Court's ruling, one public and one private, suggest the strength and force of Vesey's narratives across white communities in the southern states. A public critique came in an article in the *Charleston Courier,* just two days after the court launched its initial sessions. One of South Carolina's most respected justices and member of United State Supreme Court since 1804, William Johnson Jr. published "Melancholy Effect of Popular Excitement," describing a slave insurrection scare in Georgia that occurred in 1810. In it, he detailed the rumors of conspiracy, which led to the capture of a "single poor half-witted negro . . . crossing a field on his way home, without instrument of war."[30]

In order to appease the community, he writes, a "hastily convened Court of Magistrates and Freeholders"—one quite similar to the court that convicted and executed Denmark Vesey—also convicts and hangs the accused slave. Johnson concludes his brief history of another slave conspiracy: "contained an useful moral, and might check the causes of agitation which were then operating upon the public mind" in Charleston.[31] But rather than provide a check to balance the passions and swift actions of the Vesey Court, Johnson's public criticism produced an outcry.[32] In its formal announcement of the executions, the court publicly criticized Johnson for claiming the court "capable of committing perjury and murder" and further, for implying that he "possessed sounder judgment, deeper penetration, and firmer nerves, than the rest of his fellow citizens." The notice concludes that the court's own "purity of motives" remains intact, and any suspicion otherwise reflects a lack of integrity on the part of the accuser (and readers).[33]

The second instance of dissent from the court reveals the chronology of events with more clarity (obfuscated by *An Official Report*) and the extent to which the Vesey conspiracy became for early nineteenth-century South Carolinians what the Salem Witch Trials were for seventeenth-century Massachusetts residents. Governor Thomas Bennett had been a member of the state legislature in South Carolina since 1804, was Speaker of the House from 1814 to 1817, and was just finishing out his gubernatorial term in the summer of 1822.[34] In Bennett's *Letter to the General Assembly*, he argues that as governor he took the appropriate steps necessary for repressing the rumored insurrection by establishing a strong militia, after which the "utmost tranquility prevailed."[35] But attentive to the effects of these rumors, as "the public mind was excessively agitated," he did not immediately issue a warning to "give alarms in cases of an extraordinary character." Since the City Council of Charleston was keenly interested in the outcome, Bennett advises that a "Court of Investigation" convene an ad-hoc body of white freeman of some stature in the city that would precede the official trial. However, Bennett notes that in just a few days, the city created a "Court of alternate jurisdiction . . . in every sense . . . an usurpation of authority, and a violation of the Law." He criticizes the court for relying on testimony clearly given by accused slaves "for the purpose of self-preservation" and for not allowing the accused to face their accusers. Most of all, Bennett accuses the court of "illegal" executions and deportations.

What makes Bennett's letter unique is his conception of insurrection generally and of Denmark Vesey in particular. His letter describes a conspiracy plan that was unorganized and therefore never a threat; depicts Vesey, rather than a figure of great rhetorical powers, as an unremarkable character; and argues that slaves traditionally show loyalty to their owners, rather than each other, proven by the few who stepped forward to reveal the plan in the first place. Bennett concludes that "successful rebellions cannot occur in this state," and that "the liberal and enlightened humanity of our Fellow-Citizens produce many attachments, which operate as tricks on the spirit of insubordination." In this single document, Bennett both undermines the potential threat of Vesey's insurrection (and all insurrections) and reverses the characterization of its white and black figures. Rather than the black trickster figure whose unseen manipulations threaten every fiber of the community, an enlightened humanity, the white citizens of South Carolina, become tricksters suppressing any insubordination among its slaves. Conspicuous in Bennett's letter is the absence of any reference to Saint-Domingue. This absence is especially noticeable when compared with all the other documents circulating around the events. In these, Saint-Domingue establishes the degree and implications of the potential for violence in Charleston. If we agree with Johnson's and Bennett's assessment that the "court of alternate jurisdiction" acted preemptively by executing Vesey and his four slave compatriots on July 2, in an attempt not only to purge community fear but to establish without a doubt—in the absence of any material evidence—that the Vesey Conspiracy did exist, then Saint-Domingue and Vesey's hypothetical ties to it provide evidence, motive, and warning of future slave revolts simultaneously. The Atlantic revolutionary conflict functions as a specter, a versatile symbol working on multiple levels to instantiate the policies and practices of the white community, while continuing to dominate over its black population.

What becomes clear is how important Hamilton's *Account of the Late Intended Insurrection* and Kennedy and Parker's *Official Report* are for the circulation of images and ideas about Denmark Vesey and slave resistance more broadly. His rumored connections to Saint-Domingue and the complete erasure of his speech, especially, make visible the importance of fugitive slave narratives not only for their historical moment, but also as testimony for the future of slavery in the United States. The silence at the center of Vesey's fugitive slave narrative has critically compromised its place among more traditional forms of slave narration; however, what if we understood Vesey's silence, like Britton Hammon's, as defiant, a willful performance of resistance to—and rejection of—the court's theatrical display of state power and the false testimonies of his frightened cohorts? Such a reading would situate Vesey's narrative as a precursor to the assertion of voice in the narratives of Frederick Douglass and Harriet Jacobs. The narrative "confession" of Nat Turner goes some way toward filling this silence. Turner's defiance of slavery echoes still differently, as his voice is intertwined with the amanuensis, Thomas Gray. This multivocal narrative borrows from various literary genres in order to mediate the violence of his rebellion.

Gothic Confessions

What we know of Nat Turner is very little: we know that he was part of a slave insurrection that began with the killing of his owner, Joseph Travis, Travis's wife, and their child; that in the following twenty-four hours the approximately six original insurgents were joined by nearly forty more; and that between sixty and seventy whites of the Southampton community in Virginia were murdered. We also know that every insurgent was killed by local vigilante gangs, militia, and even federal troops; that an additional hundred or so blacks were killed; and that Nat Turner remained at large for over two months after the revolt, finally being captured on October 30, 1831. Beyond these details, his slave revolt becomes an extremely complex performance of authority, fear, domination, and repression by various actors, including Turner, his amanuensis, and the broader white community for whom the "confession" was intended. Thomas R. Gray, an elderly lawyer and owner of thirty-three slaves, clearly had "an eye for a good thing."[36] Within two weeks after Nat Turner's execution on November 11, 1831, some forty thousand copies of the *Confessions* were published and distributed by Gray, who claimed to "transcribe" Turner's confession "with little or no variation, from his own words."[37]

Denmark Vesey can be seen as an important link between the noncirculating government documents on Gabriel Prosser and the highly mediated, sensationalistic "confessions." For "Vesey's Conspiracy" proved that narrative accounts, no matter their basis in truth or law, could play a role in keeping the white population vigilant while maintaining broad support for the weakening institution. Fugitive slave narratives worked to convince those with ambivalent positions that only severe punishment and exile might dissuade other slaves from similar plans of revolution.

In the nine years following Vesey's conspiracy, some important events had taken place, heightening the panic that was beginning to grip the South. Perhaps most responsible for intensifying the alarm was the circulation of *Walker's Appeal* by David Walker in 1829.[38] No prior black writing in the United States equaled its rhetorical power or reach; in it, Walker spoke directly to slaves and free black men, demanding not only their reflection on the condition of slavery but also their participation in radical abolitionism. Walker argued, "it is no more harm for you to kill a man, who is trying to kill you, than it is for you to take a drink of water when thirsty."[39] The resulting responses to *Walker's Appeal* were passionate and contagious, especially throughout the southern states. For example, a Virginia bill was introduced in 1830, outlawing seditious writing and pronouncing that meetings of "free negroes" for purposes of literacy instruction would be punished. Similar legislation was introduced and put into law in Georgia, Louisiana, North Carolina, and Mississippi—extending the ways in which sedition was applied to the native population from the Alien and Sedition Acts of 1798.

What links *Walker's Appeal* to the *Confessions*, and distinguishes both of them from Vesey's fugitive narrative, is the explicitness and ferocity of the rhetoric, even if mediated by Turner's interlocutor, Thomas Gray. The increasing surveillance of materials related to slave rebellion helps to explain the gradual move from historical accounts of slave conspiracy to the much more literary account of Nat Turner. The fictionality of the literary confession, an Old World genre, allows for a highly mediated historical account of New World slave violence. Nevertheless, the generic contract implied by the "confession" carries with it a set of codes and signs meant to authenticate the experience of Turner and thus make official Thomas Gray's document. Reading *The Confessions of Nat Turner* today, however, I am struck by its unique blend of realism and horror, idealism and violence, slavery and liberation. The "blend" of generic features and effects, which Horace Walpole used to differentiate romance from history in his preface to *The Castle of Otranto*, underscores its mixed-generic register. The awkward editorial frame of Turner's confession, replete with spectacular collective violence, ambivalent politics, and deep anxiety about the future of the nation, draws upon the gothic romance, a genre already racially coded across the U.S. South and the American hemisphere. In conjoining features of gothic romance and confession, Gray authorizes romance through the gravitas of a confessional history and also imbues its formality with a sense of play, of possibility, and of uncertainty romance-as-form makes available.

Gothic romance is frequently defined more by what it is not than what it is. The explosion of gothic novels in 1790s Britain is critically considered collateral damage from the French Revolution, that is, they "fed off the revolutionary anxieties of its readership."[40] Its contemporary critics linked the genre to low cultural (or political) allegiances, considering gothic romances and "terror tales" thinly disguised platforms for Jacobin Terror. Such literary forms appealed to the lowest social strata, such as semiliterate mobs or women.

The early American genre, on the other hand, is more overtly counter-revolutionary working to discipline more radical energies and forms (such as the "confession"). Rather than situate its story in the past as a way of commenting on a present political moment, the early American gothic, lacking any substantive past out of which to critique its present crises, depends upon an uncertain future, threatened most immediately by institutional slavery and the free and enslaved blacks poised to topple its structure. Unable or unwilling to recognize the influence of democratic principles on its black population, and terrified of the host of unknown but certainly radical agents poised to cross over the nation's borders, Haiti provides a geographic, political, and ultimately imaginative space onto which early American fears are projected. This alternative philosophy of history, one invested in futurity rather than an historical past, emergent in the early American gothic romance helps account for what Robert Miles calls "the first law of genre: to deviate and make it new."[41]

Among the fugitive slave narratives I treat, only *The Confessions of Nat Turner* does so, deviates, clothed in the garb of a different genre, the Romantic "confession." So while writers such as Charles Brockden Brown and Blackwood's *Edinburgh Magazine* writer, John Howison, yoke Saint-Domingue to the gothic earlier in the century, the different rhetorical needs of the ostensibly authentic *Confessions* function like a Jamesonian "ideologeme": its traces of a past form lie embedded in its anticipations of a new, unstable, and unknown future. When Gray writes in his prefatory remarks to the *Confessions* that "It will thus appear, that whilst every thing upon the surface of society wore a calm and peaceful aspect; whilst not one note of preparation was heard to warn the devoted inhabitants of woe and death, a gloomy fanatic was revolving in the recesses of his own dark, bewildered, and overwrought mind, schemes of indiscriminate massacre to the whites," the generic tension between the "calm surface" of society and the unseen machinations of "a gloomy fanatic" comes to the fore, demanding that readers—like all those "devoted inhabitants" unprepared for slave rebellion—are keenly attentive.[42]

Initially, then, Gray's narrative frame compels us to look for conventions of the British Romantic form. Rousseau's *Confessions* (1782, 1789) ushered into modernity a kind of intimacy simultaneously embarrassing and thrilling to its readers. The confession as a genre discloses what Peter Brooks identifies as "hidden acts and thought in a form that reveals—[or] creates—the inwardness of the person confessing," which allows for the possibility of his "punishment, absolution, rehabilitation, [and] reintegration."[43] But "confession" as representation of hidden acts and thoughts makes it fertile ground for imaginative, often parodic, revision. In 1821, *London Magazine,* widely read in America throughout the nineteenth century, published Thomas De Quincey's *Confessions of an English Opium-Eater,* and later that year, Charles Lamb published his *Confessions of a Drunkard* under the pen name Elia. The tendency toward more and more intimate revelations in these texts occasioned the send-up confessional rhetoric. Henry Thomson (under the pseudonym "Thomas Ticklepitcher") took aim at De Quincey and Lamb in particular in his

Confessions of a Footman, published in *Blackwoods* in 1823. Thomson writes, "SEEING that the world, through the medium of the Press, is rapidly becoming acquainted with the miseries of all classes; that drunkards, hypochondriacs, water-drinkers, and opium-chewers, are alike received with sympathy and commiseration; I take leave shortly to address you upon the grievances of footmen; a set of men, I do believe, more universally persecuted than any other body of artists within his Majesty's dominions."[44] If Western cultures since Rousseau's *Confessions* "[have] made confessional speech a prime mark of authenticity," then the playfulness of Thomson's *Confessions of a Footman* ridicules the seriousness of such revelatory documents.[45] It also highlights that by 1823, the original function of the "confession" was already compromised: as parody, the genre begins to deviate, to make new. Once the Romantic "confession" appears as Blackwoodian satire, contemporary readers clearly understood its revelatory function.

The strains of using the Romantic form to narrate the violence of Nat Turner are immediately visible on the title page. In the opening authenticating "Seal" submitted to the District of Columbia Clerk, Gray describes, "the leader of the late insurrection . . . fully and voluntarily" offering his "confession" from "the prison where he was confined."[46] Readers' access to the "full" story and to Turner, however, is rendered both feeble and threatening as result of Gray's influence and the reminder of Turner's threat to society. Brooks's reading of the legal rhetoric of moral discipline makes "confession of a wrong doing . . . fundamental to morality because it constitutes a verbal act of self-recognition" or is the sole "release from interrogation."[47] Turner's *Confessions* is a remarkable instance of interiority, but it is novelistic insofar as the narrative compels us to read for the resolution of the plot, even for revenge. Turner's moral cleansing does not quite account for Thomas Gray's frame, but rather functions to discipline the leader and the impact his stray words might have on future insurrectionary schemes. Unlike the accounts of Vesey's conspiracy in which his voice is fully suppressed, Turner's confession clearly required vigilant policing of language and narrative voice.

Nat Turner's guilt was already known; moreover, absolution and reparation were undesirable—what cultural work, then, does Gray/Turner's confessional form perform? The multivocal confession draws attention to white victims and the broader slaveholding South, while it stands as a legal justification for Turner's execution aimed at Gray's popular readership. The opening of the *Confessions* presents an official "Seal"—indicating by the clerk of the district that the submission of Turner's account, as transcribed by Gray, is a "true copy" and was used as "testimony" in the trial of Nat Turner. Turner's *Confessions* acts as "testimony" or evidence of his guilt as the leader of the rebellion, as a sensational story of slave violence given as a firsthand account for an anxious public, and to secure Gray's copyright of Turner's narrative. It participates in competing public discourses—legal, literary, and commercial. Gray was well aware of the conditions of production, the demand for sensationalism in the guise of truth, and was prepared to make a significant sum from what he called "the fearful tragedy." In his introductory remarks, for example, Gray claims that the insurrection "greatly excited the public mind, and led to a thousand idle, exaggerated and mischievous reports," but immediately points to the "atrocious circumstances of cruelty and destruction, as could not fail to leave a deep impression, not only upon the minds of the community where this fearful tragedy was wrought, but throughout every portion of our country, in which this population is to be found."[48] Gray highlights his main rhetorical purpose for the circulation of the text—to instruct the public in the art of "proper" interpretation, as a corrective to excitement, idleness, and mischievousness—in the recognizable mode of confession. At the same time, however, he plays on the heightened state of anxiety in the white local communities across the South, the very same anxiety his opening remarks claim to undermine. These "atrocious" acts of "cruelty and destruction," and the vivid images of bloody white corpses, echo Bryan Edwards's popular 1797 travel narrative, *An Historical Survey of the French Colony in the Island of St. Domingo*, in which the most sensational scenes of violence appeared. This gesture of sensationalism marks one of the many tensions of Gray's narrative, one that asks to be understood as historical truth, adorned with sentiment and vivid imagery. In its sensationalism and political ambivalence *The Confessions of Nat Turner* can be fruitfully read as gothic.

Stephen Browne has argued that "to read *The Confessions* is in fact to read two texts at once, the one locating itself within a scriptural rationale for holy wrath, the other staking its claim to an emergent logic of free will and the perversities to which that will is subject."[49] He concludes that the text "sustains in uneasy and dramatic tension competing modes of understanding the source, nature, and meaning of violence."[50] To be sure, Browne's assertion that violence is at the center of the *Confessions* is undeniable; reading it today, one is struck by the horror film quality of its gore. Turner describes the axe murders as taking place by "repeated blows to the head" and the killing of a woman by nearly "sever[ing] her head from her body"; of another victim he boasts that "after repeated blows with a sword, I killed her by a blow on the head, with a fence rail."[51] In between these moments of graphic violence, Turner describes the victims' attempts to escape death, with little affect, calmly and dispassionately.

> We started from there for Mrs. Reese's, maintaining the most perfect silence on our march, where finding the door unlocked, we entered, and murdered Mrs. Reese in her bed, while sleeping; her son awoke, but it was only to sleep the sleep of death, he had only time to say who is that, and he was no more. From Mrs. Reese's we went to Mrs. Turner's, a mile distance, which we reached about sunrise, on Monday morning. Henry, Austin, and Sam, went to the still, where, finding Mr. Peebles, Austin shot him, and the rest of us went to the house; as we approached, the family discovered us, and shut the door. *Vain hope!* Will, with one stroke of his axe, opened it, and we entered and found Mrs. Turner and Mrs. Newsome in the middle of a room, almost frightened to death. Will immediately killed Mrs. Turner, with one blow of his axe. I took Mrs. Newsome by the hand, and with the sword I had when I was apprehended, I struck her several blows over the head, but not being able to kill her, as the sword was dull. Will turning around and discovering it, dispatched *her* also.[52]

There are some striking aspects of this passage: the calm silence of the rebels as they move from house to house, the use of victim's surnames, the defiance in claiming "Vain hope!" and, perhaps most startlingly, the intimacy suggested when Turner takes the hand of his victim before beating her with a dull sword. The mix of familiar and strange, the horror and dispassion, and the methodical manner in which events unfold for the reader do not in themselves, however, make the *Confessions* gothic. Gothic romance registers more in the generic mixing of Gray's interpretive frame (the confession) and Turner's spectacle of violence. The portrait of Nat Turner we find in the *Confessions* is not sympathetic, but frightening and alienating. It is not the inner "hidden truths and acts" of Turner that excite feelings in readers, but the unification of a white readership out of racial violence, made possible by Thomas Gray's interpretation and publication.

The description of Turner in Gray's conclusion illustrates his own vacillation between admiration and repulsion. He writes, "[it] is notorious, that he was never known to have a dollar in his life; to swear an oath, or drink a drop of spirits. As to his ignorance, he certainly never had the advantages of education, but he can read and write, (it was taught him by his parents,) and his natural intelligence and quickness of apprehension, is surpassed by few men I have ever seen."[53] Similarly, Gray's description of Turner as a good Christian complicates his status as a "gloomy fanatic." Rather than understanding Turner as a "trickster" figure, however, Gray locates Turner's deviance in his family line, grounded in nineteenth-century theories of scientific racism, rather than in any critique (or recognition) of systemic violence inherent to the institution. Turner's mother in particular "warped and perverted" his impressions, raising him to believe, for example, that "[he] surely would be a prophet, as the Lord had shewn [him] things that had happened before [his] birth."[54] Turner concludes: "I was intended for some great purpose."[55] Believing that he was put on earth to fight against slavery, Nat Turner became an important precursor to later abolitionists, such as John Brown, who thought his example a sign of God's will. Like the hero of Brockden Brown's *Wieland; Or the Transformation: An American Tale* (1798), Turner misreads the signs, "perverts" piety into fanaticism, and reveals the potential destructiveness of religion in the absence of tempering reason. If we understand Turner's fugitive text as an expression of unwieldy religious "enthusiasm," then Gray's text becomes an attempt to elucidate the obscurity of Turner's narrative through reason, even while he relies on romance and the spectacular to elicit sympathy for the white community of Southampton.

Despite claiming that he "shall not attempt to describe the effect of [Turner's] narrative," Gray draws a vivid portrait of Turner and of what he experienced in his presence: "The calm, deliberate composure with which he spoke of his late deeds and intentions, the expression of his fiend-like face when excited by enthusiasm, still bearing the stains of the blood of helpless innocence about him; clothed with rags and covered with chains; yet daring to raise his manacled hands to heaven, with a spirit soaring above the attributes of man; I looked on him and my blood curdled in my veins."[56] But Gray's description brings about a role reversal: Turner reflects a "calm" and "deliberate composure" while Gray sees only a "fiend" and "stains of blood." This switch elicits anxiety through its unsettling disorientation and contrast between Turner and his amanuensis. Turner's oral account to Gray is like a site of affective transmission, while Gray's description of his own reaction seems to model how the reader of *Confessions* should be similarly moved by the text, productive of yet another dynamic affective transfer. The tension between enlightenment and romance is precisely what suggests the *Confessions* is a part of the gothic romance tradition; as a narrative of slave insurrection, not just conspiracy but actual violence, the *Confessions* becomes a decisive text in a burgeoning, national tale linking blackness, fear, mystery, violence, and representation.

An important marker of its place within literary history is the sheer quantity and passion of the commentary it generated, allowing for various forms of disclosure and critique otherwise absent from the public discourse of Denmark Vesey's conspiracy. I want to briefly cover a few of the more trenchant responses to the insurrection as reported by the press, particularly the hysteria unfolding in communities across Virginia. A prominent Richmond paper that published the first article about the insurrection also wrote: "It is with pain we speak of another feature of the Southampton Rebellion. . . . We allude to the slaughter of many blacks, without trial, and under circumstances of great barbarity. How many have thus been put into death (generally by decapitation or shooting) reports vary; probably however some five and twenty and from that to 40; possibly a yet larger number."[57] The piece concludes menacingly: "Let the fact not be doubted by those whom it most concerns, that another such insurrection will be the signal for the extermination of the whole black population in the quarter of the state where it occurs." This self-conscious analysis and ambiguous warning was picked up and widely circulated by northern newspapers in Boston and New York.

Among the array of newspaper pieces associated with the *Confessions* is one entitled "Gabriel's Defeat" published in the *Richmond Enquirer,* October 21, 1831. In it, the writer is responding to an article of the same title published in the *Albany Evening Journal,* which "attempt[s] . . . to palm off such gross misrepresentations upon the public mind.—It is a silly romance from beginning to end."[58] The article spends a few pages refuting errors in the facts of Gabriel's 1800 rebellion and uses James Monroe's letter as its evidence. Of particular importance is the New York paper's assertion that Gabriel intended to sail to "St. Domingo": "a little African came into a grocery store in Richmond, and asked for a quart of rum—The grocer asked him for whom he wanted it—He said for his uncle Gabriel. The grocer asked the boy where his uncle Gabriel was. He replied in the Sally Ann, a vessel at the dock, just ready to sail for St. Domingo. . . . All romance!"[59] Although it seems an incidental reference in a peripheral notice, it was published during the height of panic and suspicion. Nat Turner's insurrection may not have been isolated, rumors suggest, but rather a piece in a larger conspiracy to overthrow slavery. In this context, even if only a "silly romance," the link between Gabriel's rebellion and "St. Domingo" raises the specter of slave violence on a mass scale and repositions it in relation to Nat Turner's insurrection. It also highlights the resilience of an imagined "St. Domingo" in its travels from an earlier insurrection to the present one, from southern states to northern newspapers and back to Virginia where, despite its recognizably fictional status, it nevertheless provides a familiar context for Virginians and other southerners in 1831. Perhaps it is no coincidence that Gabriel's (and by association, Turner's) connection to Haiti is described as a "romance"—a conjectural narrative in which past, present, and future are collapsed.

In his abolitionist paper the *Liberator,* William Lloyd Garrison spells out what had been haunting all press coverage of Nat Turner's rebellion. He writes: "What we have long predicted,—at the peril of being stigmatized as an alarmist and declaimer,—has commenced its fulfillment. . . . The first drops of blood, which are but the prelude to a deluge from the gathering clouds, have fallen." Garrison continues,

> Ye accuse the pacific friends of emancipation of instigating the slaves to revolt. . . . The slaves need no incentive at our hands. They will find in their stripes—in their emaciated bodies—in their ceaseless toil—in their ignorant minds—in every field, in every valley, on every hill top and mountain, wherever you and your fathers have fought for liberty—in your speeches and conversations, your celebrations, your pamphlets, your newspapers—voices in the air, sounds from across the ocean, invitations to resistance above, below, around them! What more do they need? [I]s it wonderful that they should rise to contend—as other "heroes" have contended—for their lost rights?[60]

Garrison makes visible the hidden subtext of all print taken up by the insurrection of Nat Turner—southern slaveholders in particular displace blame and anxiety for slave violence onto a foreign other, rather than recognize the local conditions out of which violent resistance emerges. At the same time, however, Garrison highlights the revolutionary and liberatory rhetoric circulating across the Atlantic since the 1790s. He points out the many heroes of revolutionary violence and is sufficiently abstract in his evocation to suggest a hero like Touissant L'Ouverture as much as George Washington, both contenders "for their lost rights."

William Wells Brown surely had Nat Turner in mind when he asked, "Who knows but that a Toussaint, a Christophe, a Rigaud, a Clervaux, and a Dessalines, may some day appear in the Southern States of this Union?" in his 1855 essay "The History of the Haitian Revolution."[61] The figure of Turner as a hero participates in the historiography of a nation terrified of the consequences of its own violent oppression. Throughout the many apparitions of a revolutionary slave in print culture across the nineteenth century, the Haitian Revolution was always available as the worst yet unavoidable association. Thus, while Gray's *The Confessions of Nat Turner* never mentions Saint-Domingue or its possibility in the United States, the specter of Haiti overdetermines the ways in which Turner's spectacular violence was interpreted, reproduced, and circulated throughout the nineteenth century.

In Philip Gould's interpretation of William Wells Brown's *Clotel; or The President's Daughter: A Narrative of Slave Life in the United States* (1853), he writes: "Even this brief reading of one anti-slavery novel begins to suggest the literary value that anti-slavery writing procured from its critique of slavery as an economic institution."[62] Linking literary value to the economic value of slavery for white plantation owners, Gould's analysis offers a useful grid against which fugitive slave narratives might be understood. The narratives of Gabriel Prosser, Denmark Vesey, and Nat Turner can be read as vehicles for proslavery discourse even while the fugitive narratives of the silenced or transcribed leader mitigates the extent to which readers would understand this. The narratives avoid such analyses in favor of tales of sensibility, repression, and seduction: the human cost is shifted away from that of the slave onto the innocent victims—real and imagined—in the white slaveholding community. The white man figuratively stands on the auction block, the horror of such a reversal played out in all of its macabre details for white readers at the height of debates over the future of slavery in the United States.

Displacing the rhetorical ground from the effects of ceasing the Atlantic Slave Trade to the immediate and very local sites of slave resistance, the fugitive slave narrative borrows from gothic and popular literary forms in order to make anti-abolitionist arguments most vivid. Perhaps the most compelling reason to understand these fugitive slave narratives within the tradition of antislavery narratives is the position of the conspiratorial slave around which each of the stories pivot. Without the figure of a particular slave, the disciplinary function of fugitive slave narratives would be far less effective. The regulation of slavery relies upon widespread belief that slave violence is aberrant and foreign, a belief that depends upon a single slave. At the core of Gabriel's Rebellion, Vesey's conspiracy, and Nat Turner's revolt, is that slave.

Notes

1. Davis and Gates, *Slave's Narrative*, iv.
2. Bland, *Voices*, 4.
3. See the introduction to this book for Nicole Aljoe's description of slave narratives as a "form cobbled together" and as "complex textual testimonies."

4. *Spectator,* April 9, 1864, 423.

5. Drexler and White, "Constitution," 60. Drexler and White offer several examples of black-identified writing, such as "Toussaint's Constitution," in which the authors are known to be white men. They mention Venture Smith and Sojourner Truth as two of the more famous examples of this but also highlight the inclusion of Olaudah Equiano and Phillis Wheatley in the U.S. canon of black writers in spite of their place of publication and national affiliation (2).

6. See Margaret Cohen's "Traveling Genres," for some implications of movement across geographic and temporal space for the conditions and features of literary form.

7. Timothy Dwight, from "Triumph of Democracy," January 1, 1801. In Basker, *Amazing Grace,* 488.

8. James Monroe to the Speakers of the General Assembly, December 5, 1800, *Virginia Executive Papers,* Governor's Letter Book, 1800–1803, Library of Virginia, Richmond.

9. See Jeffrey Gagnon, this volume.

10. Fischer, *Modernity* 2.

11. The *Virginia Gazette,* September 16, 1800, referred to Ben Prosser, who testified in the trial of Solomon, a co-conspirator of Gabriel's. The anonymous comment comes from the *Virginia Herald,* September 23, 1800.

12. See Fox-Genovese and Genovese, *Slavery.*

13. By novelization of slave violence I mean that chroniclers of Prosser, Vesey, and Turner both intentionally dramatize the horror of black violence and its potential for the future of U.S. slavery broadly and also foreclose—even make inevitable—the suppression of large-scale violence and the maintenance of white supremacy.

14. The term *fugitive archive* is one I am adapting from Drexler and White's concept of the fugitive slave narrative and also from Rodrigo Lazo's concept of migrant archives. See Lazo, "Migrant Archives," 2–9, 36–54.

15. Gould, "Economies," 90–91.

16. See José Guadalupe Ortega, this volume, 173.

17. I compare the two central narratives, *An Account of The Late Intended Insurrection Among A Portion of the Blacks of this City,* 1st ed., published by the Corporation of Charleston, and *Negro Plot: An Account of The Late Intended Insurrection Among A Portion of the Blacks of the City of Charleston, South Carolina,* 2nd ed., published and circulated by the mayor of Charleston, James Hamilton. The second narrative I look at is Kennedy and Parker, *An Official Report of the Trials of Sundry Negroes.*

18. In October 2001, the *William and Mary Quarterly* published the first of a two-part forum, "The Making of a Slave Conspiracy." Michael P. Johnson began part 1 with a review of the recent Denmark Vesey scholarship, entitled "Denmark Vesey and His Co-Conspirators." Edward A. Pearson's study *Designs against Charleston,* upon which I initially relied for primary documentation of the Vesey File, has been the most scholarly treatment of Vesey to date insofar as it includes the trial transcript in full, rather than relying on *An Official Report* or *An Account.* But what Johnson illustrates in his provocative and lengthy essay is that scholarship on Vesey, including Pearson's, remains marred with transcriptive, editorial, and interpretive errors.

19. See Pearson, *Designs*. See also Document I, Letter from Stephen C. Crane to John Lofton, January 27, 1983 (Crane is a relative of Captain Vesey): "In the Fall of 1781, Captain Vesey traveled to St. Thomas and St. Domingue and purchased Denmark Vesey and 389 other slaves." In the Denmark Vesey File, Vesey Archives, South Carolina Historical Society, Charleston. Also noted in John Lofton, *Insurrection*, 14.

20. Hamilton, *Account*, 1st ed., 17. Pearson suggests that there is no medical record of Vesey's epilepsy, which may mean that he used "fits" as a form of resistance while in St. Domingo. Johnson suggests that Pearson, along with Egerton and Robertson, "by imputing legal knowledge, charades, and possibly even voodoo to fits the court termed epileptic. . . . read the mentality of a wily fifty-five year old insurrectionist into the behavior of a fourteen-year old slave boy" (917).

21. Pearson, *Designs*, 38.

22. Qtd. in ibid., 39. *Manumission of Telemaque*, December 31, 1799, *Miscellaneous Records*, vol. KKK, 427.

23. Pearson, *Designs*, 41.

24. J. Hamilton Jr. Intendent, Charleston, August 16, 1822.

25. Kennedy and Parker, *Official Report*.

26. These acts are written in a preface by James Dudley, district clerk, of the district of South Carolina.

27. See Ian Watt's definition of realism: "a full and authentic report of human experience, and is therefore under and obligation to satisfy its reader with such details of the story as the individuality of the actors concerned, the particulars of the times and places of their actions, details which are presented through a more largely referential use of language than is common in other literary forms" (Watt, *Rise*, 32).

28. Although the narrative says nothing here about voodoo, Parker and Kennedy signal "his" God, a marker of separation between the black and white community, even between he and Vesey's preaching of Christianity.

29. Johnson, "Denmark Vesey," 943.

30. Qtd. in ibid., 935–36. "Melancholy Effect of Popular Excitement," *Charleston Courier*, June 21, 1822.

31. William Johnson, *To the Public of Charleston* (Charleston, July 1822), 5. Cited in M. Johnson, "Denmark Vesey," 936. This piece was meant to justify his article printed in June against the criticism he received from the court.

32. By the end of the Vesey trials, thirty-four slaves and one free black man were executed, sixty-eight were transported outside the nation, and several others were in a state of limbo, possibly to be transported outside the United States.

33. Johnson, "Denmark Vesey," 936.

34. There are at least two mitigating circumstances surrounding Bennett's private machinations to alter what he considered to be a most unethical course of the court: first, three of the first five slaves executed belonged to Bennett—Rolla, Ned, and Batteau all were hung along with Denmark Vesey on July 2, 1822, just eleven days after the initial proceedings began. Second, state power had only recently been transferred from Charleston to Columbia, and therefore any collaboration between the two regions remained extremely divisive. That Bennett

did not wholeheartedly accept the proceedings of the city of Charleston, then, makes sense in the political and historical framework of early nineteenth-century South Carolina. Nevertheless, Bennett's skillful critique of the Court turns the tale of conspiracy on its head, suggesting a bit more than a last-ditch effort to grasp power or a personal connection to those accused.

35. South Carolina Department of Archives and History, *Governor's Messages*, no. 2, Record 1328, 1328-01, Columbia, SC: November 28, 1822.

36. Tragle, *Slave Revolt*, 402.

37. Greenberg, *Confessions*, 40.

38. Walker, *Walker's Appeal*.

39. Ibid., 37.

40. Miles, "1790s," 44.

41. Ibid., 28.

42. Greenberg, *Confessions*, 41.

43. Brooks, *Troubling Confessions*, 2.

44. Tomson, "Confessions of a Footman," 1. A footnote tells us that *water drinkers* are people who abstain from drinking alcohol and that a *footman* is "A man-servant in livery employed chiefly to attend the carriage and wait at table" (*OED*).

45. Brooks, *Troubling Confessions*, 4.

46. Greenberg, *Confessions*, 39.

47. Brooks, *Troubling Confessions*, 2.

48. Greenberg, *Confessions*, 40.

49. Browne, "'This Unparalleled,'" 310.

50. Ibid., 311.

51. Greenberg, *Confessions*, 50.

52. Ibid., 49.

53. Ibid., 54.

54. Ibid., 44.

55. Ibid., 44.

56. Ibid., 54–55.

57. *Constitutional Whig*, "Southampton Affair."

58. Tragle, *Nat Turner's*, 124.

59. Ibid., 125.

60. Greenberg, *Confessions*, 69–72.

61. Brown, "History," 252.

62. Gould, "Economies," 91.

Bibliography

Aptheker, Herbert. *Nat Turner's Slave Rebellion. Together with the full text of the so-called "Confessions" of Nat Turner made in prison in 1831*. New York: Grove Press, 1968.

Basker, James G., ed. *Amazing Grace: An Anthology of Poems about Slavery, 1660–1810*. New Haven, CT: Yale Univ. Press, 2002.

Baucom, Ian. *Specters of the Atlantic: Finance Capital, Slavery, and the Philosophy of History*. Durham, NC: Duke Univ. Press, 2005.

Bland, Sterling L. *Voices of the Fugitives: Runaway Slave Stories and Their Fictions of Self-Creation.* Westport, CT: Praeger/Greenwood, 2000.

Brooks, Peter. *Troubling Confessions: Speaking Guilt in Law and Literature.* Chicago: Univ. of Chicago Press, 2000.

Brown, William Wells. "The History of the Haitian Revolution." *Pamphlets of Protest: An Anthology of Early African American Protest Literature, 1790–1860.* Ed. Richard Newman, Patrick Rael, and Phillip Lapsansky, 240–53. New York: Routledge, 2001.

Browne, Stephen Howard. "'This Unparalleled and Inhuman Massacre': The Gothic, the Sacred, and the Meaning of Nat Turner." *Rhetoric and Public Affairs* 3 (2000): 309–31.

Cohen, Margaret. "Traveling Genres." *New Literary History* 34.3 (2003): 481–99.

Davis, Charles, and Henry Louis Gates Jr., eds. *The Slave's Narrative.* New York: Oxford Univ. Press, 1986.

Drexler, Michael J., and Ed White. "The Constitution of Toussaint: Another Origin of African American Literature." In Jarrett, *Companion to African American Literature,* 59–74.

Fischer, Sybille. *Modernity Disavowed: Haiti and the Cultures of Slavery in the Age of Revolution.* Durham, NC: Duke Univ. Press, 2004.

Fox-Genovese, Elizabeth, and Eugene D. Genovese. *Slavery in White and Black: Class and Race in the Southern Slaveholders' New World Order.* Cambridge: Cambridge Univ. Press, 2008.

Gould, Philip. "The Economies of the Slave Narrative." In Jarrett, *Companion to African American Literature,* 90–102.

Greenberg, Kenneth, ed. *The Confessions of Nat Turner and Related Documents.* Ed. Kenneth Greenberg. 1831. New York: Bedford/St. Martin's, 1996.

Hamilton, James. *An Account of the Late Intended Insurrection among a Portion of the Blacks of this City.* 1st ed. Charleston, SC, 1822.

———. *Negro Plot: An Account of the Late Intended Insurrection among a Portion of the Blacks of the City of Charleston, South Carolina.* 2d ed. Boston, 1822.

Jarrett, Gene Andrew, ed. *A Companion to African American Literature.* West Sussex, UK: Wiley-Blackwell, 2010.

Johnson, Michael P. "Denmark Vesey and His Co-Conspirators." *William and Mary Quarterly* 58 (Oct. 2001): 915–76.

Kennedy, Lionel H., and Thomas Parker. *An Official Report of the Trials of Sundry Negroes, Charged with an Attempt to Raise an Insurrection in the State of South Carolina: Preceded by an Introduction and Narrative; and, in an Appendix, A Report of the Trials of Four White Persons on Indictments for Attempting to Excite Slaves to Insurrection.* Charleston, SC, 1822.

Lazo, Rodrigo. "Migrant Archives: New Routes in and out of American Studies." In *States of Emergency: The Object of American Studies,* ed. Russ Castronovo and Susan Gilman, 36–54. Chapel Hill: Univ. of North Carolina Press, 2009.

Lofton, John. *Insurrection in South Carolina: The Turbulent World of Denmark Vesey.* Yellow Springs, OH: Antioch Press, 1964.

Miles, Robert. "The 1790s: The Effulgence of the Gothic." In *The Cambridge Companion to Gothic Fiction*, ed. Jerrold E. Hogle, 41–62. Cambridge: Cambridge Univ. Press, 2002.

Pearson, Edward A., ed. *Designs against Charleston: The Trial Record of the Denmark Vesey Slave Conspiracy of 1822*. Chapel Hill: Univ. of North Carolina Press, 1999.

Scott, James C. *Domination and the Arts of Resistance: Hidden Transcripts*. New Haven, CT: Yale Univ. Press, 1990.

Tomson, Henry. "Confessions of a Footman." *Blackwood's Edinburgh Magazine* 14 (1823).

Tragle, Henry. *Nat Turner's Slave Revolt, 1831*. New York: Grossman, 1972.

Walker, David. *Walker's Appeal, in Four Articles, together with a preamble, to the coloured citizens of the World, but in particular, and very expressly, to those of the United States of America*. Boston, 1829.

Watt, Ian. *The Rise of the Novel*. Berkeley: Univ. of California Press, 1957.

"They Us'd Me Pretty Well"

Briton Hammon and Cross-Cultural Alliances in the Maritime Borderlands of the Florida Coast

Jeffrey Gagnon

THE OPENING scene of Briton Hammon's *A Narrative of the Uncommon Sufferings, and Surprizing Deliverance of Briton Hammon, a Negro Man* (1760) appears to describe yet another stereotypical eighteenth-century tale of Indian savagery and captivity. According to the text, a ship carrying the narrator is returning home to Massachusetts in late spring of 1748 with a cargo of logwood when it becomes lodged on a shallow reef off the southern Florida coast.[1] As the captain and crew debate whether to ditch the expensive cargo to lift the ship off the reef, a group of unidentified local Natives launch a marine assault on the crew in a surprise attack that leaves nearly everyone dead. Hammon is the lone survivor of the ship, and as these "inhuman savages" bring him ashore, they declare their intentions "to roast [him] alive."[2] However, instead of experiencing cannibalism or torture during his five-week stay, Hammon is surprised to discover that he is "us'd well," as his "captors" share "boil'd corn" with him, "which was what they often ate themselves."[3] Eventually they let him "escape" without confrontation by allowing him to board a passing Spanish trading vessel.[4] Of the recent scholarship that has addressed this scene, most seem to agree that it represents a rather straightforward episode of Indian captivity, and that this is how it would have been understood in the historical moment of his publication.[5] However, when taken together, these somewhat contradictory details invite speculation as to whether Hammon was ever really taken captive in the first place. This speculation is based on changing perspectives in how we read this text. Certainly, from the perspective of a British reading audience in 1760, Hammon appears to be a free British subject captured by "inhuman savages" who are predisposed to unwarranted violence. However, from the vantage point of a black man enslaved by British subjects (and presumably under the watchful care of his captain), the attack and Hammon's subsequent survival, during which time he is "us'd well," looks like something else entirely.

Instead of being captured by bloodthirsty savages, Hammon may have in fact been rescued by Natives sympathetic to the plight of transatlantic African slaves. I base this claim on newly uncovered archival research that suggests that Hammon was General John Winslow's slave (both before the trip described above and later, when he returns to Massachusetts and publishes this *Narrative*). This research challenges scholarship that interprets the ambiguous language of the extended subtitle to mean that Hammon was Winslow's free black servant and that his participation on the voyage was of his own volition.[6] Making the argument that Hammon was enslaved is essential for the second argument I make about his *Narrative*, which involves the unnamed Natives in this scene. As Daniel Vollaro has recently observed, contemporary scholarship's fascination with Hammon's ambiguous racial identity has obscured an interest in the identity of the Natives that play such an important role in this text. However, while Vollaro and I agree that further attention must be paid to these important figures, we disagree in the literary conclusions we draw about them. Pinpointing geographical, linguistic, and cultural inconsistencies in the *Narrative*, he argues that Hammon is an "unreliable witness to history" and concludes that the Natives are likely Hammon's fictional creation intended to sensationalize his account and attract readership for the publication.[7] However, I argue that the *Narrative*'s clues about these maritime Natives resonate with the work of scholars most familiar with Floridian Native peoples in this period. This research implies that these Natives were most likely the Calusa Indians, or a collection of Natives closely affiliated with the Calusa and neighboring tribes.[8] Before and after European contact, the Calusa were a powerful tribe of skilled boatmen who historically controlled territory from the Florida Keys, where Hammon's ship is likely to have run aground, to Tampa on the west coast of the Floridian peninsula. Based on a number of factors that I discuss in this essay, including the onset of disease, European and Native warfare, naval impressment, and British slavery, by 1748 they had become a small and fragile tribe that faced severe questions regarding their sovereignty and survival. To fortify their ranks, it is likely they incorporated members of other Native tribes from across the southern peninsula, as well as marooned British slaves such as Hammon. Making an exact argument for who these Natives might have been, however, is not the primary argument of this essay.

In attempting to identify these Natives and contextualize the text's portrayal of their actions, I am more interested in the text's brief but meaningful support for Hammon's cross-cultural alliance with Natives, which lacks historical and political context in the tale. By providing this context and theorizing the identity of the Natives as the Calusa, I am reorienting away from conventional readings of the text that privilege perspectives rooted in British New England. My reading of the text finds the Calusa asserting a sense of collective agency by protecting their territory and bringing ashore a possible black ally. In defending this argument, I incorporate historical and literary studies showing precedent for black-Native alliances along the Florida coast. From this angle, the Calusa rescued Hammon because they perceived him to be a victim of British slave traffickers who had historically captured and enslaved the Calusa as well.

By adopting this perspective and rereading this scene as one of alliance instead of captivity, my essay accepts the challenge proposed by Tiya Miles and Sharon Holland, who ask: "What political issues, strategies, and conflicts emerged out of their shared experience; and what creative works and cultural productions were inspired by their coming together?"[9] Hammon's *Narrative* reflects a complicated "coming together" of a subjugated black man who forged transnational bonds with sympathetic Native peoples fighting for sovereignty and survival on the margins of the circum-Atlantic world.

Hammon's Captivity among Plymouth's Elite

Conclusive facts regarding Briton Hammon's life continue to elude those interested in the intimate biographical details of his life. Nevertheless, how we interpret Hammon's class status strongly dictates how readers understand his limited sense of agency, his experiences in Florida, and his authority over his *Narrative*. As Vincent Carretta has demonstrated with his biographical research on Olaudah Equiano's birthplace, the stakes are high when it comes to a pinning down the essential details of a slave's biography. In Hammon's case, we know that he briefly entered the public stage because of a written text, only to be reclaimed by the objectivity and anonymity of a slave's life. The ambiguity over his status as slave or servant has remained unresolved since his text was reintroduced to the field by Dorothy Porter in her important anthology, *Early Negro Writing: 1760–1837* (1971). In fact, outside of the inclusion of "a Negro man—servant to General Winslow, of Marshfield, in New-England" included in the subtitle to his own story, the striking absence of racial discourse in the *Narrative* makes it highly possible that the first autobiography authored by a Black man in North America would be lost to researchers.[10] Nevertheless, despite this racial designation, his class status has remained in doubt. The extended version of his title identifies Winslow as his "good old master."[11] Other than these minor details, contemporary readers have been left to speculate—was Briton Hammon a servant or a slave to Winslow? In this regard, Carretta's anthology of Black Atlantic texts includes several valuable footnotes. He writes that the term *master* is "apparently used here in the sense of employer rather than owner. Hammon thus seems to have been a free man."[12] In contrast, John Sekora assumes that Hammon was a slave and that his work is "the earliest slave narrative."[13]

Historical uses of the two terms render it difficult to ascertain whether Hammon was a slave or servant, as these two terms were used interchangeably in the seventeenth and eighteenth centuries among New Englander slaveholders.[14] Adding to this difficulty, while very few records of any kind have surfaced regarding Hammon's life, those that researchers have found continued to use the term *servant* to classify his status. For example, Robert Desrochers located a revelatory marriage record in *Plymouth Church Records, 1620–1859* indicating that, on June 3, 1762, nearly two years to the day after he returned to Massachusetts, "Britain Negro Servt of Genl Winslow" married "Hannah, Servt of Mr. Hovey" in Plymouth's First Church.[15] Hovey was a noted barrister in Plymouth who had partnered to Winslow's brother, Edward, and the record suggests Hammon and Hannah were somehow linked through Winslow family relations. Clearly, this vital record lists both Hammon and his wife as servants to their respective masters. This usage fits with others, such as the *Vital Records of Marshfield, Massachusetts to the Year 1850*, which simply records the marriage without classification at all: "Briton Hamon of this town & Hannah Hovey of Plymouth."[16] These genealogical records seem to imply that Hammon was indeed a free servant.

However, other records suggest otherwise. *Vital Records of Plymouth, MA to the Year 1850* also records "Marriage Intentions" and lists the following entry on December 26, 1761, "A Purpose of Marriage, Between, Brittain Hammond Negro manslave, to John Winslow Esqr of Marshfield; And Hannah, Negro Woman Slave, to James Hovey, Esqr of Plymouth."[17] According to this document Hammon was, in fact, Winslow's slave.

How should we interpret these conflicting documents? And why is there a discrepancy? Do these disparate classifications reflect the whims and racial ideologies of two different recording clerks in Plymouth in the 1760s? Does the use of "servant" indicate a racially self-conscious clerk attempting to euphemize Hammon's slave status? If we accept that

Hammon was a slave, then this potential whitewashing represents the power of the archivist as "author." He or she inserted himself or herself into the process of data recording in order to distort intentionally the relationship between Hammon, Hannah, and their respective slave masters. On the other hand, if we believe that Hammon was actually a free man of color, then why would someone recording marriage intentions list him as a "manslave?" As Joanne Pope Melish argues, "Until the 1780s the great majority of people of African descent were slaves in fact, formally classified as items of property; free Africans were rare, anomalous cases."[18] Melish's claim, taken together with the marriage record, suggest a plausible conclusion that Hammon was more likely to be a slave and less likely to be a free wage laborer.

Additional research points to the fact that because multiple generations of the Winslow family owned slaves and indentured servants, there is context for perceiving Hammon as a slave. According to Karin Goldstein, records indicate that multiple generations of the family owned slaves, including John Winslow's wife, brother, father, and grand-uncle.[19] As most of Winslow's relatives owned slaves, it is likely that Hammon was part of a much larger network of slave relations when he traveled from Marshfield to Plymouth and Boston on errands for John. This network probably explains how he met his wife, Hannah, upon his return to Marshfield.

But this network was not limited to slaves of African descent. Like many prominent colonial families across the region, the Winslow family also owned Native indentured servants who worked as domestics. Goldstein's insightful archival research on the Winslow family's servants and slaves has uncovered that during the middle of the eighteenth century, Winslow owned a woman, likely Wampanoag, named Nab Nowitt.[20] Whether Nowitt was a part of the Winslow household during both of Hammon's terms in the house is hard to say, but her presence as Winslow's indentured servant is a reminder that after King Philip's War, colonial court authorities often forced Natives into contracts of involuntary servitude to pay off outstanding debts.[21] Ironically, this history reveals that Hammon was probably networking among New England Natives for most of his life before ever setting foot on Florida soil.

Ultimately, Hammon's experience of New England enslavement represents an ironic play on captivity—while the text suggests he was an Indian captive for five weeks in Florida, the archive suggests he was held captive, along with other men and women of African and Native descent, for his entire life among Plymouth's elite. Thus, the *Narrative*'s euphemistic use of the phrase "servant to General Winslow" should not be perceived as an innocent exchange of equally weighted terms. In attempting to subdue Hammon's own captivity in Plymouth, these genealogical records demonstrate some self-consciousness with regard to African slavery in Massachusetts. In this case, those editing the archive appear to recognize, and even mitigate, the idea that elite families in Plymouth were historic participants in their own version of African and Native captivity. Nevertheless, as Hammon sat down to write or share his story with eminent Boston publishers John Green and Joseph Russell, he was certainly aware of his own lived experiences of these inconsistencies.

Searching for the Voice of a Captive Author

Just as biographical questions swirl around Hammon's life, so do authorship questions hover over the writing and printing of the story itself. It is necessary to unpack these questions, as they bear weight on how we interpret pivotal scenes in the *Narrative*. It is this essay's position that the text represents a collective literary work that incorporates Hammon's own version of events in combination with the political agendas of its publishers, Green and Russell. This essay is less concerned with the historical truth of the text and more interested in how the text produces meaning based on Hammon's cross-cultural encounter in Florida.

In his analysis of Hammon's authorship, Vollaro argues that certain details in the text, such as the number of Indians who attacked the ship, were borrowed from other New England captivity narratives of the eighteenth century. He argues that Hammon intentionally selected these details and based his text on "accounts of Indian attacks that were circulating in Boston before Hammon's departure" because he wanted to appeal to the "audience's expectations of what should appear in an Indian captivity narrative."[22] In this reading, Hammon is a fully authoritative author who exercises complete command over the tone and content of the text. In addition, Hammon appears in possession of the established forms and conventions of the Indian captivity story.[23] However, as many critics have argued, it is likely that Hammon did not possess complete authority over the final printed product of his story.[24] There are also questions as to whether Hammon himself would have enjoyed widespread awareness of the cultural conventions of the captivity narrative. More likely, such overlapping was a product of the printers' understanding of the genre's forms and conventions. John Sekora's research on captivity narratives published by Green and Russell, as well as their close colleagues, Fowle and Draper, suggests that the text borrowed wording from other similarly conceived captivity narratives of the era in its title, as well as in its opening and closing lines.[25] Unfortunately, while it seems likely that his account was edited, we do not know how the editor or editors took liberties with Hammon's diction, style, tone, vocabulary, or version of events.

These vexing questions of authority are perhaps most related to the fact that Hammon was an author who was the captured property of those who represented the anticipated reading audience of his account. In other words, those who had enslaved him, maintained surveillance over him, and rendered him an unautonomous subject would represent his primary readership. Saidiya Hartman's analysis of the subjugation of the enslaved reminds us that Hammon would have had been distinctly aware of this relationship when choosing which words to include in his account, and which ones to leave out, for when it comes to slavery, "direct and simple forms of domination, the brutal asymmetry of power, the regular exercise of violence, and the denial of liberty that make it difficult, if not impossible, to direct one's own conduct."[26] She asks, "what are the constituents of agency when one's social condition is defined by negation and personhood refigured in the fetishized and fungible terms of object of property?"[27] In consideration of Hartman's poignant question, analysis of Hammon's authority as author must attend to the severe restraints placed upon him regarding what he could and could not say about his experiences. Recognizing that Winslow, Winslow's family members, and other pro-Christian, pro-English readers would be perusing the pages of the text, Hammon needed to be immensely careful in how he talked about the so-called villains in his adventures, namely the Natives, Spanish political officials, and Catholics that he encountered in his travels. Ultimately, because of his own marginalized status upon his return to New England, it is necessary to speculate whether Hammon preferred to publicly share his story in print, or whether Winslow ordered him to do so.

Ambiguities pertaining to authorship have a direct bearing on how scholars interpret the critical scenes in the text, especially Hammon's experiences in Florida. As stated at the outset, most would agree that the *Narrative* fits the captivity genre due to its representations of Native peoples. Weyler observes that despite recording instances of kindness on the part of Indian captors, captivity narratives point out the innate savagery and violent nature of Indigenous peoples, and Hammon's text fits the genre in this way.[28] The extended title characterizes the attack on Hammon's ship as the "Horrid Cruelty and Inhuman Barbarity of the

Indians."[29] And later, in Hammon's narration we find that he would rather drown than "be kill'd by those barbarous and inhuman Savages."[30] Do we believe these are Hammon's words, or those of an editor with a political agenda as well as a racial and religious bias against Native people? If we can assume that Green and Russell were probably responsible for writing the extended title, then it seems plausible to suggest that similar wording located within the body of the *Narrative* may also have been the work of the editors. The fact that the text was published in the middle of the Seven Years' War (1756–63) also provides essential context for negative anti-Native sentiments offered in these characterizations. In other words, political context of the era, combined with the political leanings of the editors, makes it possible that representations of Native savagery, as well as Hammon's captivity, are more the work of the pro-Christian, pro-English editors than Hammon himself.

Nevertheless, advancing this claim does not mean that in his re-creation of events, Hammon was completely and totally subjected. As Rafia Zafar has argued, "Domination by the white editor, no matter how significant, can never be complete. Whether or not the black narrators or their white editors meant to do so, the inclusion of slaves within American captivity narratives marked an inroad into and adaptation of white literary and popular culture."[31] This consideration means we also need to consider the ways he may have chosen to remain silent about certain details in his text that would not have been seen as favorable by this audience. She adds, "The facts selected by the black tellers may be suspect, for the same reason that a slave's smiling face and tuneful whistle did not necessarily indicate happiness, simple-mindedness, or unconcern."[32] In other words, despite his status, Hammon still possessed some control over what he wanted to write or say and what not to say about his story.

The text suggests Hammon may have done just that. Toward the end of the *Narrative*, readers find a "surprising" revelation that Hammon intentionally withheld important facts, details, events, and his personal feelings about them, as he crafted his tale: "I think I have not deviated from Truth, in any particular of this my Narrative, and tho' I have omitted a great many Things, yet what is wrote may suffice to convince the Reader, that I have been most grievously afflicted, and yet thro' the Divine Goodness, as miraculously preserved, and delivered out of many Dangers; of which I desire to retain a grateful Remembrance, as long as I live in the World."[33] That Hammon has "omitted a great many Things" is a critical admission. Where are these omissions and what information was withheld from the original account? Could they be read as Hammon's sly acknowledgment that he purposefully withheld key details that would not have pleased Winslow, Green and Russell, and the anticipated pro-English readership?

One possibility is that Hammon intentionally silenced himself. This approach to his story resembles what Patricia Laurence would describe as acts of resistance found in the self-silencing of female authors. For Laurence, literary silences are not merely signs of consent or complicity with dominant ideologies or oppressive institutions, but rather they are active expressions of voice and "presence."[34] Such silences circumvent socially dangerous or unconventional ideas or expressions, and remain like "a text, waiting to be read."[35] When pairing Laurence's rereading of female novelists with Hammon's admission of intentional omission, we can read his silences as active insertions into his story. After all, as is discussed in an upcoming section of this chapter, how could he adequately explain to a pro-British reading audience that he may have found sanctuary from British slavery within a community of "savage heathens" in Florida?

Naval Captivity in Massachusetts

Just as critics have debated Hammon's access to agency and autonomy, so too have they speculated on just how he ended up on a Plymouth sloop bound for the Caribbean in 1747. What is missing from this analysis is historical context pertaining to a form of brutal captivity feared by white and Black sailors alike in this era—naval impressment. As context demonstrates, it is likely that Hammon owed his presence on a ship bound for the Caribbean because free sailors possessed the agency and autonomy to decline an invitation. As a slave, he had to do what his master commanded.

The *Narrative* maintains that it was his "intention" to head to sea: "On Monday, 25th Day of December, 1747, with the leave of my Master, I went from Marshfield, with an Intention to go a Voyage to Sea, and the next Day, the 26th, got to Plymouth, where I immediately ship'd myself on board of a Sloop, Capt. John Howland, Master, bound to Jamaica and the Bay."[36] Picking up on the text's use of the word *intention,* W. Jeffrey Bolster speculates that Hammon possessed some type of agency in choosing to head to sea. He writes:

> Prompted by memories of luxuriant Jamaican alternatives to sleety nor'easters, he negotiated the right for a voyage when his master Winslow's frozen fields were untellable, and earned a brief sojourn in the black tropics—the productive

heartland of the Anglo-American plantation system. Winslow, of course, pocketed most of the wages.[37]

Bolster's analysis of Hammon positions him as a liminal figure—a slave who was able to "negotiate" his place on Howland's ship. However, as personal correspondence between the Winslow brothers reveals, Hammon probably lacked much agency, "intention," or ability to negotiate when it came to his presence on the sloop. In fact, he would have probably never been a crew member at all had it not been for an uprising of Bostonian maritime workers just thirty miles north of Plymouth who were rebelling against their own experiences of unjust captivity—British naval impressment.

On November 19, 1747, Edward Winslow sat down in his office in Plymouth and composed an anxious letter to his brother, Captain John Winslow in Boston.[38] John, a native of nearby Marshfield, was in Boston serving as Plymouth's representative to the colonial government. Edward was concerned with the recent events in Boston that had maritime workers and political leaders around the Atlantic buzzing. On November 17, a mob of three hundred to several thousand unruly sailors rebelled against the press gangs sent by British commander Charles Knowles. Thomas Hutchinson described the event as "a tumult in the Town of Boston equal to any which had preceded it."[39] The riots were the culmination of years of impressments up and down the Atlantic seaboard. They ended with Governor William Shirley in hiding and sailors burning a barge in front of the governor's mansion in Boston's town common. Despite the tumult, fears of press gangs had a ripple effect throughout New England port cities. As a result, local sailors, particularly from Hammon's hometown of Plymouth, wanted nothing to do with sailing to Boston. Naval impressment among the British navy was a form of captivity unwelcomed by those sailors who valued just compensation for their labor, as well as respect for their health and safety.

Therefore, Edward was worried that his wife's cousin, Captain John Howland, would not find enough able seamen to sail his sloop north to Boston before heading south to the Caribbean and the Gulf of Mexico. He writes, "I fear Capt. Howland will meet with difficulty in getting hands to bring up the sloop, as I cannot prevail with those that are here to go to Boston for fear of the press."[40] As a remedy to this dilemma, Edward proposed sending John's able-bodied slave, Briton, to work as an extra sailor, and the letter requested permission to do so: "I wrote him to mention it to you to let Briton come in her, not knowing but she may be ready to come at the time it would suit for Briton to come and it will be easier for him than to foot it, however I knew there could be no damage in proposing it."[41] From this letter we learn that Hammon's trip was not the result of a personal desire to work aboard a ship or even to flee the cold New England winters. Instead, Hammon experienced a type of maritime impressment, for being a slave, he was in no position to resist the Winslow's needs. He was going to have to help fill the crew by working onboard Howland's ship. Whether John ever replied is not known, but he must have authorized Edward's plan, for on December 25, Briton Hammon said goodbye to his friends and loved ones, walked ten miles south to Plymouth, and stepped aboard Howland's sloop. While other sailors were fortunate to resist Knowles's impressment, as Winslow's personal slave, Hammon was subject to his own local version of it.

Rescuing Briton Hammon from Captivity

Hammon's status as enslaved property, and the provocative "omissions" withheld from the text, work together to complicate the scene that many have described as Indian captivity. A close reading suggests that after shipwreck, the Calusa were rescuing what they perceived to be a racialized slave of African descent, rather than capturing a free black British subject. This claim suggests that instead of being captured by "barbarous and inhuman Savages," Hammon was brought ashore by a more sophisticated group of coastal Natives with a very specific political agenda rooted in a historical moment. This analysis provides an important look into cross-cultural reciprocal exchanges between Florida Native people, European imperialists, and marooned black subjects on the margins of maritime empires.

As I argue at the outset of this essay, coastal Natives with maritime skill and diplomatic political and economic ties with the Spanish Crown in Havana accurately describe several Floridian Indigenous groups at the time, but particularly the Calusa. According to historian Jerald T. Milanich, the Calusa were probably the largest and most powerful and influential Native group in pre-Columbian southern Florida.[42] Primarily, they were skilled fishermen and aggressive warriors who maintained a powerful authority over other Native tribes in the southern peninsula of Florida. Among archeological and historical scholars they are probably best known for their early resistance to Spanish imperialism and for their historical salvaging of wrecked ships on the keys.[43] Between the sixteenth and eighteenth centuries the Calusa increasingly participated in the European mercantile trade, particularly with the Spanish in Cuba. It is known that the Spanish made several attempts throughout the centuries to convert the Calusa to Christianity. In fact, it seems as though the Calusa used this tactic to their advantage, often promising to allow missionaries to practice in the region in exchange for military protection and commercial trade options. However, it is known that they also relied on Spanish ships for seasonal tribal migration along the coast. By the mid-seventeenth century, they had become adept at using their longstanding political alliances with Spain in exchange for protection from English slave traders and English Native allies, such as the Yamasee and the Creeks.

Native fears of enslavement provide at least one substantial reason explaining the Calusa surprise attack on Hammon's English ship in 1748. Analysis of English slave practices in the southeast region of the continent suggest that the Calusa had grave reasons to fear English ships sailing along the coast. By the mid-eighteenth century, when Hammon's sloop struck a reef, the region from the southern tip of Florida to Georgia and the Carolinas was becoming an increasingly contested space among Spanish missionaries, English slaveholders, shipping companies on both sides, and scores of Indian tribes with divided loyalties. Historian Amy Turner Bushnell argues that throughout this region, "Native hatred of the English ran deep. The real cause was that the English treated the wild coast like a labor pool, seizing the natives at will and taking them to distant places where they were forced to labor under dangerous conditions that few would survive."[44] British attacks on Native settlements were a real threat to the sovereignty of tribes such as the Calusa at this time, and those that did not politically ally with the British were vulnerable to military assaults, including surprise attacks on their communities. In the words of plantation owner and English military commander Thomas Nairne of Charlestown, the English "destroy'd the whole Country, burnt the Towns, brought all the Indians, who were not kill'd or made Slaves, into our own Territories, so that there remains not now, so much as one Village with ten Houses in it, in all Florida, that is subject to the Spaniards."[45]

Nairne's comments suggest that due to English enslavement practices, the Calusa probably comprised some part of the cheap labor force on Carolinian plantations in the late seventeenth and early eighteenth centuries. Because of English-led incursions along the coast, many Florida Indians were taken to various plantations across the region, especially those in the Carolina territories. According to Florida historian Patrick Riordan, "Indian slaves became the fastest-growing segment of the South Carolina population in the 1708 census."[46] Spanish documents support the claim that early eighteenth-century slaving raids decimated the Calusa population. These attacks caused a major shift in Calusa political policy with Spain, including the migration of 270 Calusa to Havana.[47] If Spanish documents are accurate, then the Calusa owed part of their decline to English-based slavery and warfare. This history suggests that when Hammon's ship struck the reef, Calusa warriors and boatmen took action perhaps in order to stave off a potential English attack or even a slave raid.

In the captivity narratives that were popular in New England and elsewhere during the Seven Years' War, the origin of the story usually involved an unsuspecting attack on an isolated farm or village located somewhere on the periphery of English colonial territory. In these stories, the conflict begins with a violent, unprovoked attack on supposedly innocent English settlers. However, as the history regarding English enslavement of the Calusa and other Native populations of Florida demonstrates, from the Calusa perspective, the origins of the conflict, and of captivity, go back much further than an assault on a single mercantile ship in 1748.

Nevertheless, my arguments for how to explain the attack on the ship do not clarify the decision to take Hammon ashore. One theory is that they realized that African slaves such as Hammon needed to be rescued from British enslavement. Due to the fears of their own possible enslavement, as well as the circulation of news and political developments across the region, the Calusa must have been fully aware of the growing English dependence on African slave labor, particularly in nearby Carolina territories. Such news would likely have come from passing Spanish ships, such as the one that eventually picked up Hammon in Florida and brought him to Cuba. In fact, because they were situated in the maritime circuits between Spanish-held St. Augustine and Havana, the Calusa may have heard news of English dependence on slavery with the proliferation of runaway black slaves fleeing colonial English plantations in the Carolinas beginning in the late seventeenth century. As Jane Landers has examined in detail, these slaves often fled to St. Augustine, where, in exchange for services and conversion to Catholicism, they could enjoy relative freedom.[48] Partly due to the escalation of military tensions with the English, by 1738, St. Augustine governor Manuel de Montiano granted unconditional freedom to all fugitives from Carolina. This act coincided with the establishment of a Florida refuge for escaped slaves, Gracia Real de Santa Teresa de Mose, located adjacent to St. Augustine. This context suggests that the Calusa perceived Hammon to be a captured British slave from the Carolina region. In other words, from the Calusa perspective, taking Hammon from the ship and preserving his life was more about helping to free a Black man from the clutches of widely circulated, notorious British slave practices. And if we return to the fact that Hammon was technically Winslow's slave who was temporarily working for Howland at Winslow's request, then Hammon was technically freed from slavery in the Calusa's attack on the ship. This fact could not have been lost on Hammon, whether he was happy to be in Florida or not.

By attempting to better understand the Calusa's attack on the ship and their reasons for bringing Hammon ashore, I am calling into question whether this text really belongs in the genre of Indian captivity narratives. For authors such as Weyler, Sekora, and Keith Green (included in this anthology), whether Hammon was captured by Natives is a precursor to a larger argument surrounding the multiple forms of captivity, including slavery, Spanish imprisonment, and naval impressment, to which black seamen such as Hammon were subjected. As Green convincingly argues, the *Narrative* is "not only a slave narrative, but a signification upon Indian captivity narratives, tales of slave incarceration, accounts of maritime shipwreck and abduction, and representations of African American child indentured servitude."[49] Nevertheless, these arguments continue to fall back upon basic characterization of the text as that of Indian captivity. In doing so, they inadvertently close off possibilities for more complex forms of power relations between Hammon and the Calusa. By reorienting my reading away from colonial New England to the shores of Native Floridian space, I find reasons to consider the text as a signifier of anti-imperialist, black-Native alliances with long histories in the region.

Literary and historical documentation supports the view that Native tribes in Florida were historically hospitable to outsiders, particularly men of color. Landers's research pinpoints an established history of relations between marooned slaves, free blacks, and the Calusa (and their allies) beginning almost as soon as Europeans began entering Florida.[50] These accounts include the African slave Estevan, one of the four survivors of the Panfilo de Narvaez expedition to La Florida in 1528. According to Cabeza de Vaca's account of the failed incursion, Estevan was able to quickly learn local Indigenous languages and thus became an interpreter for the shipwrecked survivors.[51] In addition, Conquistador Hernando de Soto's expedition included several slaves. In one story, a slave named Gomez helped the female leader of an unidentified Native group in northern Florida escape capture by the Spaniards. Gomez later became her husband, left the de Soto party, and ran away with her to live in what is known today as Camden, South Carolina.[52]

Perhaps the most compelling story documents black-Native racial mixing among the Calusa in southern Florida. Hernando D'Escalante Fontaneda was a Spanish shipwreck survivor who, like Hammon, survived a wreck on the Florida Keys and came to live with the Calusa for a period. Sometime after 1575, he published an account of his experiences among the Calusa entitled *Memoir of Hernando D'Escalante Fontaneda, On the Country and Ancient Indian Tribes of Florida, 1575.* According to Fontaneda, when he arrived in Florida an unidentified black man named Luis, himself a former shipwreck survivor, was already an intimate member of the tribe and a strong ally to the Cacique, Carlos. Luis plays a pivotal role in Fontaneda's story, for he was fluent in the local language and had become the Calusa's translator to outsiders. He was also a close relation to the cacique Carlos. In fact, during a pivotal moment in Fontaneda's story, when the Cacique Carlos is preparing to decide whether to kill Fontaneda and members of his party, Luis intervenes and saves Fontandeda's life.

Despite being published much later, David George's *An Account of the Life of Mr. David George, from Sierra Leone in Africa; given by himself in a Conversation with Brother Rippon of London, and Brother Pearce of Birmingham* (1793) offers a complicated look at the possibilities and pitfalls of escaped slaves living in Native spaces. He describes his decision to leave his South Carolina plantation and "[run] away up among the Creek Indians."[53] The Creek welcome George, but they relegate him to an ambiguous form of servitude. He lives among them for less than a year, during which time he "worked hard," but "the people were kind to me," a declaration that strongly resembles Hammon's characterization of being "us'd well."[54] However, while George experiences more humanizing conditions than he did among white slaveholders in Virginia, he is still not a fully free man. After his master's son tracks George to Creek territory, he runs away again, this time to live among the Natchez. Welcomed by yet another Native community, he learns to "mend deer skins."[55] Later, he marries Phillis, a Creek woman. For George, opportunities for freedom take place in the confines of southeastern Native circles, even as he experiences a modified form of liberty among them.

Many scholars working with Hammon's text have noted the similarities with John Marrant's *A Narrative of the Lord's Wonderful Dealings With John Marrant, A Black* (1785). Similar to the tale in Hammon's

Narrative, it is widely accepted that Marrant was the captured prisoner of the Cherokee Nation. The scene begins when a Cherokee hunter in the wilderness outside of Charleston, South Carolina, stumbles upon the lost and starving Marrant, who has wandered into the woods. After an initial confrontation, the two become unlikely travel companions. They hunt for over ten weeks, engage in "constant conversation," and in the process, Marrant receives "a fuller knowledge of the Indian tongue."[56] His linguistic skill becomes essential to his survival, for when he returns with the hunter to the leaders of the Cherokee Nation, they view him as an enemy to execute, not once, but twice. According to the story, God's divine intervention and Marrant's own linguistic dexterity save him from death. In the first part of the scene, he prays in the Cherokee language, "which wonderfully affected the people."[57] Marrant's last-minute prayer moves his captors to temporarily free him. Shortly thereafter, he finds himself ready to be executed again for offending the Cherokee chief. This time, divine intervention causes the chief to relent, and "all my enemies to become my great friends."[58] In this revelation, Marrant's "great friends" among the Cherokee signify a less obvious example of the "Lord's wonderful dealings," just as Hammon being "us'd well" represents his "surprising deliverance" among the Calusa.

Collectively, these documented histories of black-Native mixing throughout the Southeast provide a valuable lens through which to speculate as to why Hammon might have been taken from the ship and positively received by the Calusa. Hammon was certainly not the only or even the first black man to find refuge and even cross-cultural acceptance among Native peoples.

Re-creating Social Life among the Calusa

In temporarily rescuing Hammon from the legal conditions of British slavery and bringing him ashore, the Calusa granted him a sense of subjectivity and community that he did not enjoy as a colonial New England slave. The recognition of his subjectivity coincides with the Calusa's own fragile sense of community and sovereignty. With this context in mind, Hammon's connection with the Calusa may be seen as a temporary, cross-cultural alliance. This alliance would be based on experiences of mutual vulnerability in response to the socially destructive practices of European imperialism.

Saidiya Hartman's analysis of nineteenth-century "networks of affiliation" among plantation slaves in the United States provides the theoretical underpinnings for claims of an alliance between Hammon and the

Calusa.[59] A major feature of her argument concerns slaves' social gatherings and late-night dances, wherein "pleasure is central to the mechanisms of identification and recognition that discredit the claims of pain but also to those that produce a sense of possibility—redress, emancipation, transformation, and networks of affiliation under the pressures of domination and the utter lack of autonomy."[60] These networks were not defined by the sharing of racial identity or even the shared conditions of slavery. Rather, this distinction locates the importance of "affiliation" and "community" in the "connections forged in the context of disrupted affiliations, sociality amid the constant threat of separation, and shifting sets of identification particular to site, location and action."[61] Hartman's claim raises important possibilities for reconfiguring Hammon's experience among the Calusa. I am not specifically arguing that what Hammon experiences in Florida can be classified as "pleasure" in any sense—he does not provide enough clues to suggest this possibility. What he does emphasize, however, and what this essay has worked to establish up to this point, is that his experience among the Calusa should be understood within the framework of "networks of affiliation." What makes this network so compelling is the way it transcends racial and cultural boundaries that were central to European-rooted discourses on the rigidity of racial difference. These discourses, based in Enlightenment philosophy and the growing emphasis on scientific racism, worked to prohibit the mingling of subaltern racial groups. Hammon's unexpected participation in the networks of affiliation between circum-Caribbean Indigenous and marooned slaves represents a disruption of these imperial modes of domination and subjection.

The Calusa's recognition of Hammon as something more than a slave, as a human being worthy of emancipation, gestures to what Hartman calls the "sense of possibility" in such networks. The "possibility" is being identified by others as a human subject not situated on some type of hierarchical scale of humanness. The Calusa's recognition of Hammon as a potential ally resembles a slave's hunger for reciprocity and the sharing of pain. These needs hold the potential for "creating and experiencing supportive, enjoyable and nurturing connections."[62] It provides us a fresh lens for unraveling the complex representations of cross-cultural encounter in Hammon's account.[63]

In consideration of relational possibilities, did Hammon replace an experience of English slavery—the terror of surveillance, a lack of autonomy, and an objectified humanity—with a more empowering form of affiliation among the Calusa? To take this question a step further, did Hammon emerge into a space of possibility when his vulnerability merged with the Calusa's own fragile position? The Calusa's vulnerability was based on their precarious position at the epicenter of European conquest, which was more in jeopardy than ever. The continued dwindling of their population, combined with the growing threat of Spanish and English naval power in the region, would have created a very real threat of destruction. In fact, this was a cultural razing that would become nearly complete by the time Hammon returned to Boston in 1760.

Thus, an additional theory posits that Hammon was rescued to fortify the dwindling numbers of the Calusa. Captivity scholar Gordon Sayre argues that many Native captives in early North America were not taken for ransom or to punish the captives.[64] They were not taken as random acts of "terrorism."[65] In many cases, they were taken for other reasons, such as to enhance the tribe or the nation. Sayre writes: "Captives were valuable human lives who could add to the strength of a village; thus they were integrated into the tribe of their captors through a process so foreign to European notions of identity that captivity narrators often failed to understand it."[66] Through this lens, the Calusa shared a sense of connection with Black slaves they encountered on wrecked ships, particularly English ones. This form of connection, however transient, offered a mutual sense of relief in the form of shared struggle and solidarity.

This point provides a community-building context for the seemingly unremarkable instance of food sharing in this scene. Unlike other captivity narratives, Hammon is surprisingly silent about his experiences during the approximately five weeks he spends among his Native hosts. One detail is that the Calusa share "boil'd corn, which was often what they ate themselves."[67] The Calusa's apparent willingness to share what they eat with Hammon invites deeper speculation about their positive treatment of him. That the Calusa shared a dish made of boiled corn may have both literal and symbolic meaning for Hammon. Skeptical readers may conclude that by giving him "boil'd corn, which was often what they ate themselves," the Calusa were simply feeding a prisoner to keep him alive. However, symbolically, they could also have been inviting him to participate in a ritual of community building and social hospitality.

Native practices of food sharing resembles what Lisa Brooks has called the "common pot." Brooks centers her study on eighteenth- and nineteenth-century, northeastern Native networks of affiliation. She focused on the Abenaki word for dish, *Wlogan*, or "common pot."[68] The metaphor of the shared dish describes the "conceptualization of a cooperative, interdependent Native environment that emerges from within

Native space as a prominent trope in the speeches and writings of the eighteenth and nineteenth centuries."[69] It was a historical term, but it began to be used more frequently by tribal leaders as colonial control over Native people and lands increased. It was also a symbolic term meant to signify the nourishment of a tribal body or a network of inhabitants through the sharing of resources and, most importantly, ideas around reciprocity and interdependence. Brooks writes, "The Common Pot is that which feeds and nourishes. It is the wigwam that feeds the family, the village that feeds the community, the networks that sustain the village."[70] As Brooks indicates, food sharing was both a literal and metaphorical feature of Native life. Sharing a common pot extended to the sharing of values, ideologies, resources, and even romantic intimacies. These affiliations were built and nurtured as households of slaves shared a common dish, passing it from person to person as they conversed. They also resemble the political mixing that occasionally threatened the governing of intimacies. Alliances among Black and Native slaves in southern Massachusetts in the eighteenth century grew as many slaves and free-Blacks found refuge among southern New England Native groups.

Certainly Brooks's study is more focused on the employment of this concept in the writings of northeastern U.S. Native groups. However, evidence suggests that southeastern Native groups may have held similar beliefs. Creek, Seminole, and Cherokee peoples had a shared dish of corn (and occasionally meat) called the *sofkee* or *safki*."[71] Derived from the Creek word *osafki,* meaning "Hominy," the sofkee pot was a common feature in most homes, and family members and visitors would eat from it throughout the day. This traditional dish was an essential feature of family bonding and strengthening community networks. An example of the importance of the sofkee pot to southeastern Indigenous peoples was recorded by William Bartram (1739–1823) in his eighteenth-century travels throughout this region. As he described it, "the most favorite dish the Indians have amongst them is Corn thin Drink seasoned with hicory nut Oil."[72] In visiting one Seminole family, Bartram, as a visitor, was invited to partake in the dish: "in this bowl is a great wooden ladle; each person takes up in it as much as he pleases, and after drinking until satisfied, returns it again into the bowl, pushing the handle towards the person in the circle, and so it goes round."[73] Although Bartram's description of the sofkee as a communal common pot was practiced among northern Florida Natives, Hammon's *Narrative* suggests that they developed a similar practice. In other words, when Hammon ate "corn" during his five-week stay in Florida, he was participating in ceremonies designed to welcome him into the community or, at the very least, intended to recognize him as a welcome outsider.

If this is true, it provides a more critical insight into the Calusa's hospitality toward Hammon. They were sending him the message that he was welcome, secure, and liberated from the bonds of slavery. His text attributes the preservation of his life and their kind hospitality to the work of God: "But the Providence of God order'd it other ways, for He appeared for my Help, in this Mount of Difficulty, and they were better to me than my Fears."[74] However, it was perhaps the cultural acceptance of free Black men and marooned slaves among the Calusa that was most responsible for his positive reception. After all, from his perspective, he may or may not have even been able to interpret why he was taken from the ship and why he was treated well. Perhaps those tribal members who communicated in "broken English" could have shared the meaning and symbolism behind their sharing of the common pot with him. We will never know.

The significance of incorporating the notion of the common pot to this analysis resonates with scholar Tiya Miles's observations on nineteenth-century Black-Native relations. She co-hosted a conference at Dartmouth in 1998 entitled "'Eating Out of the Same Pot': Relating Black and Native (Hi)stories." She took this name from a quote given in an interview in a 1940 Works Progress Administration (WPA) interview by a black man formerly held as a slave by Creeks. In the interview he was asked to compare his slave experience with that of African Americans enslaved by whites. He responded, "I was eating out of the same pot with the Indians, going anywhere in this country I wanted to, while they was still licking the master's boots in Texas."[75] For Miles, this quotation illustrates "the ways that people of African descent transported and transformed cultures, created intersectional communities, and built metaphysical as well as physical homes on Native lands and within Native cultural landscapes. In the process, they altered their interior worlds as well as those of Native peoples."[76] The arguments of Miles and coeditor Sharon P. Holland support the point I wish to make here, which is that texts such as Hammon's *Narrative* exist at the intersection of African diasporic and Native American experience in North America. To be clear, I am not suggesting that Hammon's five-week experience was personally or culturally transformative, either for him or the Calusa. There is simply not enough evidence to support this contention. Nevertheless, I am arguing that his text represents a cultural production that belongs in the growing realm of these studies. When Miles and Holland argue that "Native America has been and continues to be a critical site in the histories and lives of dispersed African peoples," they are challenging scholars to reconsider how we view instances of so-called captivity in texts such as Hammon's.[77] In other words, whether he intends to do so or not, when Hammon discloses that the Calusa "gave me boil'd corn, which was often what they ate themselves," his revelation evokes the metaphor of the "common pot" that has been so integral to black-Native cultural histories.

Epilogue

My reading complicates the oversimplified critique that Hammon was simply a captive of savage and barbarous heathens. Instead, it reimagines the Calusa as agents acting not only in their own political and cultural interests, but also in the interests of other vulnerable subjects circulating in the circum-Atlantic maritime space of coastal Florida. This alternative reading of Hammon's experiences in Florida is based on the notion that vulnerable black and Native peoples in the eighteenth century sometimes formed temporary alliances designed to mediate the oppression and exploitation of slavery and domination.

IN MARSHFIELD, Massachusetts, the Winslow house is now a historically preserved heritage site where visitors can tour the home of a distinguished, highly venerated colonial English family with ancestral roots dating to the Mayflower. Built in 1699 by John Winslow's father, Isaac, the home features an impressive collection of furniture, dishware, books, and artwork assembled throughout the years, many of which date to General John Winslow's life on the estate. Just inside the entryway, the Jacobean stairway represents a unique example of eighteenth-century craftsmanship and art. It leads visitors to a second floor, where stately bedrooms feature the wonders of carved wooden beds, beautifully decorated linens, and even a display of eighteenth-century children's toys. It is clear to any visitor that despite the challenges of living in eighteenth-century Massachusetts, the Winslow family enjoyed a degree of comfort and pleasure.

Upstairs, in the back corner of the second floor, are two simple rooms that lack the homey, nostalgic feel of the others. They also lack the basic amenities, such as the fireplaces that can be found in nearly every other room in the house. Curators have included a simple, rustic bed with a straw mattress, dated to the period in which servants and slaves lived among the splendid opulence collected by several generations of Winslow wealth and power. It is in these rooms that Briton Hammon, Nab Nowitt, and many others rested their heads at the end of the day.

In the quiet cold of these rooms, a small community of African and Native slaves shared the intimate confines of captive space. Like his sharing of "boiled corn" among the Calusa, perhaps these men and women passed a common pot, a simple but meaningful dish to share among a cross-cultural community of marginalized others. And just as Hammon described being "us'd pretty well" in his *Narrative,* perhaps this small community formed meaningful interpersonal bonds that echoed those that he briefly formed among a strange but hospitable people living precariously on the distant shores of a Floridian coastline.

Notes

I would like to thank Dr. Nicole Tonkovich and Dr. Sara Johnson for their critical encouragement of this paper, the ideas of which first emerged in Dr. Tonkovich's graduate seminar. I would also like to thank Dr. Anna Brickhouse for her early support for the work. I also extend my gratitude to the Massachusetts Historical Society for access to their archives, as well as to Winslow historians who generously shared their research and ideas with me along the way. These include Mark Schmidt, the executive director of the Winslow House in Marshfield, Massachusetts, Cynthia Krusell, and Dr. Karin Goldstein, curator at Plimoth Plantation. And a special thanks to Dr. Jim Power who helped me locate several important archival documents in my research stages.

  1. Probably the Florida Keys, islands located south of present-day Miami.
  2. Hammon, *Narrative* 22.
  3. Ibid.
  4. Ibid.
  5. Foster 42; Sekora, "Briton Hammon" and "Red, White and Black"; Bolster 9; Weyler 42; Green. For those such as Foster and Sekora, this debate spills into the question of whether Hammon's Indian captivity places his *Narrative* as a precursor to the nineteenth-century slave narrative. Green's essay also includes a thorough overview of the scholarship on the debates regarding the text's place in the canon of slave narratives. See Green, this volume, 119–20, note 1.
  6. Carretta 24; Sekora, "Briton Hammon" 133; Bolster 8.
  7. Vollaro 134, 144.
  8. Hann; Marquardt; Milanich; Worth.
  9. Miles and Holland, introduction 7.
  10. Hammon 20.
  11. Ibid.
  12. Ibid., 24n3.
  13. Sekora, "Briton Hammon" 143.
  14. Kawashima 404, Melish; Demos.
  15. Desrochers; *Plymouth Church Records* 493.
  16. Sherman and Sherman, *Vital Records of Marshfield* 179. Plymouth and Marshfield are nearby towns in Plymouth County, Massachusetts.

17. Sherman and Sherman, *Vital Records of Plymouth* 251.

18. Melish 76.

19. Goldstein 317–27. Among members of Winslow's immediate family, his father, Judge Isaac Winslow, owned several indentured servants and African slaves. Both Goldstein and Winslow historian Cynthia Hagar Krusell unearthed research confirming that John Winslow's wife, Mary Little, was born into a family that owned slaves for multiple generations. In fact, in his will her father Isaac bequeathed to Mary a female slave named Belah (322). Belah would have become Winslow's property upon marriage to Mary, and it is also likely she lived with and knew Hammon. Goldstein notes that Winslow is listed in the 1754 Massachusetts Slave Census as having one "female servant for life" (322). Records also indicate that Winslow also owned a black slave named Cato who would have been a part of the homestead in Marshfield when Hammon returned in 1760 (330). Winslow's brother Edward, who lived in Plymouth and worked in the legal system, owned at least one female slave named Esther, as well as her enslaved children, Philip and Eunice.

20. According to the diary of his great-granddaughter, Anna Green Winslow, Nowitt died of some unidentified illness in the Winslow house in 1773. Reflecting on her visit to see relatives in Marshfield, she writes, "Mr. Shaw went to the General's & prayed with an Indian woman who is sick there. . . . The General has lost another of his family to day (sic)—an Indian woman named Nab Nowitt" (qtd. in Goldstein 322).

21. Silverman 197–224.

22. Vollaro 135.

23. Ibid., 133.

24. Andrews; Zafar; Sekora, "Briton Hammon" and "Red"; Weyler.

25. Sekora, "Red" 100.

26. Hartman 55.

27. Ibid., 52.

28. Weyler 42.

29. Hammon 20.

30. Ibid., 21.

31. Zafar 54.

32. Ibid.

33. Hammon 24.

34. Laurence 157.

35. Ibid., 158.

36. Hammon 20.

37. Bolster 7–8.

38. Winslow.

39. Qtd. in Linebaugh and Rediker 215.

40. Winslow.

41. Ibid.

42. Milanich 38.

43. Ibid., 40–44.

44. Bushnell 56.

45. Qtd. in Riordan 127.

46. Riordan 27.
47. Hann.
48. Landers 22–26.
49. Green, this volume, 118.
50. Landers 13.
51. Ibid.
52. Ibid., 14.
53. George 334.
54. Ibid.
55. Ibid.
56. Marrant 117.
57. Ibid., 118.
58. Ibid., 120.
59. Hartman 59.
60. Ibid., 58.
61. Ibid., 59.
62. Ibid., 60.
63. Therefore, I would like to make one qualification to avoid overromanticizing Hammon's communal experience in Florida so as to avoid characterizing it as unequivocally "utopian" in any sense. It is not safe to assume that European colonialism and imperial practices produce a shared experience of collectivity in the region. Native groups across the region made (and frequently switched) their own alliances with European powers. These alliances occasionally put them at odds with other Native groups. In addition, the Creeks and, later, the Cherokees participated in their own version of African slavery. Taken together this context provides a challenge to any utopian notions of alliance building.
64. Sayre 6.
65. Ibid.
66. Ibid., 8.
67. Hammon 22.
68. Brooks, *Common* 3.
69. Ibid., 3.
70. Ibid., 3–4.
71. Qtd. in Braund 44.
72. Ibid.
73. Ibid.
74. Hammon 22.
75. Qtd. in Miles xvi.
76. Miles and Holland, introduction 2–3.
77. Ibid., 3.

Bibliography

Andrews, William. *To Tell a Free Story: The First Century of Afro-American Autobiography, 1760–1865*. Urbana: U of Illinois P, 1988.
Bolster, W. Jeffrey. *Black Jacks: African American Seamen in the Age of Sail*. Cambridge: Harvard UP, 1997.

Braund, Kathryn Holland. *Field of Visions: Essays on the Travels of William Bartrum, 1739–1823*. Tuscaloosa: U of Alabama P, 2010.

Brooks, Lisa. *The Common Pot: The Recovery of Native Space in the Northeast*. Minneapolis: U of Minnesota P, 2008.

Bushnell, Amy Turner. "Escape of the Nickaleers: European-Indian Relations on the Wild Coast of Florida in 1696, from Jonathan Dickinson's Journal." *Coastal Encounters: The Transformation of the Gulf South in the Eighteenth Century*. Ed. Richmond F. Brown, 31–58. Lincoln: U of Nebraska P, 2007.

Carretta, Vincent, ed. *Unchained Voices: An Anthology of Black Authors in the English-Speaking World of the Eighteenth Century*. Lexington: UP of Kentucky, 1996.

Carretta, Vincent, and Philip Gould, eds. *Genius in Bondage: Literature of the Early Black Atlantic*. Lexington: U of Kentucky P, 2001.

Demos, John. *A Little Commonwealth: Family Life in Plymouth Colony*. New York: Oxford UP, 1970.

Desrochers, Robert, Jr. "'Surprizing Deliverance?' Slavery and Freedom, Language and Identity in the Narrative of Briton Hammon, 'A Negro Man.'" Carretta and Gould 153–74.

Fogelson, Raymond D., and William Sturtevant, eds. *The Handbook of North American Indians*, vol. 14, *Southeast*. Washington: Smithsonian Institute, 2004.

Fontaneda, Hernando D'Escalante. *Memoir of Hernando D'Escalante Fontaneda, On the Country and Ancient Indian Tribes of Florida, 1575*. Ed. David O. True. Trans. Buckingham Smith. Coral Gables: Glade House, 1944.

Foster, Frances Smith. *Witnessing Slavery: The Development of Ante-bellum Slave Narratives*. Washington: Howard UP, 1988.

George, David. *An Account of the Life of Mr. David George, from Sierra Leone in Africa; given by himself in a Conversation with Brother Rippon of London, and Brother Pearce of Birmingham*. 1793. Carretta 333–50.

Goldstein, Karin. "Parlors and Garrets: The Winslow Families and their Servants." *Mayflower Quarterly* 64.4 (1998): 316–36.

Hammon, Briton. *A Narrative of the Uncommon Sufferings, and Surprizing Deliverance of Briton Hammon, a Negro Man,—Servant to General Winslow, of Marshfield, in New-England; Who Returned to Boston, After having been Absent almost Thirteen Years: Containing an Account of the Many Hardships He Underwent from the Time He Left His Master's House, in the Year 1747, to the Time of His Return to Boston—how He was Cast Away in the Capes of Florida;—the Horrid Cruelty and Inhuman Barbarity of the Indians in Murdering the Whole Ship's Crew;—the Manner of His being Carry'd by them into Captivity. Also, an Account of His being Confined Four Years and Seven Months in a Close Dungeon,—and the Remarkable Manner in which He Met with His Good Old Master in London; Who Returned to New-England, a Passenger, in the Same Ship*. 1760. Carretta 20–25.

Hann, John, ed. and trans. *Missions to the Calusa*. Gainesville: U of Florida P, 1991.

Hartman, Saidiya. *Scenes of Subjection: Terror, Slavery, and Self-Making in Nineteenth-Century America*. New York: Oxford UP, 1997.

Kawashima. "Indian Servitude in the Northeast." *Handbook of North American Indians*, vol. 4, *History of Indian-White Relations*. Ed. Wilcomb E. Washburn and William C. Sturtevant. Washington: Smithsonian Institute, 1988.

Krusell, Cynthia Hagar. *The Winslows of Careswell in Marshfield*. Marshfield Hills: Historic Research Associates, 1992.

Landers, Jane. *Black Society in Spanish Florida*. Urbana: U of Illinois P, 1999.

Laurence, Patricia. "Women's Silence as a Ritual of Truth: A Study of Literary Expressions in Austen, Bronte, and Woolf." *Listening to Silences: New Essays in Feminist Criticism*. Ed. Elaine Hedges and Shelley Fisher Fishkin. Oxford: Oxford UP, 1994. 156–67.

Linebaugh, Peter, and Marcus Rediker. *The Many-Headed Hydra: Sailors, Slaves, Commoners, and the Hidden History of the Revolutionary*. Boston: Beacon P, 2000.

Marquardt, William H. "Calusa." Fogelson and Sturtevant 204–12.

Marrant, John. *A Narrative of the Lord's Wonderful Dealings with John Marrant, A Black*. 1785. Carretta 110–33.

Melish, Joanne Pope. *Disowning Slavery: Gradual Emancipation and "Race" in New England, 1780–1860*. Ithaca: Cornell UP, 1998.

Milanich, Jerald T. *Florida Indians and the Invasion from Europe*. Gainesville: UP of Florida, 1995.

Miles, Tiya. "Eating out of the Same Pot?" Preface. Miles and Holland xv–xviii.

Miles, Tiya, and Sharon Holland, eds. *Crossing Waters, Crossing Worlds: The African Diaspora in Indian Country*. Durham: Duke UP, 2006.

———. Introduction. Miles and Holland 1–24.

Mulroy, Kevin. "Seminole Maroons." Fogelson and Sturtevant 465–77.

Plymouth Church Records, 1620–1859. 2 vols. Boston: Society, 1920–23. *Heritage Quest Online*. Web. 1 Dec. 2010.

Riordan, Patrick. "Finding Freedom in Florida: Native Peoples, African Americans, and Colonists, 1670–1816." *Florida Historical Quarterly* 75.1 (1996): 24–43. Web. 13 Oct. 2010.

Sayre, Gordon. *American Captivity Narratives: Selected Narratives*. Boston: Houghton Mifflin, 2000.

Sekora, John. "Briton Hammon, the Indian Captivity Narrative, and the African American Slave Narrative." *When Brer Rabbit Meets Coyote: African-Native American Literature*. Ed. Jonathan Brennan. Urbana: U of Illinois P, 2003. 141–57.

———. "Red, White and Black: Indian Captivities, Colonial Printers, and the Early African-American Narrative." *A Mixed Race: Ethnicity in Early America*. Ed. Frank Shuffelton. Oxford: Oxford UP, 1993. 92–104.

Sherman, Robert S., and Ruther Wildern Sherman, eds. *Vital Records of Marshfield, Massachusetts to the Year 1850*. Plymouth: Society of Mayflower Descendants, 1970.

———, eds. *Vital Records of Plymouth, Massachusetts to the Year 1850*. Plymouth: Society of Mayflower Descendants, 1993.

Silverman, David J. *Faith and Boundaries: Colonists, Christianity, and Community among the Wampanoag Indians of Martha's Vineyard, 1600–1871*. Cambridge: Cambridge UP, 2005.

Vollaro, Daniel. "Sixty Indians and Twenty Canoes: Briton Hammon's Unreliable Witness to History." *Native South* 2 (2010): 133–47. Web. 14 Oct. 2010.

Weyler, Karen A. "Race, Redemption, and Captivity in *A Narrative of the Lord's Wonderful Dealings with John Marrant, a Black* and *A Narrative of the Uncommon Sufferings and Surprizing Deliverance of Briton Hammon, A Negro Man.*" Carretta and Gould 39–53.

Winslow, Edward. Letter to John Winslow. 19 Nov. 1747. *Winslow Family Papers, 1690–1887.* Massachusetts Historical Society. MS.

Worth, John. "The Social Geography of South Florida during the Spanish Colonial Era." *"From Coast to Coast": Current Research in South Florida Archaeology.* Proc. of 71st Annual Meeting of the Society for American Archaeology Conf., 30 Apr. 2006. San Juan, Puerto Rico.

Zafar, Rafia. *We Wear the Mask: African Americans Write American Literature, 1760–1870.* New York: Columbia UP, 1997.

Uncommon Sufferings

Rethinking Bondage in *A Narrative of the Uncommon Sufferings, and Surprizing Deliverance of Briton Hammon, a Negro Man*

Keith Michael Green

ALTHOUGH IT has often been recognized as the first slave narrative published in North America,[1] Briton Hammon's *Narrative of the Uncommon Sufferings and Surprizing Deliverance of Briton Hammon, A Negro Man* (1760) is actually a quintessential example of several kinds of captivity, but not explicitly or even especially of chattel slavery. The fourteen-page document relates the Atlantic seaman's many fantastic adventures, detailing his departure from New England aboard a trading vessel, his shipwreck off the coast of Florida, his subsequent capture by Florida Natives, his paradoxical rescue and semicaptivity by the Cuban governor, his detention by a Spanish press gang, and his imprisonment for four and a half years in a Havana "Dungeon." What is more, the text renders sensationalized descriptions of the "barbarous and inhuman savages" who kill Hammon's fellow seamen, explores the "deplorable Condition" he lives in while in the jail, and recounts his various attempts at "escape" from the governor's oversight.[2] Even more provocatively, it ends when Hammon is reunited with his New England owner, a General John Winslow, whom he calls "my good master," a seemingly puzzling appellation for readers of nineteenth-century slave narratives who are accustomed to bondspeople's scathing remarks about the cruelty and hypocrisy of their white owners.[3]

The research of such scholars as John Sekora, Robert Desrochers Jr., and Jeffrey Gagnon has gone a long way toward explaining these anomalies, revealing that Hammon was a New England slave who was forced by his owner, Winslow, to leave his family on a Christmas Day shipping expedition bound to Jamaica and Campeche Bay. His apparent enthusiasm after being reunited with this "good master" is probably a function of the kind of story Winslow permitted him to tell and the kind of story his New England audience wanted to hear. Hence, the chauvinistic language used against Native Americans and the complimentary remarks made in reference to Winslow are likely symptomatic of Hammon's lack of authorial control and the ideological imperatives of mid-eighteenth-century publishing. Gagnon's incisive analysis, in fact, suggests that Hammon's "captivity" to the coastal tribe of the Calusa might have actually been liberatory, given the fact that the Calusa were repeated targets of English raids for Native slaves and potentially perceived Hammon, still a slave of the English, as a fellow victim.[4] But the *Uncommon Sufferings* was not the venue for that kind of suffering, at least not openly. In the interest of sales to, and sympathy with, a white New England audience, Hammon could only tell the story of his captivities to foreign agents, and not to domestic ones.

One of the many implications of this purposeful silencing is that Hammon's narrative tells us just as much about the unexpected entanglements between various forms of captivity writing as it does about any one particular story of bondage. As John Sekora has noted:

> Briton Hammon's presence as a subject for a captivity for a time expands the scope of the captivity tale, but at the same time it creates the terms of possibility for the slave narrative. As a slave writing, a captivity undermines that form but strengthens alternative life stories for other slaves, so the meaning of one narrative is sometimes another one. The earlier tale of Indian captivity is easily turned to the later story of southern bondage. One escape teaches another.[5]

This confluence of seemingly unrelated species of bondage produces a fascinating enigma at the proverbial "beginning" of African American slave narratives: while Briton Hammon's *Uncommon Sufferings* "creates the terms of possibility" for the genre of the slave narrative," it is not exclusively or even chiefly concerned with mapping the historical, social, and psychological dimensions of chattel slavery.

I read this as a productive confusion, what Philip Gould has elsewhere referred to as an "enabling ambiguity."[6] That is, the generic instability present at the inauguration of the slave narrative offers a singular opportunity to reimagine what narratives of black bondage are and how we might read them, to think more critically about the kinds of bondage Hammon's narrative recounts and its implications for the genre of the slave narrative. Read closely, I argue, the tale discloses a subtle, yet significant, fact about "slave" narratives and black life in the New World: even in the context of chattel slavery—perhaps the most conspicuous, influential, and menacing historical reality of the New World—multiple kinds of captivity, confinement, and bondage structured the lives and stories of people of African descent. In Hammon's case, this truth comes to us at the cost of a straightforward narrative about his bondage to New England white subjects, which might make us leery of the price of such knowledge. However, the means by which this more varied story of black bondage and experience comes to us should not disqualify its validity or import. Rather, it should teach us that stories of captivity often vie for attention, displace one another, and disavow their own vexed relationships to other kinds of bondage. Furthermore, they carry their own particular theories of power, models of history, notions of identity, and formulas for resistance. As a result, to ignore any aspect of black bondage is to deny African and African American subjects full participation and agency in the contradictory and ever-unfurling complexity that is the social world.

If slave narratives constitute "the ground on which later black writing is based," as Sekora argues, much depends on appreciating this complexity.[7] During Hammon's time, "slavery" could signify any number of conditions in which a person's property within themselves was compromised or denied. C. B. Macpherson more precisely explains, "The individual, it was thought, is free inasmuch as he is proprietor of his person and capacities. The human essence is freedom from dependence on the wills of others, and freedom is a function of possession."[8] Olaudah Equiano famously emblematizes this definition of slavery and freedom when he exclaims in his *Interesting Narrative* that "I who had been a slave in the morning, trembling at the will of another, now became my own master," paradoxically communicating his personal autonomy through the language of mastery and possession.[9] The "will of another" defined his bondage, and conversely, his ownership of his own will defines his freedom. Following this line of thinking suggests that the hardships of unfreedom were not just particular to African and African American bondspeople, but to a wide range of subjects. Servants, sailors, apprentices, wives, children, the unpropertied, and even supposedly "free-born" white men could all potentially find themselves subject to the will of others, even as they might have limited or denied the ability of other subjects to actuate their wills. It was for this reason that American colonists, roughly a decade and a half after the publication of Hammon's narrative, could speak of their "slavery" to the British without a touch of intentional irony. *Uncommon Sufferings* transmits this flexible and eclectic definition of bondage to later narratives of black captivity by presenting "an Atlantic world," in Desrochers's reading of the narrative, "governed by hierarchies of servitude."[10]

However, as opposed to reveling in the "hierarchies of servitude" that mark the account, two approaches have typically structured analyses of the text. The first has been to acknowledge promptly and astutely the irregularity of Hammon's narrative with respect to later slave narratives, and then to insist on the text's centrality to that genre. As codified in John Sekora's earlier statement, the "captivity" recounted in Hammon's tale "undermines" the tradition, and yet it also "creates the terms of possibility for the slave narrative."[11] The other approach has been to isolate *Uncommon Sufferings*'s specific relationship to Indian captivity narratives, easily its most talked-about feature, and then to consider how later African American writing processes or revises this particular aspect.[12] Bracketing both of these moves, at least for the moment, I would like to pause at and pursue Sekora's first observation: "Briton Hammon's presence as a subject for a captivity for a time expands the scope of the captivity tale." What exactly does this mean? In what ways does Hammon's narrative continue, expand, and revise the "captivity tale"? What is more, if Hammon's narrative "undermines" the slave narrative, then for what kind of narrative does it lay the foundation? If "one escape teaches another," then what narratives of escape does *Uncommon Sufferings* teach?

I would argue that the narrative of escape that the text teaches is a conflicted but persistent story of African American captivity, one that refracts multiple locations and disparate agents of bondage; though these stories of captivity may certainly be informed by the logic and logistics of chattel slavery, as is the case with Hammon's narrative, they are not ultimately reducible to and congruent with the experience of lifelong bondage to whites in America. Rather, they are animated by competing, contested, and overlapping sites and systems of mastery. In the process, Hammon's narrative expands what a "captivity tale" might look like and mean, placing a black subject at the center of a narrative tradition that presumes white privilege, motivations, and identity. As is suggested by the potential rescue precipitated by Hammon's "captivity" to the Calusa, such appropriations of the "captivity tale" do not only expand it but also repurpose and even deconstruct it. Read in this way, *Uncommon Sufferings* does more than "create the terms of possibility for the slave narrative"; it inaugurates a multifaceted tradition of black captivity writing that exists both inside and in excess of American narratives of slavery.

This essay is an initial gesture toward outlining this unarticulated tradition. Reading the *Uncommon Sufferings* as a scene of instruction for black captivity writing, broadly conceived, it revisits the sundry captivities refracted in Hammon's foundational text as they signify on depictions of black bondage found in contemporaneous, early nineteenth-century, and antebellum African American autobiographical writing. In doing so, it situates black American bondage within a larger and more nuanced network of images, vocabulary, narratives, and histories related to confinement and coercion in the New World, a world made out of assorted, far-reaching, and counter-intuitive relationships to bondage.

Transnational Captivities

Perhaps the most conspicuous difference between *Uncommon Sufferings* and the typical "plantation narrative," to use William Tynes Cowan's apt phrase, is its transnational vision of bondage; it is not bound to the American South but inhabits a world born out of, in Paul Giles's words, "traversals between national territory and intercontinental space."[13] Hammon's captivity is not to any single nation, but to isolated and, at other times, overlapping systems and techniques of confinement that work within and without imperial boundaries. By the second sentence of *Uncommon Sufferings,* Hammon already finds himself in Jamaica, and just a few short statements later he is "captive" to Natives in Spanish Florida. Hammon spends roughly five weeks with them, after which he is transferred to a "Spanish Schooner" and taken to Cuba.[14] Later, Hammon becomes the personal ward of the Cuban governor, Francisco Antonio Cagigal de la Vega, until he is imprisoned for almost five years in a Havana jail when he refuses to serve in a Spanish press gang, thereby making him a prisoner of the Spanish empire. Since his imprisonment occurs without the governor's knowledge, this suggests that Hammon is also a captive of local systems beyond the empire's or, at least, the governor's purview. Eventually, a sympathetic Englishman intercedes on his behalf, and he is delivered into the governor's more lenient custody, at which time he makes a successful escape from the island after three tries.

For the class of subjects Hammon represents here, African American seafarers, such intersections of African American bondage and Atlantic captivity were probably frequent enough, though their simultaneity in the experience of one subject and in one narrative is noteworthy. As

W. Jeffrey Bolster explains in *Black Jacks: African American Seamen in the Age of Sail*, "Slaves were drawn increasingly into the maritime labor market of the northern colonies during the middle of the war-torn eighteenth century, when seamen were often in short supply," and "sailed regularly to Europe, the West Indies, and Africa."[15] Hence, Hammon's maritime movements marked him as a "citizen of the world," and with that, exposure to the varied forms of captivity such citizenship presented. To be sure, his status as a bondsperson certainly tempers our understanding of the level of mobility he enjoyed—his "travels" from one locale to the next are often under duress, as with his forced removal from New England on Christmas Day—but it nonetheless suggests that his appreciation of the condition of servitude went well beyond New England versions of that experience.[16] As a captive to Native Americans in coastal Florida, a prisoner to Spanish interests in a Havana jail, and a ward of the governor of Cuba, Hammon knew that bondage took polymorphous forms across and within varied geographical locations.

Other eighteenth-century slave narratives bear out the unexceptional nature of black bondage beyond American shores. *A Narrative of the Most Remarkable Particulars in the Life of James Albert Ukasaw Gronniosaw, an African Prince, As Related by Himself* (1770), *The Interesting Narrative of Olaudah Equiano Gustavas Vassa, Written by Himself* (1789), and Venture Smith's *A Narrative of the Life and Adventures of Venture, a Native of Africa, but Resident Above Sixty Years in the United States of America. Related by Himself* (1798) all detail scenes of extranational captivity, beginning first with the domestic slave trade practiced in West Africa. Although domestic African slavery had already become complicit with the techniques and agents of the Atlantic slave trade, these narratives take pains to underscore the differences between the bondage occurring in Africa and the slavery later experienced by captives in the New World. Equiano's narrative,[17] for example, compares the status of slaves to Africans and of those to Europeans in this way, "Those prisoners which were not sold or redeemed we kept as slaves: but how different was their condition from that of the slaves in the West Indies!," corroborating Paul E. Lovejoy's assertion that in African domestic slavery bondspeople "could become full members of these groups, or they could be kept as voiceless dependents," but there "was no class of slaves."[18] Slavery inhered in specific relations of dependency, not in particular groups of people. Hence, Gronniosaw's, Equiano's, and Smith's depictions of African slavery diversify the locations and captive formations that we might typically associate with the "slave narrative."

James Albert Gronniosaw, for instance, first enters captivity when he is tempted away from his Nigerian hometown by a seemingly benign African merchant who promises to show him "houses with wings" that could "walk upon the water" and "white folks."[19] Though the merchant promises to "bring [him] safe back soon," the merchant carries him over a thousand miles away from his place of birth, at which point the young Gronniosaw is nearly beheaded by a local ruler.[20] Likewise Olaudah Equiano's first introduction to bondage is at the hands of Africans; while he and his sister were still children among the Igbo, Equiano writes, "two men and a woman got over our walls, and in a moment seized us both."[21] This experience of West African captivity is replicated several times before he gets to the Atlantic coast, as he explains that he "had often changed masters" before seeing any Europeans.[22] As in Hammon's narrative, captivity here is temporary and episodic; the captive tumbles from one form of bondage into another and at the hands of different and differently motivated agents. Similarly, Venture Smith's first captivity occurs when another band of Africans, also working at the behest of coastal slave-trading interests, capture his mother, father, and remaining family and then subsequently murder his father. Suggesting the competition and unique motivations of each of these separate groups and captors, this band is then defeated by another band, at which point, Smith explains, "I was then taken a second time."[23] Though they are sometimes framed as mere prelude to New World bondage in these texts, stories of domestic slavery in Africa constitute their own complex representational histories and concerns that complicate the nature of bondage in the slave narrative.

True to the logistics of the Atlantic slave trade, bondage in early slave narratives is often set in the Caribbean. Venture Smith's first stop is "Barbadoes," as is the case with both Gronniosaw and Equiano.[24] It is in Barbados, in fact, that Gronniosaw finds a purchaser who eventually transfers him to New England.[25] Likewise, Barbadian slavery is the backdrop of Venture Smith's narrative when he notes that of the two hundred bondspeople who made it through the Middle Passage, all but four were sold "to the planters there," underlining David Eltis's observation that "the continent of North America received fewer slaves in total than did the tiny island of Barbados alone."[26] In this context, the West Indian locations to which Hammon's narrative alludes by way of his compelled journeys to Jamaica and Cuba are hardly exceptional within black New World experience, but quite consistent with the historical realities and narrative representations of eighteenth-century black bondage.

An early nineteenth-century example of the geographical diversity that marks narratives of black bondage can be found in *The Narrative of Robert Adams, a Sailor, who was Wrecked on the Western Coast of Africa, in the Year 1810, was Detained Three Years in Slavery by the Arabs of the Great Desert, and Resided Several Months in the City of Tombuctoo* (1816). This Barbary captivity narrative recounts the transatlantic adventures of Robert Adams, or Benjamin Rose as he might have been known in the United States, a biracial sailor who was captured by Moors somewhere off the coast of Senegal in 1810.[27] The text is peculiar within the genre of the Barbary captivity narrative, however, because it also includes the tale of Adams's abduction by a band of "negroes" headed to the famed city of Timbuktu—a tale that is, to put it mildly, highly suspect. Even so, the narrative clearly relies on the well-known historical realities of Barbary captivity and the domestic African slave trade to frame the not-so-familiar story of the unlucky seaman. Robert J. Allison estimates that nearly seven hundred Americans were captured in North Africa between 1789 and 1817, and of that number at least a handful were persons of African descent.[28] Their experience was not the lifelong, intergenerational captivity outlined in the traditional slave narrative, as "[t]heir captors hoped to ransom the men and vessels back to either their friends or government."[29] Nonetheless, North African captivity constituted a historical form of black bondage that demands further critical investigation and, more to my point, represented a reality powerfully, if obliquely, suggested by Hammon's intercontinental adventures.

Adams's narrative recounts extranational events that have their counterparts in Hammon's account, particularly the story of shipwreck and captivity caused by an incompetent captain. In chapter 1, Adams sets off from New York (for Hammon, New England) on a British trading vessel bound for the Island of May (for Hammon, Jamaica and Campeche Bay). Eventually, the vessel runs aground off the coast of Senegal (for Hammon, Florida), due to the ineptitude of the captain. In Adams's account "the captain did not know where he was steering," and in Hammon's "the captain was advised, intreated, and beg'd on, by every Person on board," to unload the too-heavy cargo.[30] Upon swimming ashore, Adams and his compatriots encounter racial and linguistic outsiders, Moors, who take them as prisoners; likewise, Hammon is held for five weeks by "Indians" who behave "like so many Devils."[31] Sometime thereafter, Adams is taken by a band of "Negroes" and taken to Timbuktu. During his six-month stay, he becomes the cherished captive and houseguest of the "King and Queen" and receives the mildest treatment of his captivity anywhere; he is essentially free to roam the city. Similarly after his incarceration, Hammon becomes the ward of the governor in Cuba and is free go where he pleases, except off the island.[32] Finally, in chapter 4, Adams finds his way to London, where he is "completely destitute"; likewise, Hammon is "left in very poor circumstances" in the capital city and fortuitously finds passage back to America.[33]

Published over fifty years after *Uncommon Sufferings,* Adams's account indicates that narratives of black captivity continued to be shaped by multiple international locales, and especially by the historical realities and concerns of (black) seafaring populations. Though the regimented hierarchies, intensive labor, and deferred compensation of maritime occupations made seafaring a risky proposition, what Paul A. Gilje has termed "a life akin to slavery," many sailors often understood their perambulations in "the wooden world" as a refuge from the typical strictures of eighteenth-century society.[34] Peter Linebaugh and Marcus Rediker have shown that seamen established their own systems of rule, codes of conduct, and modes of expression that confounded the fictions of national allegiance, cultural superiority, and racial privilege that prevailed on land, what they term a "hydrarchy."[35] As such, a life before the mast could open singular opportunities for black subjects, even for those who were enslaved. Vincent Carretta's reading of Equiano's experience on the high seas and in the Royal Navy bears this out: "At sea, artificially imposed racial limitations would have destroyed everyone, white and black."[36] Consequently, "black sailors ate the same food as their white counterparts, wore the same clothes, shared the same quarters, received the same pay, benefits, and health care, undertook the same duties, and had the same opportunities for advancement."[37] Refracting the relatively egalitarian social order of eighteenth-century nautical life, accounts of black maritime experience and captivity make available a quite different story of bondage than those narratives that are bound to the continental United States.

Native American Captors

Hammon's narrative also explores the possibility of Native American captors. As Frances Smith Foster has already noted, with Hammon's account "the first narrative by a Black Indian captive exists."[38] Jeffrey Gagnon's revelation that the Florida Natives Hammon encounters may have believed they were liberating Hammon from the English, rather than capturing him certainly complicates this claim.[39] It demands a consideration of Hammon's experiences alongside other moments of Afro–Native American collaboration, such as Spain's failed attempt to establish a colony in eastern South Carolina in 1526. Christened San Miguel de Gualdape by its founder, Lucas Vasquez de Ayllon, the settlement collapsed after Ayllon died, disputes over power ensued, and the enslaved Africans brought to provide cheap labor revolted and fled to sympathetic Natives in the South Carolina woods.[40] This story of the "first foreign colony on U.S. soil" anticipates the terms of cooperation that would structure fugitive slaves' memorable flights to the Seminole Indians in Florida during the early nineteenth century: "A common foe, not any special affinity of skin color, became the first link of friendship, the earliest motivation for alliance."[41] An uncanny reprise of Hammon's potentially fortuitous encounter with the Florida Calusa, the Seminole's coalition with and defense of escaped slaves in Florida points to the enduring tradition of Afro-Native resistance to white domination.[42]

At the same time, the text's references to the "inhuman Savages," "hallowing like so many Devils," also convincingly installs the account within the more sensational tradition of the colonial Indian captivity narrative, what Richard Slotkin has termed "the starting point of an American mythology."[43] Hammon and his editors appear to be fully aware of this tradition, and the narrative directly aligns itself with it, concluding by rejoicing that Hammon was "freed from a long and dreadful Captivity," a word that expresses the incredible variety and complexity of his many harrowing experiences.[44] Following the lead of Francis Smith Foster, John Sekora, and Karen A. Weyler, I too read Indian captivity as the "generic context" in which Hammon's account would have been read.[45]

Indian captivity narratives were an established and profitable form by which to articulate a particular kind of human experience, and Hammon's narrative drew much of its appeal from that genre. The leading Boston firm for publishing Indian captivity narratives, Fowle and Draper, was closely connected by "family and business" to John Green and Joseph Russell, the company that published Hammon's narrative.[46] Moreover, at the time of the account's publication, public discourse surrounding the Seven Years' War (1756–1763) fomented anti–Native American sentiment by framing the French and their Native American allies as persecutors of the British colonists.[47] In reading Hammon's miraculous tale, then, the most important difference for mid-eighteenth-century British colonists might not have been between white and black, at least immediately, but between the British colonies and competing European and Native

American constituencies. Hammon's text might therefore be profitably explained through the ignoble cultural tradition of "Indian hating," as Herman Melville called it in *The Confidence Man*. In this context, it is not wholly unexpected that Hammon directs his most disparaging words not at General Winslow, his actual captor, but at the "Indians" allegedly allied with the Spanish in Florida. Hammon's description of them as "barbarous" and willing to "roast [him] alive" clearly issues from these local and historically specific matters of publication, historical context, and the more general tradition of anti-Indian prejudice.[48]

A look at the contemporaneous *Narrative of the Lord's Wonderful Dealings with John Marrant, a Black* (1785) similarly reveals the complex relationship of black bondage to Native American captivity in early African American writing. This Methodist-sponsored tract chronicles the sinful childhood and adolescent conversion of Marrant, who was born free in New York and who eventually relocated to South Carolina after his father's death. Soon after hearing and meeting the transatlantic preacher George Whitefield and being converted, Marrant wanders off into the woods, where he encounters a Cherokee scout and continues on with him into the countryside. Later in the narrative, he becomes a captive and is nearly beheaded at a Cherokee encampment. If not for his ability to pray in their language, the account maintains, Marrant would have surely died and, more importantly, would have been unable to convert the souls of the both the Cherokee executioner, the Cherokee chieftain, and his daughter.

Even if the equation of sin and captivity, salvation and freedom, is here in inchoate form—the formula that structured later slave narratives—Marrant's narrative is not strictly defined as a slave narrative, but, more properly, a narrative about his simultaneous obliteration and appropriation of Cherokee culture. He effectively domesticates what he calls the "wilderness" of the South Carolina forest through his conversion of the Cherokee to Christianity, even as he inhabits Native American difference through his manipulation of their language and dress.[49] As "the text's ventriloquist," to invoke Henry Louis Gates Jr.'s phrasing, Marrant impersonates and parodies Cherokee subjects only to displace them.[50] Accordingly, when he returns from captivity to the white settlements, he notes this of his own clothing: "the skins of wild beasts composed my garments, my head was set out in the savage manner, with a long pendant down my back, a sash round my middle without breeches, and a tomahawk by my side."[51] Despite the seemingly unfavorable connotation of "savage" here, Marrant does not represent himself as corrupted by his encounter with

Native Americans. Instead, his putative "savagery" allows him access to a John the Baptist–like experience with God in the Georgia "wilderness," thereby bolstering his right of entry to Christian experience and buttressing the requisite separation from secular humanity embedded in the spiritual conversion narrative. This is what we hear so tellingly in Hammon's generic and baldly chauvinistic reference to the "devilish" howling of the "Indians." As Karen Weyler contends, "Hammon's and Marrant's narratives create for their subjects identities marked not by race, but by piety."[52] Native American representation mediates between white civilization and black inferiority by triangulating the relationship of blacks to whites, thereby humanizing African Americans at the expense of Native Americans.

These ideologically freighted representations of African American captivity to Native Americans anticipate the picture of Cherokee slaveholders presented in Henry Bibb's *The Life and Adventures of Henry Bibb, An American Slave* (1849). Just as Hammon writes that "the *Indians* on board the sloop betook themselves to their Canoes, then set the vessel on Fire, making a prodigious shouting and hallowing like so many Devils,"[53] Bibb invokes the sensational language found in many Indian captivity narratives during his rendition of an "Indian frolic": "Their dress for the dance was most generally a great bunch of bird feathers, coon tails, or something of the kind stuck in their heads, and a great many shells tied about their legs to rattle while dancing. Their manner of dancing is taking hold of each others hands and forming a ring around the large fire in the centre, and go stomping around it until they would get drunk or their heads would get to swimming, and they would go off and drink, and another set come on."[54] In Hammon's account, the more "devilish" the Indians behave, the more refined, Anglo-American, and human he appears to be; in Bibb's account, the more exotic the dress of the "frolicking" Indians, the more self-possessed and even sophisticated he appears to his middle-class, white, northern readership. Rafia Zafar explains: "Bibb swings between the idea of the Indian as interesting foreigner . . . and that of the Native American as a debased individual."[55] In the process, he becomes an ethnographic authority through his masterful observations of idiosyncratic or depraved Indian behavior. As with Hammon and Marrant, representations of reprobate Native American captors help an African American narrator negotiate his precarious position in a white world.

Although Bibb's is the only sustained representation of African American enslavement to Native Americans in the antebellum slave narrative, there were thousands of African American slaves held by southeastern

Indians in the first half of the nineteenth century.[56] The research of
Laura Lovett reveals that roughly 12 percent of all Works Projects Administration slave narratives come from African Americans who identified themselves as Indians or were descendants of Indians, and many of
these accounts recall experiences of enslavement by members of the Five
Nations.[57] Compared to Hammon's and Bibb's narratives, of course, the
WPA texts are more involved and relate the accounts of those who were
born Indian slaves or spent much of their lives in that condition. They
speak to what Celia Naylor identifies as an "African Indian" subjectivity
forged in continued and complex relationships with Native Americans;[58]
both Hammon and Bibb, on the other hand, make it a point to distinguish their subject positions from their "devilish" captors.[59] Still, both
texts reveal the continued linkages between African American captivity
and Native Americans—a reality and rhetorical ploy that is alluded to by
Hammon's many-sided account.

Imprisonment

Along with being a de facto prisoner in several locales and to different kinds of people, Hammon is also quite literally a prisoner, for "four
years and seven months," in a Havana "prison" for his refusal to join
a Spanish press gang.[60] Despite its spare treatment in the narrative—he
never describes the conditions of the structure or his activities there in
any detail—his incarceration is chronologically the longest single form
of bondage the text recounts. He spends nearly five years in the jail; his
next longest captivity is for five weeks at the hands of Calusa Natives.
Furthermore, it is distinguished in the narrative by the relative lack of
the physical mobility that he enjoys, even while a captive, throughout
the rest of the narrative. While he is a ward of the Cuban governor, for
example, he is free to "walk about the City" and "do work for [him]
self," but while he is in the "close Dungeon" people are compelled to ask
the "Keeper" for permission to see him.[61] Thus, one might imagine that
imprisonment figured as the most traumatic form of bondage among the
constellation of captivities that made up Hammon's nearly thirteen-year
absence from his New England "master." Moreover, despite their significantly different historical contexts, Hammon's representation of Cuban
imprisonment is highly suggestive of the antebellum experience of black
Americans, who were often simultaneously victims of the penal system
and of the slave system.

Particularly in urban areas, such imprisonment in jails and workhouses formed a regular component of African American enslavement

and free black life in the South. As Richard C. Wade makes clear in *Slavery in the Cities,* "In the metropolis . . . official agencies took over large areas of [slave] control—and this was inevitable. . . . enforcement of ordinances necessarily fell to the local police and municipal courts."[62] Slave imprisonment appears to have occurred most frequently in the context of the domestic slave trade, the intrastate and interstate trading system in which more than two million slaves, Walter Johnson speculates, were transported during the antebellum era, mostly from the upper South to the lower South.[63] County jails and other penal structures were used in this system as spaces for "safekeeping." Between 1837 and 1857 in Baltimore, for instance, nearly 500 slaves were imprisoned, many of whom were recaptured runaways.[64] Similarly, slave traders lodged 452 slaves at the District of Columbia jail between 1824 and 1828.[65] Certainly, such tactics were not the first or even the most desirable options in slave discipline, as it denied the owners of slaves (if nothing else) the labor of their bondspeople. But whether it was for disciplining wayward slaves, holding intransigent ones until sale, or housing them on the journey south, jails and workhouses had an important place in southern slavery.

The reality of simultaneous enslavement and incarceration is well reflected in antebellum slave narratives. Henry Bibb, who was noted earlier for his remarkable rendition of Indian slavery, was also a "four time loser," incarcerated in Kentucky's Bedford jail, Covington jail, Louisville jail, and Louisville workhouse for his repeated attempts to rescue his family from the South. Likewise, the narratives of Frederick Douglass, Solomon Northup, Henry Box Brown, and Lunsford Lane, to cite only the most recognizable examples, also reflect the frequency of slave and black incarceration in antebellum life.[66] In particular, Harriet Jacobs's *Incidents in the Life of a Slave Girl* is frequently cited for Jacobs's seven-year confinement in her grandmother's attic, but what is often left unacknowledged is the literal imprisonment members of her family experience while in slavery.[67] The narrative relates, for example, her brother's incarceration in the Chowan County jail for six months after a failed escape attempt, and the imprisonment of her daughter, son, aunt, and uncle for another two months as a means of extorting information from them after Jacobs's disappearance. As with Bibb's depiction of Indian slavery in his autobiography, this is not an incidental episode; a close reading of this moment reveals that it is the children's incarceration that ultimately triggers the set of events that leads to their emancipation. After Flint is unable to afford the continued costs of detaining the children in the Chowan County jail, he reconsiders his vow never to sell them. "My brother and the children," Jacobs explains, "had now been in the jail two months, and that also was some expense. My friends thought it was a favorable time to work on [Dr. Flint's] discouraged feelings."[68] Once he does decide to sell them, the children's grandmother arranges for an ally slave trader to purchase them and sell them to the children's father, who subsequently buys them and relinquishes them to their grandmother. The convergence of slave power and penal structures here results in the cracking of the armor, a rupture in the ability of the slave power to lock in slaves. Again, this intersection of varied systems of constriction might appear "surprising," but it was fairly well anticipated (if only in oblique form) by Hammon's 1760 account.

Indentured Servitude

All of Hammon's experiences of captivity and bondage, however, are contextualized by the fact that Hammon was, what the text calls, a "servant" to General Winslow at the beginning of his travels. We are now fairly confident that Hammon was actually Winslow's slave, and not just his employee or servant, but the interchangeability of the words *servant* and *slave* in the mid-eighteenth century alerts us to the fact that indentured servants and slaves led disturbingly similar lives in the colonial era.[69] Jeffrey Gagnon reveals the saliency of this point when he notes that Hammon likely worked and lived beside Native American indentured servants in the Winslow household, thus having contact with North American Natives well before his encounter with the Calusa through the shared experience of service to whites.[70] Black indentured servitude, in fact, frequently took up where slavery left off. After northern states passed acts of emancipation, Ira Berlin explains, many former bondspeople were compelled to accept "long-term indentureships as part of the price of freedom," which meant that they "left bondage and entered servitude in the same motion."[71] As such, black indentured servitude exists as another underappreciated form of captivity obliquely signified on by the *Uncommon Sufferings*.

In the edited collection *Children Bound to Labor: The Pauper Apprenticeship System in Early America,* Ruth Wallis Herndon and John E. Murray outline the pervasive nature of indentured servitude, particularly for children, from the mid-eighteenth century until the first half of the nineteenth century. For youths who had been born out of wedlock, raised by only one parent (usually the mother), abandoned by their parents, or simply reared by parents who were deemed otherwise unfit to take care of them, "binding out," as it was then called, was a likely fate. Their personal care, occupational training, and basic education would be entrusted to another family until they reached adulthood, usually eighteen for girls and twenty-one for boys.[72] Herndon and Murray speculate that the practice was so common that "it may have functioned in some places as a system of bound labor second only in importance to slavery."[73] Though established as an efficient and humane way of alleviating the economic burden of indigent children on orphanages and other publicly supported institutions, pauper apprenticeship sometimes meant equally poor, if not worse, treatment with new families. Herndon and Murray note that children were already understood as a "form of property," and pauper apprenticeship could exacerbate this condition, particularly when it was compounded by race. "Girls of color," the authors note, "benefited the least from the system," and the presence of slavery and racism, in both the North and the South, probably systematically crippled African American parents' ability to protect their children from and within this system.[74] Child apprenticeship thus provides yet another important frame of reference for thinking about African American bondage in provocative ways, especially as it concerns the suffering of children, whose abuse and compulsion have often been elided by appeals to stewardship, guardianship, and paternalism.

We need look no further than the spiritual autobiographies collected in William L. Andrews's *Sisters of the Spirit: Three Black Women's Autobiographies of the Nineteenth Century* to appreciate the force and nature of indentured servitude in African American life writing. Though a "free"-born black, the spiritual autobiography of Jarena Lee, *The Life and Religious Experience of Jarena Lee, A Coloured Lady, Giving an Account of her Call to Preach the Gospel* (1836), begins with a proclamation of her unfreedom: "I was born February 11, 1783, at Cape May, state of New Jersey. At the age of seven years, I was parted from my parents, and went to live as a servant maid, with a Mr. Sharp, at the distance of about from the place of my birth."[75] Likewise, the narrative of Zilpha Elaw's spiritual conversion, *Memoirs of the Life, Religious Experience, Ministerial Travels and Labours of Mrs. Zilpha Elaw, An American Female of Colour* (1846), begins by explaining that after her mother dies, "My father, having placed my younger sister under the care of her aunt, then consigned me to the care of Pierson and Rebecca Mitchel, with whom I remained until I attained the age of eighteen."[76] Both Elaw and Lee provide skeletal terms with which to flesh out their experiences; Lee is a "servant maid" and Elaw is "consigned" to the services of other adults. Moreover, as spiritual autobiographies, and not records of material histories, the overarching theological imperative of these texts prevent them from providing any substantial commentary on the conditions and meanings of their apprenticeship, or how they might have compared to slavery. Instead, they provide fairly normative narratives of spiritual conversion (as is the case with Lee)—a reprobate heart (27), sin sickness (28), thoughts of suicide (28, 30)—but not any explication of the conditions of servitude.[77] Like the "servitude" that frames Hammon's 1760 account, their narratives are perhaps purposely ambiguous about these details in order to highlight more emphatically the captivity that is really at stake in the narrative: the servitude of people to sin, not of children to adults.

One narrative, however, in which the latter form of captivity is still legible, despite its clear commitment to spiritual autobiographic aesthetics, is Julia Foote's *A Brand Plucked from the Fire* (1879). Like those of Elaw and Lee, the narrative begins with a statement announcing an arrangement whereby the young child will become the ward of another family. In the third chapter, Foote reveals: "When I was ten years of age I was sent to live in the country with a family by the name of Prime. They had no children, and soon became quite fond of me. I really think Mrs. Prime loved me."[78] However, in chapter 5, Foote fails to find some baked goods that should have been deposited in the attic, and for this offense, her new guardians "brought a rawhide. This Mrs. Prime applied to my back until she was tired, all the time insisting that I should confess that I took the cakes. This, of course, I could not do."[79] After this assault, Foote describes what is essentially her escape from the abusive family: "It was a long, lonely road, through the woods; every sound frightened me, and made me run for fear someone was after me."[80] When the Primes come to reclaim Foote from her biological parents, they are asked to explain the reason for the severe beating, but Foote is, tellingly, still bound out to the Primes for another year. More to my point, this is done, as Foote is sure to point out, "very much against my will."[81] If *unfreedom* means the violation of another person's will, the abuse or misuse of a person's property within themselves, then Foote clearly inhabited some relation of captivity to the Primes, a captivity that might have been in excess of the narrative of spiritual conversion that she was authorized to tell that nonetheless leaks out in these striking moments.

We find a partly fictionalized and more sustained autobiographical exploration of childhood apprenticeship through Harriet E. Wilson's *Our Nig; or, Sketches from the Life of a Free Black* (1859), a novel largely based on the author's own experience of childhood indenture in New Hampshire as told through the character Frado. Though P. Gabrielle Foreman's 2009 introduction of the text claims that "indenture is not an appropriate model through which to understand Frado's experience" and that the novel is better understood through the framework of "life stories published by and about former slaves,"[82] *Our Nig*'s emplotment, characterization, and thematics accord with the essential realities of antebellum, child indentured servitude.[83] Like the historical Wilson, the biracial child Frado is abandoned by her parents and forced to toil as the servant of a white, middle-class family, the Bellmonts. Frado's life with this new family begins when her parents fall on hard economic times, which is compounded by the fact that Mag Smith, Frado's mother, is already understood as a social pariah for having had children out of wedlock and for marrying a black man. Speculating on the chances of binding out the child, her mother's male companion notes, "There's Frado six years old, and pretty, if she is yours, and white folks'll say so. She'd be a prize somewhere."[84] Soon after this conversation, Frado is left at the Bellmonts' "large, old fashioned, two story white house," suggesting the improved economic possibilities for the young girl.[85] However, Frado is terribly mistreated as a servant, particularly by Mrs. Bellmont, who is described as a "she-devil."[86] She violently kicks Frado, wedges objects into her mouth, and shaves off her hair. Though *Our Nig* mimics much of the physical and psychological abuse found elsewhere in 1850s slave narratives, it still holds out the promise of an eventual and definitive freedom, a requisite feature of narratives of indentured servitude. At one especially trying moment when Frado contemplates killing her mistress, the narrator reminds the reader: "But she was restrained by an overruling Providence; and finally decided to stay contentedly through her period of service, which would expire when she was eighteen years of age."[87] Though "slavery's shadows fall even there," as the novel's extended title famously declares, Frado's childhood and life in New England is structured by the logic and timetable of indentured servitude, not just slavery.

I HAVE argued that Briton Hammon's *Uncommon Sufferings* is not a typical slave narrative or, more to the point, is not only a slave narrative but also a signification upon Indian captivity narratives, tales of slave incarceration, accounts of maritime shipwreck and abduction, and representations of African American child indentured servitude. As such, it is a text that lives in excess of the meanings scholars have ordinarily attached to black bondage. This is an observation that has far-reaching consequences. Though Sekora argues that Hammon's text challenged the parameters of the captivity narrative "for a time,"[88] the complex lives and narratives of Harriet Jacobs, Henry Bibb, Harriet Wilson, and Robert Adams in the nineteenth century bear witness to the fact that captivity for people of African descent did not die with Hammon but, if anything, might have taken on an added and even more robust life than it had before. In this light, it is interesting to note that Robert Desrochers Jr. states that Hammon might have made his last appearance in the historical record in 1790;[89] this is the same year in which the first U.S. penitentiary was constructed, the Walnut Street jail. African Americans made up as much as 44 percent of the prison population in late eighteenth-century prisons.[90] At the present moment, scholars have variously labeled the explosion of prisons and detention facilities in the United States (and the West) as a prison industrial complex, suggesting the ways in which prisons and other correctional facilities arrange and impact the organization of our cities, social policy, and even models of subjectivity.[91] Even more than this, we currently live in a world characterized by the presence of military detention camps (Guantanamo Bay), child slavery (*restavek* in Haiti), Somali piracy, sex trafficking, debt slavery (bonded labor), and prison labor, just to name a few formations of present-day bondage. Captivity, confinement, and coercion are everywhere, from our historical realities to our political metaphors. Hammon's captivities may appear remarkable in the context of the slave narrative, but in the context of these conditions, his narrative appears eerily familiar, if not prophetic. If he were alive today, it is conceivable that the historical Hammon may not have been surprised at the shape of the world in which we live. Having lived a life marked by so many disparate instances and systems of bondage, he may have found them, in contrast to his title, quite common.

Notes

1. In her pioneering *The Slave Narrative: Its Place in American History* (1981), Marion Wilson Starling identifies "the first slave narrative" as Adam Negro's Tryall (1703), the court record of a New England slave's freedom suit against his master, John Saffin. Starling names Hammon's account as "the next slave narrative" in the tradition (52). However, most scholars tend to identify Hammon's account either as the first slave narrative or, unsure about Hammon's status as a slave, the earliest prototype of the genre. In *The Slave's Narrative* (1985), Charles T. Davis and Henry Louis Gates Jr. begin their bibliography of slave narratives with the *Uncommon Sufferings,* and in "Briton Hammon's Narrative: Some Insights into Beginnings" Frances Smith Foster argues that "its

content and form are the direct antecedents of the slave narrative" (179). Similarly, *Call and Response: The Riverside Anthology of the African American Literary Tradition* dubs the account the "forerunner of the African American slave narrative" (112). *The Oxford Companion to African American Literature* sums up these sentiments when it concludes that Hammon's text is "generally regarded as the first African American slave narrative" (337). Speaking to the implications of Hammon's account for African American literature writ large, Rafia Zafar calls *Uncommon Sufferings* "this first African American narrative" ("Capturing" 28), and William Andrews anoints Hammon's narrative "the opening statement of black autobiography in America" (32). Following these interpretations, Philip Gould places Hammon among the "first black autobiographers" ("Rise" 12) in his discussion of early slave narrators.

2. Hammon 22.

3. Ibid., 24.

4. Gagnon, this volume. Intriguingly, Daniel Vollaro has argued that the Indian captivity narrative portion of Hammon's narrative was likely fabricated, as suggested by the geographical inconsistencies, chronological impossibilities, and lack of cultural specificity with respect to Hammon's "Indians." Vollaro's observations shed light on the many stock elements of Hammon's portrayal of the Florida Natives, but Gagnon's historical analysis convincingly demonstrates how they might have been grounded in the realities of circum-Caribbean life.

5. Sekora, "Red" 103.

6. Gould, "Free" 663.

7. Sekora, "Black" 482.

8. Macpherson 3.

9. Equiano 137.

10. Desrochers 159.

11. In an almost identical move, Frances Smith Foster notes that *Uncommon Sufferings* is "not really a part of the genre," yet its "content and form are the direct antecedents of the slave narrative, the first Afro-American literary genre" (179).

12. See Zafar; Weyler.

13. Cowan; Giles 63.

14. Hammon 22.

15. Bolster 26, 27.

16. Ibid., 9.

17. It should be noted that scholars have challenged Equiano's claim that he was born in Africa. See Carretta, "Questioning the Identity of Olaudah Equiano, or Gustavus Vassa, the African."

18. Equiano 40; Lovejoy 13.

19. Gronniosaw 31.

20. Ibid. 32.

21. Equiano 47.

22. Ibid., 51.

23. Smith 11.

24. Ibid., 13; see also Gronniosaw 34; Equiano 60.

25. Gronniosaw 34.

26. Smith 13; Eltis 354.
27. See Adams 17.
28. Allison 107.
29. Ibid., 110.
30. Adams 214; Smith 21.
31. Smith 21.
32. Hammon 23.
33. Adams 245; Hammon 24.
34. Gilje 69. The phrase "wooden world" comes from N. A. Rodger's magisterial *The Wooden World: An Anatomy of the Georgian Navy.*
35. Linebaugh and Rediker 144.
36. Carretta, *Equiano* 74.
37. Ibid., 74–75. According to Carretta, Equiano's promotion by Pascal, his master, to "able seaman" effectively frees him since it was a paid position, and slaves could not be compensated for their labor (82–83), further underscoring the upward mobility blacks found at sea. This argument is undercut, however, by the fact that Pascal then refuses to grant Equiano his liberty, ignoring the Royal Navy's typical refusal to countenance "the legality of slavery" on its vessels (85).
38. Foster 186.
39. Gagnon, this volume, 84.
40. Katz 22–26.
41. Ibid., 22, 29.
42. See Mulroy for an insightful ethnohistorical assessment of African and African American escape to the Seminole and the subsequent communities that emerged from these partnerships.
43. Hammon 21; Slotkin 97.
44. Hammon 24.
45. Weyler 42.
46. Sekora, "Red" 97.
47. Ibid., 96–97.
48. Hammon 21, 22.
49. Marrant 83, 87.
50. Gates 146.
51. Marrant 88.
52. Weyler 43.
53. Hammon 21.
54. Bibb 154.
55. Zafar, *We Wear* 75–76.
56. Halliburton 39.
57. Lovett 195.
58. Naylor 145.
59. I do not want to overstate this point, however. Bibb also withholds the name of his Cherokee master from the reader, explaining that he received kinder treatment from him than all of his previous owners. Consistent with later WPA narratives of Cherokee slavery, Bibb's account argues that southeastern Native American slavery is milder and more humane than slavery to southern whites. See Minges for a sample of these narratives.

60. Hammon 22.
61. Ibid., 21, 22.
62. Wade 97.
63. Johnson 7.
64. Wade 219.
65. Bancroft 53.
66. In the 1845 version of his narrative, Frederick Douglass records his detainment for an unspecified amount of time (but at least for a couple of weeks) in St. Michaels's Easton jail after a failed escape attempt by him and three other compatriots (60–61). Also see the curious case of Native Americans who assist whites in the recapture and eventual imprisonment of fugitive slaves in Solomon Northup's *Twelve Years a Slave*, 242.
67. Douglas Taylor's "From Slavery to Prison: Benjamin Rush, Harriet Jacobs, and the Ideology of Reformative Incarceration," for instance, notes the important connections between the prison discourse of the late eighteenth century and Harriet Jacobs's representation of slavery in the mid-nineteenth century. However, he fails to acknowledge the literal imprisonment of Jacobs's children and relatives in Edenton's Chowan County jail as well as the actual threat of imprisonment under which Jacobs lives as a fugitive. Similarly, in Anita Goldman's "Harriet Jacobs, Henry Thoreau, and the Character of Disobedience," which attempts to compare the political value of Thoreau's imprisonment and Jacobs's, she neglects the literal imprisonment of Jacobs's family and only focuses on the de facto prison created by Jacobs's seclusion in her grandmother's garret.
68. Jacobs 117.
69. See Carretta, *Unchained* 24–25 for a reading of Hammon as servant. For a discussion of the similarities and differences between the conditions of white indentured servants and slaves, see Jordan and Walsh 111; Waldstreicher 22–23.
70. Gagnon, this volume, 78.
71. Berlin 104, 105.
72. Herndon and Murray 17.
73. Ibid., 18.
74. Ibid., 14, 16.
75. Lee 27.
76. Elaw 53.
77. Ibid., 27, 28, 30.
78. Foote 18.
79. Ibid., 175–76.
80. Foote 176.
81. Ibid.
82. Foreman xxxvi.
83. For a discussion of *Our Nig* as it compares to a contemporaneous account of child indentured servitude, see Kete.
84. Wilson 11.
85. Ibid., 13.
86. Ibid., 12.
87. Ibid., 60.
88. Sekora, "Red" 103.

89. Desrochers 168.
90. Lawrence-McIntyre viii.
91. See Gordon, "Globalism."

Bibliography

Adams, Robert. *Narrative of Robert Adams, a Barbary Captive: A Critical Edition*. Ed. Charles Hansford Adams. Cambridge: Cambridge UP: 2005.

Allison, Robert J. *The Crescent Obscured: The United States and the Muslim World, 1776–1815*. New York: Oxford UP, 1995.

Andrews, William L., ed. *Sisters of the Spirit: Three Black Women's Autobiographies of the Nineteenth Century*. Bloomington: Indiana UP, 1986.

———. *To Tell a Free Story: The First Century of Afro-American Autobiography, 1760–1865*. Urbana: U of Illinois P, 1986.

Andrews, William L., Frances Smith Foster, and Trudier Harris, eds. *The Oxford Companion to African American Literature*. New York: Oxford UP, 1997.

Bancroft, Frederic. *Slave Trading in the Old South*. Baltimore: J. H. Furst, 1931.

Berlin, Ira. *Generations of Captivity: A History of African- American Slaves*. Cambridge: Harvard UP, 2003.

Bibb, Henry. *Narrative of the Life and Adventures of Henry Bibb, an American Slave, Written by Himself*. Intro. by Charles J. Heglar. Madison: U of Wisconsin P, 2001.

Bolster, W. Jeffrey. *Black Jacks: African American Seamen in the Age of Sail*. Cambridge: Harvard UP, 1997.

Carretta, Vincent. *Equiano, the African: Biography of a Self-Made Man*. Athens: U of Georgia P, 2005.

———. "Questioning the Identity of Olaudah Equiano, or Gustavus Vassa, the African." *The Global Eighteenth Century*. Ed. Felicity Nussbaum. Baltimore: Johns Hopkins UP, 2003. 226–35.

———, ed. *Unchained Voices: An Anthology of Black Authors in the English-Speaking World of the Eighteenth Century*. Lexington: UP of Kentucky, 1996.

Cowan, William Tynes. *The Slave in the Swamp: Disrupting the Plantation Narrative*. New York: Routledge, 2005.

Davis, Charles T., and Henry Louis Gates Jr., eds. *The Slave's Narrative*. New York: Oxford UP, 1985.

Desrochers, Robert, Jr. "'Surprizing Deliverance'? Slavery and Freedom, Language and Identity in the Narrative of Briton Hammon, 'A Negro Man.'" *Genius in Bondage: Literature of the Early Black Atlantic*. Ed. Vincent Carretta and Philip Gould. Lexington: UP of Kentucky, 2001. 153–74.

Elaw, Zilpha. "Memoirs of the Life, Religious Experience, Ministerial Travels and Labors of Mrs. Zilpha Elaw." Andrews 49–160.

Eltis, David. "The U.S. Atlantic Slave Trade, 1644–1867: An Assessment." *Civil War History* 54.4 (2008): 347–78.

Equiano, Olaudah. *The Interesting Narrative and Other Writings*. Rev. ed. (London, 1789.) Ed. Vincent Carretta. New York: Penguin, 2003.

Foote, Julia. "A Brand Plucked from the Fire: An Autobiographical Sketch by Mrs. Julia Foote." Andrews 161–234.

Foreman, P. Gabrielle, ed. Introduction. *Our Nig; or, Sketches from the Life of a Free Black,* by Harriet E. Wilson. New York: Penguin, 2009.

Foster, Frances Smith. "Briton Hammon's Narrative: Some Insights into Beginnings." *CLA Journal* 21 (1977): 179–86.

Gates, Henry Louis, Jr. *The Signifying Monkey: A Theory of African-American Literary Criticism.* New York: Oxford UP, 1988.

Giles, Paul. "Transnationalism and Classic American Literature." *PMLA* 118.1 (2003): 62–77.

Gilje, Paul A. *Liberty on the Waterfront: American Maritime Culture in the Age of the Revolution.* Philadelphia: UP of Pennsylvania, 2004.

Gordon, Avery F. "Globalism and the Prison Industrial Complex: An Interview with Angela Davis." *Race and Class* 40.2–3 (1998): 145–57.

Gould, Philip. "Free Carpenter, Venture Capitalist: Reading the Lives of the Early Black Atlantic." *American Literary History* 12.4 (2000): 659–84.

———. "The Rise, Development, and Circulation of the Slave Narrative." *The Cambridge Companion to the African American Slave Narrative.* Ed. Audrey Fisch. Cambridge: Cambridge UP, 2007. 11–27.

Gronniosaw, James Albert Ukawsaw. "A Narrative of the Most Remarkable Particulars in the Life of James Albert Ukawsaw Gronniosaw, an African Prince, as Related by Himself." Potkay and Burr 27–63.

Halliburton, Richard, Jr. *Red over Black: Black Slavery among the Cherokee Indians.* Westport: Greenwood P, 1977.

Hammon, Briton. "Narrative of the Uncommon Sufferings and Surprizing Deliverance of Briton Hammon, A Negro Man." *Unchained Voices: An Anthology of Black Authors in the English-Speaking World of the Eighteenth Century.* Ed. Vincent Carretta. Lexington: UP of Kentucky, 1996. 20–25.

Herndon, Ruth Wallis, and John E. Murray. "'A Proper and Instructive Education': Raising Children in Pauper Apprenticeship." *Children Bound to Labor: The Pauper Apprentice System in Early America.* Ed. Ruth Wallis Herndon and John E. Murray. Ithaca: Cornell UP, 2009.

Hill, Patricia Liggins, Bernard W. Bell, Trudier Harris, William J. Harris, R. Baxter Miller, and Sondra A. O'Neale, eds. *Call and Response: The Riverside Anthology of the African American Literary Tradition.* Boston: Houghton Mifflin, 1998.

Jacobs, Harriet. *Incidents in the Life of a Slave Girl, Written by Herself.* Ed. Nellie Y. McKay and Frances Smith Foster. New York: W. W. Norton, 2001.

Johnson, Walter. *Soul by Soul: Life inside the Antebellum Slave Market.* Cambridge: Harvard UP, 1999.

Jordan, Don, and Michael Walsh. *White Cargo: The Forgotten History of Britain's White Slaves in America.* New York: New York UP, 2008.

Katz, William Loren. *Black Indians: A Hidden Heritage.* New York: Aladdin Paperbacks, 1997.

Kete, Mary Louise. "Slavery's Shadows: Narrative Chiaroscuro and Our Nig." *Harriet Wilson's New England: Race, Writing, and Region.* Ed. JerriAnne Boggis, Eve Allegra Raimon, and Barbara A. White. Durham: U of New Hampshire P, 2007. 109–22.

Lawrence-McIntyre, Charshee Charlotte. *Criminalizing a Race: Free Blacks during Slavery.* New York: Kayode, 1992.

Lee, Jarena. "The Life and Religious Experience of Jarena Lee." Andrews 25–48.

Linebaugh, Peter, and Marcus Rediker. *The Many-Headed Hydra: Sailors, Slaves, Commoners, and the Hidden History of the Revolutionary Atlantic.* Boston: Beacon P, 2000.

Lovejoy, Paul E. *Transformations in Slavery: A History of Slavery in Africa.* Cambridge: Cambridge UP, 1983.

Lovett, Laura. "African and Cherokee by Choice: Race and Resistance under Legalized Segregation." *Confounding the Color Line: The Indian-Black Experience in North America.* Lincoln: U of Nebraska P, 2002. 192–222.

Macpherson, Crawford Brough. *The Political Theory of Possessive Individualism: Hobbes to Locke.* Oxford: Clarendon Press, 1969.

Marrant, John. "A Narrative of the Lord's Wonderful Dealings with John Marrant, a Black." Potkay and Burr 67–105.

Minges, Patrick, ed. *Black Indian Slave Narratives.* Winston-Salem: John F. Blair, 2004.

Mulroy, Kevin. *Freedom on the Border: The Seminole Maroons in Florida, the Indian Territory, Coahuila, and Texas.* Lubbock: Texas Tech UP, 1993.

Naylor, Celia E. *African Cherokees in Indian Territory: From Chattel to Citizens.* Chapel Hill: U of North Carolina P, 2008.

Northup, Solomon. "Twelve Years a Slave: Narrative of Solomon Northup, a Citizen of New-York, Kidnapped in Washington City in 1841, and Rescued in 1853." 1853. *Documenting the American South: North American Slave Narratives.* Ed. William Andrews. http://docsouth.unc.edu/fpn/northup/menu .html.

Potkay, Adam, and Sandra Burr, eds. *Black Atlantic Writers of the Eighteenth Century: Living the New Exodus in England and the Americas.* New York: St. Martin's P, 1995.

Sekora, John. "Black Message/White Envelope: Genre, Authenticity, and Authority in the Antebellum Slave Narrative." *Callaloo* 32 (1987): 482–515.

———. "Red, White, and Black: Indian Captivities, Colonial Printers, and the Early African-American Narrative." *A Mixed Race: Ethnicity in Early America.* Ed. Frank Shuffleton. New York: Oxford UP, 1993. 92–104.

Slotkin, Richard. *Regeneration through Violence: The Mythology of the American Frontier, 1600–1860.* Middletown: Wesleyan UP, 1973.

Smith, Venture. "A Narrative of the Life and Adventures of Venture, a Native of Africa, but Resident Above Sixty Years in the United States of America. Related by Himself." 1798. *Documenting the American South: North American Slave Narratives.* Ed. William Andrews. http://docsouth.unc.edu/neh/venture/ menu.html.

Starling, Marion Wilson. *The Slave Narrative: Its Place in American History.* Boston: G. K. Hall, 1981.

Vollaro, Daniel. "Sixty Indians and Twenty Canoes: Briton Hammon's Unreliable Witness to History." *Native South* 2 (2009): 133–47.

Wade, Richard C. *Slavery in the Cities: The South, 1820–1860.* New York: Oxford UP, 1964.

Waldstreicher, David. *Runaway America: Benjamin Franklin, Slavery, and the American Revolution.* New York: Hill and Wang, 2005.

Weyler, Karen A. "Race, Redemption, and Captivity in the Narratives of Briton Hammon and John Marrant." *Genius in Bondage: Literature of the Early Black Atlantic.* Ed. Vincent Carretta and Philip Gould. Lexington: UP of Kentucky, 2001. 39–53.

Wilson, Harriet E. *Our Nig; or, Sketches from the Life of a Free Black.* Ed. P. Gabrielle Foreman and Reginald H. Pitts. New York: Penguin, 2009.

Zafar, Rafia. "Capturing the Captivity: African Americans among the Puritans." *MELUS* 17 (1992): 19–35.

———. *We Wear the Mask.* New York: Columbia UP, 1997.

Narrating an Indigestible Trauma

The Alimentary Grammar of Boyrereau Brinch's Middle Passage

Lynn R. Johnson

FROM THE late eighteenth through the nineteenth centuries, African survivors of the Middle Passage publicly exposed the traumas of the Atlantic slave trade through oral and published autobiographical testimonies. As direct witnesses to the various machinations of slave trafficking, they undoubtedly understood that they were the most effective agents in rallying to end the human victimization and cultural decimation that were endemic to the business. Like other writers of trauma literature, they reasoned that "if they could only make [the world] see what they have seen," it "too could be changed."[1] In making their experiences of slavery real to global citizens, these survivors fashioned discourses on the Atlantic slave trade that allowed them, first, to acknowledge the integrity of their native cultures in order to dismantle the myths of African savagery that slavers overdramatized in their journals, and then to disclose the conditions of colonial domination that Africans often resisted and survived. By appropriating this narrative agency, these survivors/authors proved, literally and metaphorically, "that the hatches cannot be permanently secured, that the decks do not demarcate permanent separations of power, that at any moment the repressed and their signifiers may seize the vehicle."[2]

Mahommah Gardo Baquaqua, an African from the Kingdom of Zoogoo in central Africa who was sold into the slave trade, claims that African survivors of the Middle Passage possess a distinct narrative agency in recalling life aboard slave ships. While contemplating the image of the slaver on which he was brought to the New World, Baquaqua claims that "none can so truly depict its horrors as the poor unfortunate, miserable wretch that has been confined within its portals."[3] Embedded within this declaration are two critical arguments: 1) outsiders can neither fully imagine nor narrate the Middle Passage; and 2) slavers, although insiders of the trade as well, cannot comprehensively represent Africans' Middle Passage experiences since they never occupied the holds. Despite the truth of Baquaqua's assertions, Africans' success in seizing and maintaining narrative agency relied on both their ability and their willingness to remember life on the slave ships.

Many African survivors of the voyage express ambivalence about psychically returning to the oceanic world. Jerome S. Handler's study of fifteen African survivors' narratives hints at this reluctance in that nine of the accounts provide no details, five offer minimal details, and one, the autobiography of Olaudah Equiano, gives maximal details of the transatlantic journey.[4] Like scholars Wolfgang Binder and Toni Morrison, Handler speculates that the lack of particularity in these narratives' depictions of the Middle Passage might indicate forgetting, silencing, or abolitionists' editorial practices.[5] However, one may discover that additional commentaries on the transoceanic journey and Africans' responses to it may have been embedded within the visual imagery of African suffering that appears in the texts.

Boyrereau Brinch's memoir serves as a revealing case in point. In *The Blind African Slave; or, Memoirs of Boyrereau Brinch, Nicknamed Jeffery Brace* (1810), Brinch, a native of the Bow-Woo community of Mali who is kidnapped and sold into Black Atlantic slavery at the age of sixteen, situates his story of childhood trauma on the slave ship within food imagery and references to eating. As I argue here, once he assumes narrative agency from abolitionist Benjamin F. Prentiss (who transcribed and to some extent edited Brinch's oral memoir), Brinch establishes a grammar of food, or an alimentary grammar—a body of statements about the slave trade experience that he creates from dietetic lexica—which transcends the formulaic Middle Passage food narratives of European slavers and other African survivors. Although he follows the script in recounting the two meals they were given as daily sustenance, he deviates from the narrative formula by remaining silent about Africans' refusal to eat during the voyage either as a signal of their bodies' biological and emotional responses to captivity (as Equiano does in his autobiography) or as a display of resistance against domination (as slaver Captain Theodore Canot and slave ship doctor Alexander Falconbridge do in their accounts).[6] My principal claim, however, is that Brinch's alimentary grammar effectively assists him in vocalizing the impact that the politics of hunger and water deprivation has—specifically on African children who endured the transatlantic voyage. With this grammar, he also extends the capacity of caricature, which he deploys in his sketch of the slave ship captain, to portray visually the revulsions of human consumption that are part and parcel of slave trafficking. And while Brinch utilizes this alimentary grammar to bear witness to the magnitude of African children's gastronomic suffering en route to the New World, he further communicates that this corporeal punishment is psychically indigestible for him or anyone who gains knowledge of it. Certainly, this disciplinary measure can never be understood or justified as a necessary practice.

Essentially, Brinch's alimentary grammar possesses cognitive and tropological functions. Gian-Paolo Biasin explains that "as a cognitive pre-text, food is used to stage the search for meaning that is carried out every time one reflects on the relationship among the self, the world, and others."[7] Throughout his account of the Middle Passage, Brinch vividly portrays the various ways in which food mediates interpersonal relations on the ship between the enslaved and the enslavers. He also demonstrates the dynamic shifts in the uses and meanings of food according to the contexts in which these interactions occur. That is, Brinch's narrative reveals a metamorphosis of food from literal sustenance to tropological or metonymic expressions of cannibalism, erotic desire, authoritarianism, and intellectual reckoning as he recalls various shipboard encounters. While doing so, Brinch conveys "the passing of time" on the slave ship, as readers are "[introduced to] characters on the scene of narration" and are then able "to follow them in their movements" through oceanic space.[8]

In recounting his journey through the Atlantic world, Brinch first introduces his readers to the most innocent of the passengers, the African child, who was "borne away from native innocence, ease, and luxury into captivity, by a [Christian] people, who [preached] humility, charity, and benevolence."[9] With this introduction, Brinch implies that, like the sentimentalized working-class European child of Romantic literature, the African child is forced into, exploited by, and deprived of care within a capitalist system.[10] Alan Richardson has argued that at the beginning of the Romantic era, the ideal notion of the child—its innocence, vulnerability, and need for schooling—was formed by bourgeois ideology; however, when "child labor was becoming more rather than less economically valuable" during the period of industrialization, "the democratization of this ideal" was effected by social reformers and "inextricably bound up with the changing representation of childhood in the early nineteenth century." "The literary 'sentimentalization' of childhood" is one such representation that Richardson speculates "may have been a necessary condition for taking children out of the workforce."[11] In exactly this fashion, Brinch places the African child at the center of his abolitionist agenda, developing more specialized sentimental portraits of enslaved African children than found in, say, Mary Stockdale's poem "Fidelle; or the Negro Child" (1789), which depicts an enslaved African girl who focuses not on her own suffering during the Atlantic slave trade but on the emotional suffering of her father, who still resides in Africa, or William Blake's song of innocence, "The Little Black Boy" (1798), which depicts an enslaved African boy's internalization of lessons in racial ideology and Christian submission. The African children whom Brinch highlight are not only torn away from their families and robbed of their innocence, but they also endure an educative process on the slave ships that is geared not toward full enculturation but toward normalizing their subjugation.

Brinch illuminates the regulatory nature of this educational process of subjection through his memory of listening to "little girls and boys, not more than six or seven years of age . . . shut up in a pen or stye [sic] crying for food and water and their fathers and mothers" (120) while on the slaver. He shows that the basic needs of survival usually provided by their parents are denied to these children in a cruel expression of the slavers' power. Indeed, food and water deprivation were measures used to domesticate, like animals, even young African prisoners. Analogous to the confined kid goat that is "starved for want of food" and becomes "tame with being hungry" in Daniel Defoe's 1719 novel, *Robinson Crusoe,* the human kids that are penned like animals in Brinch's memoir are meant to be transformed early in their lifetimes into docile and self-regulatory beings by the slavers' exercise of extreme food rationing.[12] Put simply, they are supposed to adapt to the state of hunger. In effect, these mariners, as Alex Mackintosh argues in regard to Crusoe, tried to create "a protodisciplinary relationship in which the animal [read: enslaved African child] regulates—albeit to a limited extent—its own body and mind."[13]

Brinch's description of a seven-year-old boy's concerns about his family's survival in Africa reveals that European mariners' "form of power through 'care,'" as illustrated above, is a patriarchal apparatus that impacts African children's experiences of hunger not only within the Black Atlantic world, but also within their native communities.[14] While tending to his family's goats, the boy relates that he was kidnapped, and in his present circumstances he imagines the despair of his mother and siblings. His unrelenting fear is that "his little brothers and sisters would starve, as he was the oldest child and there was no one to drive the goats, as his father was taken away before, therefore there was no one to help [his mother] now" (120–21). Here, Brinch connects this African boy's life with that of the working-class child imagined by Romanticism, for both become laborers out of necessity. Ironically, the boy is endowed with "power through care" by the very economic system that lays claim to his father's life. As the oldest child, the boy assumes the position of his displaced father, and his ability and willingness to perform adult masculine duties determine whether or not his family will eat. It is his *willingness* to provide that controls his family's experiences with hunger. At the point of his capture, the boy immediately loses his form of "power through care"; this power is reabsorbed by the institution of Black Atlantic slavery, which once again normalizes the family's hunger by taking away another male provider. The boy reasonably speculates, then, that his siblings will starve because of his mother's inability to sustain them.

As signified by these depictions of hungry and suffering youth, Atlantic slavers' "power through care" does not accommodate the feeling of compassion. In wielding this power, slavers defy the developmental theory that "children require the irrational involvement of one or more adults over and above basic care and instruction."[15] On the slave ship, only the community of enslaved Africans expresses sympathy for the boy and the other children who are "crying for bread and water," while "no white soul paid any attention" (122). Brinch, however, seeks to command his white Christian readers' attention at the end of this story by quoting passages from the Gospels of Matthew and Luke to speak more ardently about children's hunger and man's responsibility for them and for one another. He tacitly asks these readers the same questions as the speaker in Matthew 7:7–12: "Or of what man is there of you, whom if his son ask bread, will he give him a stone? Or if he ask a fish, you will give him a serpent? If ye, then, being evil, know how to give good gifts unto your children, how much more will your Father in heaven give good things to them that ask him" (122). Brinch subsequently reminds his audience of the golden rule of humanity—"therefore all things whatsoever ye would that men should do to you, do ye even so to them"—and the scriptural allegory of the Good Samaritan found in the book of Luke; the traveling Samaritan "shewed mercy on [a man]" who is beaten and left to die by thieves (122). Through these biblical passages, he reminds his readers that Christians must accommodate their neighbors, whoever they may be, with the means of survival, just as their heavenly Father does for them. When identifying the neighbor as the African child, we discover that Brinch's message to this audience resonates with Romanticism's belief that if society continues to "abandon [the child] . . . to early immersion in the workforce, or to inadequate institutions, [they will] have blighted the image of God or [their] own best selves."[16]

By combining the lexicon of caricature with eighteenth- and nineteenth-century philosophies of physiognomy, Brinch manifests this blighted image of the self through his elaborate sketch of the slave ship captain. According to Judith Wechsler, caricature "draws on and develops a two-fold tradition: that of physiognomics, the classification of people into character types according to outward bodily signs, such as the shape of the eyes, forehead, mouth and so on; and that of pathognomics, the interpretation of changing emotions by facial and bodily expression."[17] As Brinch recalls at length, the appearance of the captain is as grotesque as his deportment:

> He was about five feet two inches in height, duck legged, high shoulders and hollow backed, his hair being red as scarlet, cued down his back, to his hips, which were broad and prominent, his nose aquiline, high cheek bones, with a face about the color of what we call crimson grapes, but what is more familiar to our ideas his complexion was that of a beet. His nose eclipsed it. His eyes resembled a bowl of cream in a smoky house sprinkled with white ashes and hemlock tan with a chin that defied them to examine his laced vest which encompassed a huge paunch that would astonish a Bishop or host of a London porter house. His mouth had destroyed about one third of his face, and each wing was about attacking his ears, with ammunition within, called teeth, that represented gourd seeds. His lips were about the thickness of the blade of a case knife and appeared as if they had been at variance for many years, for the barrier between them bid defiance to a union. His hat resembled a triangle being cocked in the ancient mode, with three sharp corners, brim laced with gold, and gold laced loops. Time had made some impression upon its former beauty; but the ostentation of the wearer made up for all deficiencies . . . his mind agreed with his appearance, and his dress emblematic of his feelings, which were bedaubed with iniquity and grown very stale. (124)

As seen through this satirical rendering of the captain, Brinch adopts eighteenth- and nineteenth-century caricaturists' practice of coupling human physical traits with animalistic features in portraits that deride an individual's turpitude.[18] Indeed, he fashions this image in juxtaposition to those of the starving African children the captain confines aboard the slaver, for short duck legs support the heavy weight of an apparently well-fed captain. To nineteenth-century physiognomers such as Samuel R. Wells, the captain's "aquiline nose" would also signal the psychological quality of acquisitiveness. Wells wrote that "people noted for their love of gain and ability to acquire property" possessed "commercial noses"; these noses were said to be "arched or hawk-like" as characteristic of most birds of prey and stereotypically associated with Jews.[19] The "brim laced gold and gold-laced hoops" (124) that adorn the captain's hat are perhaps further evidence of the captain's greed. Just as medieval caricaturists coupled "exaggerated hats and grotesque faces" in order to critique societal extravagance, Brinch associates the commander's gold-laced hat with the insolence of slave traders.[20]

Although Brinch may have borrowed from the long tradition of physiognomic caricature to vivify the moral corruption of the Atlantic slave trade, he extends the vocabulary of caricature through a symbology of consumption in order to subvert pseudoscientific claims of African bestiality and cannibalism. Alan Rice asserts that Enlightenment thinkers "such as Hegel, Hume, and Kant . . . [saw] a much narrower gap between the bestial and Africans than that between the bestial and the civilized European"; they "compared Africans to animals and denied their ability to think rationally, implying a bestiality that was linked directly to cannibalism."[21] In their narratives, Brinch and other African child survivors of the Middle Passage, such as Olaudah Equiano and Quobna Ottobah Cugoano, reverse this scientific racism when they figure the white men with "horrible looks, red faces and loose hair" as a distinct race intent on eating them.[22] For instance, Cugoano states, "According to our notion as children in the inland part of the country," whites were cannibals and were therefore feared.[23] Employing the gastronomic vocabulary of his native community and that of Europeans, Brinch details the unusual physical racial markers of these monstrous men. In privileging his African community's food lexicon, he initially describes the captain's complexion as "about the color of what we call crimson grapes" (124); according to Prentiss, these grapes, called *Otua* in Brinch's native language, "are most extraordinary and bear no resemblance to the grapes of any of the European countries or those produced in any part of the United States" (103). With a white audience clearly in mind, Prentiss then suggests that "what is more familiar to our ideas, his complexion was that of a beet" (124), a crop grown throughout Europe.

William Pierson writes that "[in] many African languages, the word for 'white' people is more literally translated as red" and that this historically connoted a sinister coloration that, for Angolans specifically, connected them directly to the cannibalistic followers of "Mwene Puto, Lord of the Dead who processed the bodies of the black captives, making oil of their fat, wine from their blood, cheese from their brains, and gunpowder from their bones."[24] Similarly, Brinch's description of the captain's eye color is sinister in connotation and implies the processing of meat and animal hides. Just as his skin color is not purely white, his eyes are not either, but "resembled a bowl of cream" that has been discolored by direct contact with white ashes and the brown tannins of hemlock in a smoke house. In the eighteenth and nineteenth centuries, meats were often cured in smoke houses, ashes were often used as salt for meat, and hemlock was often used to tan leather. As a corollary to the unique racialization of these men using this food imagery, a more direct correlation between the bestial and the cannibalistic tendencies of slavers evolves as Brinch focuses more closely on the corporeality of the slave ship's captain.

More so than Equiano and Cugoano, Brinch develops a commentary on cannibalism through his comic yet uncanny image of the captain's body. Although the verbal sketch of the slave ship captain appears, superficially, comical to the reading audience, I would suggest that the sketch is not intentionally constructed to be so, as M. Dorothy George contends about eighteenth-century English political caricature. Instead, one may argue that Brinch deploys physical deformity and mockery as rhetorical devices of social protest, ones that ultimately evoke the disgust of his readers toward those involved in the slave trade by revealing, as political caricaturists do, the "very essence of [the slaver's] personality."[25] Brinch evokes the readers' disgust and exposes the captain as a perfidious man by first representing the slaver's "huge paunch that would astonish a Bishop or host of a London porter house" (124) as an emblem of sinful gluttony as well as a signifier of the conspicuous consumption of bodily flesh that is both violent and terrifying.[26] Heather Blurton's assertion that cannibalism is "marked by the violence, fear, and revulsion evoked by the image of one person eating another" may be applied to Brinch's subsequent characterization of the captain's mouth as the primary weapon of destruction. His mouth not only incorporates the flesh of others but also destroys the flesh of its bearer; it turns on its self.[27] For, the captain's mouth "destroyed about one third of his face, and each wing about attacking his ears, with ammunition within called teeth, that represented gourd seeds" (124). The captain's lips are also compared to culinary weaponry; Brinch describes their thickness like that "of the blade of a case knife." (In the nineteenth century, a case knife was another name for a kitchen utensil used to cut food.) Indeed, these images suggest that cannibalism "is not simply a destructive act; rather, it is an act that targets the fundamentals of identity" of both the consumed and the consumer. Politically, the violence associated with the metaphorical cannibalism portrayed through these same images mirrors "the violence of the situation it describes"—the iniquity of preying on humans strictly for economic gain.[28]

Brinch exposes the treachery of this "economic cannibalism" as Pierson terms it—the preying on and consumption of Africans to sustain the New World plantation economy—when he shares the story of the kidnap of the entire village of Yellow Bonga.[29] Framing this account with a trope of ingestion, he dramatizes the traumas of consumption and confinement that these Africans experience. As the ship's interpreter relates to him and others in the hold, the villagers of Yellow Bonga prepared "public feasts for [the sailors'] amusement and entertainment"(83) and brought the eatables on board, as it was considered "a civility due from that deluded people to the officers of the vessel" (83). With this gifting of food, Africans sought to nullify the insider/outsider dichotomy by establishing congenial relations with the sailors. As Susan Brownwell has argued, "food is used to transform an outsider into an insider."[30] The sailors, however, never sought to formulate an interracial community but wanted to assert their supremacy despite being outsiders. In so doing, they served liquors, which they altered with laudanum, to the Yellow Bonga villagers. Once incorporated, "[a] general intoxication and sound sleep soon prevailed, and insensibility was the consequence. These dexterous dealers in iniquity seized upon the moment, fastened with implements already prepared, each individual down upon their backs, with poles across their breasts and legs, with hands and feet drawn up by cords to certain loop holes therein. In this situation they were obliged to lie during a six months voyage, fed like hogs in the stye [*sic*] by their drivers" (125). Here, Brinch highlights the destruction of identity that economic cannibalism effects, for at the moment of ingestion, the villagers experience a conversion of social status; they are no longer figured as humans, but as the bestial that slavers "fed like hogs in the stye" and treated inhumanely.

Brinch extends the range of the trope of ingestion to accentuate the difficulty in symbolically digesting, or assimilating into his and the readers' psyches, these harrowing scenes of subjugation. Yolanda Gampel writes that we often make connections between "what goes on in emotional experience with the 'digestion' involved in thinking," and she specifically highlights W. R. Bion's argument that "we use some of the same terms for our thinking process and ingesting and digesting food."[31] When Brinch insists that his readers "[behold] three hundred men, women, and children, who, twelve hours before, enjoyed the purest freedom that nature herself could bequeath to her natural offspring, who were untainted by vice, save only that corruption which those people had introduced among them" (125), he forces them to witness the magnitude of European perfidy involved in the slave trade economy even though it is fundamentally incomprehensible. As an indigestible traumatic event, the sailor's feast on human flesh cannot be rationalized, but can only be reported as an extreme display of the usurpation of individuals' subjectivity.

As Brinch focuses on the direct impact that the slavers' power has on the African body, he unveils the more daunting politics of consumption and deprivation. In *Discipline and Punish,* Michel Foucault posits that the subjugated body becomes "directly involved in a political field; power relations have an immediate hold upon it; they invest it, mark it, train it, torture it, force it to carry out tasks, to perform ceremonies, to emit signs."[32] Foucault's contention that the body is politicized once it is subdued is suggested by Brinch's disclosure of a peculiar "eating order" that he discovers after the ship sails from the village of Guingana. He relates that only once the officers satiated their sexual appetites by choosing young women "to sleep with them in their Hammocks . . . and introduced into their several apartments," did "they [make] arrangements for the keeping and feeding of the slaves" (126). In this instance, the female body is a metonym for food that articulates the relationship between "need-desire and desire-satisfaction both in a strictly alimentary sense and in the area of eroticism."[33] Additionally, Brinch's commentary on the abused African body anticipates Mary Douglas's assertion that "the body is a model which can stand for any bounded system. Its boundaries can represent any boundaries which are threatened or precarious."[34]

In order to justify their control of the African mind and body through food distribution, the European mariners in Brinch's narrative appear to have developed a philosophy of necessity. According to Brinch, they reasoned that since the enslaved were merely sitting or lying down during most of the transatlantic voyage and since their "exercises were not much . . . it was concluded, that [they] could do with little food" (126). They resolved to supply only "two scanty meals per day, which consisted of six ounces of boiled rice and Indian corn each meal, with an addition of about one gill of fresh water" (126). By enforcing this strict disciplinary food policy, the sailors heightened the Africans' desperation for sustenance. For example, Brinch recalls vying for scraps of goat's meat with another boy named Guy. After Guy grabs and "swallows it as soon as a hound," Brinch seeks physical redress for what he considers his "right" to have the meat since it was tossed nearest to him. Instead of the sailors ending this altercation, an elder compatriot intercedes and reminds the boys of their African beliefs in justice and dignity. Brinch relates, "One of our comrades admonished us . . . and said it was extremely wrong for us to contend, as we had no parents or friends to take our parts, and could only bring disgrace upon ourselves . . . [W]e desisted and mutually exchanged forgiveness" (126–27). Significantly, it is this African-based disciplinary code that humanizes Brinch and Guy, in spite of the mariners' attempt to dehumanize the boys by promoting this food competition.

These politics of power are not only manifested in the mariners' feeding practices but are also preserved within the physical spaces of the slave ship (deck/hold) where food and water are distributed and excreted. This point is conveyed through Brinch's memory of African children's experiences of dehydration. In particular, he recalls being so "famished for water"—Africans were given two gills (one cup) of fresh water per day—to the point that he and Guy pleaded for a drink of salt water, despite knowing it would "run through [them] like salts" (88). When a sailor discovers that someone "was so indecent as to drop some . . . on the white man's deck," his response is to discover and punish the culprit. Although Guy is the offender, another boy is blamed and is given forty lashes. The sailor's response reveals the monitoring and preservation of the hierarchical spatial boundaries that were devised on the ship, for the deck of the ship represented the pristine domain of European supremacy, while the hold was conceived as a dark, earthy space of African submission. Consequently, the sailor interprets Guy's urination on the "white man's deck" instead of in the black hole as an act of "scatological rebellion" against this hierarchy and not simply as a result of biological urgency.[35] Moreover, the sailor's response implies that the literal or physiological processing of food "can become the occasion or the pretext to affirm or establish positions of authority or subordination or of rebellion."[36]

Brinch emphasizes enslaved African children's experiences of hunger and water deprivation on transatlantic slavers in order to underscore the critical imperative to end this pernicious system of exploitation and abuse. Guy's death from dehydration and malnourishment three days after the incident on deck develops this argument. Brinch avers that "the cries of the innocent African boy . . . if they reached the ears, could not penetrate the heart of a Christian, so as to cause him to bestow a morsel of bread upon this infant captive, even enough to save his life" (128). Yet, the author does stop here. He also relays that the disregard for the African boy's body persists after death, as it was "thrown into the sea . . . [and] made food for sharks, as they continually followed [the ship], being

well baited by the frequent deaths on board" (127). For abolitionists of
the time, the shark was an apt "symbol of the violence and the terror of
the trade"; it became part of the machinery of destruction.[37] The ultimate
irony, then, is that the sharks of the Atlantic were heartily fed by the trade
in Africans while "[many] of the children died with hunger, pent up in the
same ship where midnight and beastly intoxication bloated the miserable
owner" (128).

As made evident in *The Blind African Slave,* Brinch establishes food as
more than daily sustenance; it is a philological mechanism that effectively
translates the racial histories, physiological and psychological desires,
and cultural contestations that inform Black life and survival during the
transatlantic Middle Passage. As tools of translation in this work, food
and food imagery maintain the paradoxical burden of communicating
and containing enslaved African children's traumatic encounters in the
oceanic world. The native of Mali, however, negotiates this paradoxical
function by fashioning an alimentary grammar that transfigures particular food stuffs and associations into signifiers of these children's emotive
and bodily experiences of extreme hunger and dehydration. In effect,
Brinch's alimentary grammar allows for the articulation of these disturb-
ing incidents, while also creating a safe space in which to confront them
through literary discourse.

Moreover, by refiguring food and symbologies of consumption as ap-
paratuses for visual and verbal translation, Brinch produces a unique
gastrological vocabulary for Black portraiture construction of the Middle
Passage participants and experiences. Indeed, this new vocabulary provides the means with which he is able to mediate the development of the
reading audience's social consciousness about Black Atlantic subjectivity and subjection within a transnational context. Essentially, as Jeffrey
Gagnon also conveys in his discussion of Briton Hammon's enslavement,
food has consistently signified in narratives of African captivity, whether
it has communicated sentiments of hospitality and the attempts to preserve life[38] or has indicated social exclusion and the politics of hegemonic
power.

Notes

1. Tal, *Worlds of Hurt,* 131.
2. Nielson, *Writing between the Lines,* 103.
3. Baquaqua, *Biography of Baquaqua,* 27.
4. See Table 1 ("African Autobiographical Accounts") in Handler, "Survivors
of the Middle Passage," 27. Besides Equiano's text, Handler examines the works

of Abraham Ashey, Abu Bakr, Belinda Royall, James Bradley, Ottobah Cugoano, James Gronniosaw, John Joseph, Archibald Monteith, Abdul Rahahman, Omar Said, Sibell, Venture Smith, and Ofodobendo Wooma. His study, however, excludes Boyrereau Brinch, who also gives a detailed account of the Middle Passage. One must acknowledge, moreover, that literary scholar Vincent Carretta has called into question Equiano's account of his African roots and Middle Passage experience. Carretta writes in *Equiano the African:* "Baptismal and naval records say that he was born in South Carolina around 1747. If they are accurate, he invented his African childhood and his much-quoted account of the Middle Passage on a slave ship" (xiv). In this statement, Carretta makes clear that these records may not constitute definitive evidence that Equiano fabricated his tale for the abolitionist cause. Thus, Carretta avers that although "conflicting evidence exists," one must "remember that reasonable doubt is not the same as conviction. We will probably never know the truth about the author's birth and upbringing" (xv). Since Equiano's autobiography has not been conclusively disputed by any texts and since Equiano provides the sole text of his life story, I, like Carretta, "have chosen to treat it . . . as if it were true" (xvi).

5. See Binder, "Uses of Memory"; Morrison, "Site of Memory."

6. See Equiano, *Interesting Narrative;* Canot, *Adventures of an African Slaver;* and Falconbridge, *Account of the Slave Trade.*

7. Biasin, *Flavors of Modernity,* 17.

8. Ibid., 17, 13.

9. Brinch, *Blind African Slave,* 119. Subsequently page references to this work appear parenthetically in the text.

10. The exploitation of enslaved African children was often compared with that of boy chimney sweeps in Britain. Lauren Henry argues that both the biological and occupational "little black boys" had "to do their best to make sense of a senseless society in which children are not only sold and enslaved, but also are taught to believe that it is their duty to serve and suffer" ("'Sunshine and Shady Groves,'" 80). Political opponents of child labor in chimney sweeping also realized this connection, as they "borrowed the rhetoric of the abolitionist movement" and poems by Romantic writers in producing propaganda calling on "Britons to ban the little chimney sweeping black boys just as they abolished the slave trade" (Fulford, Lee, and Kitson, *Literature, Science and Exploration,* 228).

11. Richardson, "Romanticism and the End," 24, 25.

12. Defoe, *Robinson Crusoe,* 124.

13. Mackintosh, "Crusoe's Abattoir," 28.

14. Ibid.

15. Richardson, "Romanticism and the End," 33.

16. Ibid., 26.

17. Wechsler, *Human Comedy,* 15.

18. Books on physiognomy were widely read in the eighteenth and nineteenth centuries. According to Judith Wechsler, Johann Caspar Lavater's *L'Art de connaitre les homes par la physionomie* (1794), which "maintained the tradition of animal-human parallels as a basis for moral interpretation," found its way into private homes and was "consulted when hiring staff, making friends, and

establishing business relations (*Human Comedy,* 24). It is possible, but not certain, that Brinch and Prentiss had access to this text.

19. Wells, *How to Read Character,* 61.
20. Wright, *History of Caricature and Grotesque,* 101.
21. Rice, "'Who's Eating Whom,'" 115, 110.
22. Equiano, *Interesting Narrative,* 55. According to William Pierson, Africans "reversed the stereotype of African cannibalism, believing that it was whites who were the cannibals, buying slaves in order to eat them. The tradition of the insatiable white man-eaters explained why no one ever returned after being purchased on the coast" (*Black Legacy,* 4). John Thornton also relates that "[these] bloody fears were nearly ubiquitous among Africans forced to cross the Atlantic during the period of the slave trade" ("Cannibals, Witches and Slave Traders," 274).
23. Cugoano, *Thoughts and Sentiments,* 14.
24. Pierson, *Black Legacy,* 10.
25. George, *English Political Caricature,* 11.
26. In *Religion in the Popular Prints,* John Miller conveys that "attacks on clerical gluttony" consistently registered in English visual satire. Samuel Lyons's "A Parish Feast Humbly Inscribed to the Church Wardens, Vestrymen, Questmen, and Parish Officers" (1741) linked bishops with taverns, "[alleging] that parsons and parish officials embezzled or drank away parish funds." In the late eighteenth century, the social criticism of clerical gluttony evolved when "the price of food rose substantially," and the clergy was able to collect larger amounts of tithes from prosperous farmers. "A General Fast in Consequence of the War!!" (1794) represents this "strong element of social criticism" by comparing the obese archbishop of Canterbury's elaborate feasting in Lambeth Palace with the image of thin, starving weavers at their homes in Spitalfields (47). Essentially, this graphic articulates the "social gulf between priests and people" that "was widened by lawsuits about tithes and property matters." Analogously, Brinch's caricature suggests that slavers' gastrological and economic gluttony engendered the social gaps between Europeans and enslaved Africans.
27. Blurton, *Cannibalism in High Medieval English,* 9.
28. Ibid., 8, 9.
29. "Africans knew the voracious labor demands of the white world were consuming millions of their countrymen . . . as a mythopoeic analogy, it does not seem farfetched to portray chattel slavery as a kind of economic cannibalism; and in that sense, a mythic sense, stories of white man-eaters were true enough" (Pierson, *Black Legacy,* 12).
30. Brownwell, "Food, Hunger and the State," 253.
31. Gampel, "Reflections on the Prevalence," 62.
32. Foucault, "Discipline and Punish," 468.
33. Biasin, *Flavors of Modernity,* 14.
34. Douglas, *Purity and Danger,* 115.
35. I am borrowing the phrase *scatological rebellion* from Petra ten-Doesschate Chu's discussion of Marieluise Jurreit's Freudian analysis of children's bedwetting as a "protest against parental treatment" (Chu, "Scatology and the Realist Aesthetic," 41).

36. Biasin, *Flavors of Modernity,* 15.
37. Rediker, "History from below," 286.
38. Gagnon, this volume, 91.

Bibliography

Baquaqua, Mahommah Gardo. *Biography of Mahommah G. Baquaqua, a Native of Zoogoo, in the Interior of Africa . . . Written and Revised from His Own Words.* Ed. Samuel Moore. Detroit: Geo E. Pomeroy, 1854.

Biasin, Gian-Paolo. *The Flavors of Modernity: Food and the Novel.* Princeton, NJ: Princeton Univ. Press, 1993.

Binder, Wolfgang. "Uses of Memory: The Middle Passage in African-American Literature." In *Slavery in the Americas,* ed. Wolfgang Binder, 539–64. Würzburg: Verlag Konigshausen und Newman, 1993.

Blurton, Heather. *Cannibalism in High Medieval English Literature.* New York: Palgrave Macmillan, 2007.

Brinch, Boyrereau. *The Blind African Slave; or, Memoirs of Boyrereau Brinch, Nicknamed Jeffery Brace* (1810). Ed. Kari J. Winter. Madison: Univ. of Wisconsin Press, 2004.

Brownwell, Susan. "Food, Hunger, and the State." In *The Cultural Politics of Food and Eating: A Reader,* ed. James L. Watson and Melissa L. Cadwell, 251–58. Malden, MA: Blackwell, 2005.

Canot, Captain Theodore. *Adventures of an African Slaver.* New York: Dover, 1969.

Carretta, Vincent. *Equiano the African: Biography of a Self-Made Man.* Athens: Univ. of Georgia Press, 2005.

Chu, Petra Ten-Doesschate. "Scatology and the Realist Aesthetic." *Art Journal* 52 (1993): 41–47.

Cugoano, Quobna Ottobah. *Thoughts and Sentiments on the Evil and Wicked Traffic of Slavery.* Ed. Vincent Carretta. New York: Penguin, 1999.

Defoe, Daniel. *Robinson Crusoe.* London: Penguin Books, 1965.

Douglas, Mary. *Purity and Danger: An Analysis of the Concepts of Pollution and Taboo.* London: Routledge & Kegan Paul PLC, 1966.

Equiano, Olaudah. *The Interesting Narrative and Other Writings.* Ed. Vincent Carretta. New York: Penguin, 2003.

Falconbridge, Alexander. *An Account of the Slave Trade on the Coast of Africa.* London: J. Phillips, 1788. Anti-Slavery Collection, Boston Public Library. https://archive.org/details/accountofslavetr00falc.

Foucault, Michel. "Discipline and Punish." In *Literary Theory: An Anthology,* ed. Julie Rivkin and Michael Ryan, 464–87. Malden, MA: Blackwell, 1998.

Fulford, Tim, Debbie Lee, and Peter J. Kitson. *Literature, Science and Exploration in the Romantic Era: Bodies of Knowledge.* Cambridge: Cambridge Univ. Press, 2004.

Gampel, Yolanda. "Reflections on the Prevalence of the Uncanny in Social Violence." In *Cultures under Siege: Collective Violence and Trauma,* ed. Marcelo Suarez-Orozco and Antonius C. G. M. Robben, 48–69. Cambridge: Cambridge Univ. Press, 2000.

George, M. Dorothy. *English Political Caricature to 1792: A Study of Opinion and Propaganda.* Oxford: Clarendon Press, 1959.

Handler, Jerome S. "Survivors of the Middle Passage: Life Histories of Enslaved Africans in British America." *Slavery and Abolition* 23 (2002): 25–56.

Henry, Lauren. "'Sunshine and Shady Groves': What Blake's 'Little Black Boy' Learned from African Writers." In *Romanticism and Colonialism: Writing and Empire, 1780–1830,* ed. Tim Fulford and Peter Kitson, 67–86. Cambridge: Cambridge Univ. Press, 1998.

Lavater, Johann Caspar. *L'art de connaître les hommes par la physionomie* (1794). Ed. Jacques Lortie Moreau de la Sarthe. Paris: Depelafol, Libraire-Éditeur, 1835.

Mackintosh, Alex. "Crusoe's Abattoir: Cannibalism and Animal Slaughter in Robinson Crusoe." *Critical Quarterly* 53.3 (2011): 24–40.

Miller, John. *Religion in the Popular Prints, 1600–1832.* Cambridge: Chadwyck-Healey, 1986.

Morrison, Toni. "The Site of Memory." In *Inventing the Truth: The Art and Craft of Memoir,* ed. William Zinsser, 103–24. New York: Mariner Books, 1987.

Nielson, Aldon L. *Writing between the Lines: Race and Intertextuality.* Athens: Univ. of Georgia Press, 1994.

Pierson, William. *Black Legacy: America's Hidden Heritage.* Amherst: Univ. of Massachusetts Press, 1993.

Rediker, Marcus. "History from below the Water Line: Sharks and the Atlantic Slave Trade." *Atlantic Studies* 5.2 (2008): 285–97.

Rice, Alan. "'Who's Eating Whom': The Discourse of Cannibalism in the Literature of the Black Atlantic from Equiano's *Travels* to Toni Morrison's *Beloved.*" *Research in African Literatures* 29.4 (1998): 107–21.

Richardson, Alan. "Romanticism and the End of Childhood." In *Literature and the Child: Romantic Continuations, Postmodern Contestations,* ed. James Holt McGavran, 23–43. Iowa City: Univ. of Iowa Press, 1999.

Tal, Kali. *Worlds of Hurt: Reading the Literatures of Trauma.* Cambridge: Cambridge Univ. Press, 1996.

Thornton, John. "Cannibals, Witches, and Slave Traders in the Atlantic World." *William and Mary Quarterly,* n.s., 60.2 (2003): 273–94.

Wechsler, Judith. *A Human Comedy: Physiognomy and Caricature in 19th-Century Paris.* Chicago: Univ. of Chicago Press, 1982.

Wells, Samuel R. *How to Read Character: A New Illustrated Hand-Book of Phrenology and Physiognomy for Students and Examiners: with a Descriptive Chart.* New York, 1873.

Wright, Thomas. *A History of Caricature and Grotesque in Literature and Art.* New York: Frederick Ungar, 1968.

"The Most Perfect Picture of Cuban Slavery"

Transatlantic Bricolage in Manzano's and Madden's *Poems by a Slave*

R.J. Boutelle

As THE only extant slave narrative from Spanish America, the memoir of Juan Francisco Manzano marks a foundational contribution to both the Cuban and Afro-Caribbean literary traditions.[1] Because of the Spanish colonial government's strict management of dissenting discourse and strategic censorship of potentially incendiary materials, however, it was not until 1937—over a century after the text's composition—that Cuban historian José Luciano Franco finally dusted off a surviving manuscript and published *Autobiografía, cartas y versos de Juan Francisco Manzano* in Havana. The primary vehicle for the narrative's dissemination in the mid-nineteenth century was Irish abolitionist Richard Robert Madden's *Poems by a Slave in the Island of Cuba, Recently Liberated; Translated from the Spanish, by R.R. Madden, M.D. With the History of the Early Life of the Negro Poet, Written by Himself; to Which Are Prefixed Two Pieces Descriptive of Cuban Slavery and the Slave-Traffic, by R.R.M.* (1840). As its lengthy title suggests, Madden's English translation of Manzano's narrative ("Life of the Negro Poet") and a sampling of the ex-slave's poems were compiled along with the abolitionist's own writings on Cuban slavery and two interviews he conducted with Cuban literary mogul Domingo del Monte; together, these pieces were assembled as a bound octavo, which was sold for five shillings at the office of the British and Foreign Anti-Slavery Society in London.[2] In many ways, the memoir's publication abroad and its consequent translation situate the textual nexus of *Autobiografía/Poems by a Slave* as representative of politicized Caribbean writing during the early nineteenth century.[3] From a critical perspective, however, these publications are exceptional: archival access to both Manzano's Spanish language manuscripts and Madden's English language publication have provided scholars with a unique opportunity for comparative "before and after" analysis, unveiling the editorial dynamics between the enslaved author and his white sponsors/publishers.[4] That is, where readings of white editors'/coauthors'/amanuenses' influences on transcribing oral slave testimonies or on the creative process of the ex-slave author remain largely conjectural for most other slave narratives from the Atlantic world, critics of *Autobiografía/Poems by a Slave* have been able to engage in rigorous side-by-side readings of the text's multiple versions, thereby rendering visible Madden's revisions, excisions, and occasionally tenuous grip on his nonnative language.

In a departure from these contrastive readings of the Spanish and English publications, this essay focuses almost exclusively on *Poems by a Slave* and the intratextual discourse on Cuban slavery that emerges within its pages.[5] What follows is a detailed diagramming of the volume's composition and a close examination of its oft-neglected reception history in the British abolitionist public sphere, both of which call for a rereading of the text's generic form. By foregrounding this print cultural history, we come to view *Poems by a Slave* not strictly as a problematic translation of Manzano's slave narrative that dramatizes the pitfalls of appropriation and the excesses of white authentification. Alternatively, the circulation and reception of *Poems by a Slave* suggest it functions as a heterogeneous, multiauthor mode of representing slavery that I call the *bricolated slave narrative*.[6] Here, *bricolated* plays on both the idea of *bricolage*—the scavenger-like, artistic assembly of variegated source texts from what happens to be available—and the idea of a *bricole*—a billiards shot in which the cue ball hits the object ball, followed by the cushion, and then the carom ball. This reading strategy locates Madden's role as that of a *bricoleur* or anthologizer: accumulating and organizing available works as mutually authenticating documents and complementary evidentiary support in a narrative of Cuban slavery to be represented for an international audience. Through the productive interplay of these related terms, the bricolated slave narrative provides an analytic vocabulary that accounts for the multiple perspectives in the texts comprising *Poems by a Slave* and its ricocheting trajectories through the Atlantic world, bouncing off different authors, editors, translators, cultural sites, and readers throughout the course of its publication and circulation.

The stakes of decentering Manzano in this reading are, of course, paramount and require careful attention. The irony that my approach risks reenacting the idiosyncratic obfuscation of an Afro-Cuban voice by a well-intentioned white author that characterizes *Poems by a Slave* is not lost on me; I invite those critiques, and I remain deeply invested in the politics undergirding them. To be clear, in situating *Poems by a Slave* as an anthology of sorts, this essay does not suggest that those authors consented to this representational mode, nor does it argue that their perspectives and writings are weighted equally within Madden's compendium—indeed, it remains Madden's compendium. Instead, this essay continues to interrogate the privilege afforded to the author function in slave narrative studies, a standard that maps the Romantic, European epistemology of "author-as-genius" onto texts that actively resist this formulation.[7] In her groundbreaking work on embedded slave narratives from the British West Indies, Nicole N. Aljoe reminds us that "the 'classic' paradigm of the self-written slave narrative cannot account for the overwhelming majority (6,000+) of slave narratives in the archive, which exhibit the more hybrid forms of the dictated and translated slave narrative."[8] These *creole testimonies,* as Aljoe terms them, are inherently polyvocal and mediated, each representing a "collaborative construction of several different voices working *together* to create the performance of a single, narrating first-person voice understood to be the 'slave narrator,'" (original emphasis) rather than a single-authored, autobiographical text.[9] *The History of Mary Prince* (1831) serves as an exemplar for this archive. In addition to the choral collaboration of voices resulting from Susana Strickland's service as amanuensis and Thomas Pringle's "pruning" of "the narrator's repetitions and prolixities," Prince relates her experience of slavery with a slippery "I" and an inclusive "we," which, for Aljoe, unveil her attempts to speak as a representative West Indian slave and to provoke sympathetic identification from the British public.[10] How could we even begin to measure such a text against Romantic touchstones of authorial singularity, originality, and independent genius?

Unlike the polyvocal collaboration of voices in *The History of Mary Prince,* Madden's volume evinces little interest in synthesis. *Poems by a Slave*'s multiple authorial perspectives on Cuban slavery do not "work together" to formulate a central narrating persona like "Mary Prince," but instead preserve many of the frictions and tensions among its constitutive texts. In doing so, *Poems by a Slave* clearly announces that Manzano's memoir is not intended as a central slave narrative around which Madden's poems and essays serve as authenticating documents.[11] For instance, whereas Pringle's "Supplement" explicitly aims to corroborate Prince's account and to counter her former master's vitriolic accusations against her character, the texts surrounding "Life of the Negro Poet" make no effort to verify the facts of Manzano's testimony. Although Madden hopes in his preface that he has "done enough to vindicate in some degree the character of the negro intellect," the nonspecific nature of this "vindication" bespeaks the anthology's disinterest in affirming the details of Manzano's narrative or vouching for his character beyond this universal redemption of "the negro intellect."[12] Instead of operating within the traditional paradigm of black authorship and white authentication that characterizes the slave narrative genre, the writings of Manzano, Madden, and Del Monte become mutually authenticating. Collectively, they provide a mosaic portrait of the island's peculiar institution, variously highlighting slave interiority, the plantation economy, the illegal slave trade and the Atlantic ripples of Cuban slavery; collectively, they exceed the influence, scope, and circulation that any of these could enact individually.

In a further departure from *The History of Mary Prince* or myriad other Caribbean slave testimonies, Manzano's narrative was not dictated but was written by himself. Accordingly, in lieu of extending Aljoe's conceptualization of polyvocal creole testimonies into a Hispanophone West Indian field or operating within Mikhail Bakhtin's related polyphonic framework, where "*a plurality of consciousnesses, with equal rights and each with its own world,* combine but are not merged in the unity of the event" (original emphasis), this essay's print cultural methodology shifts us away from the figurative language of vocality/voice that dominates slave narrative studies.[13] As both theoretical concepts and metaphors, "voice" and "writing" are, of course, inextricably interwoven—and rightfully so. Again, my intention is not to eschew or undermine the theoretical/metaphorical trope of "voice," but rather to distinguish my own argument from a polyphonic framework that might suggest "equal rights," "collaboration," or even "authenticity" among the distinct contributing voices of *Poems by a Slave*. By underscoring the multiauthor representational mode of the volume and its material assembly, this intratextual reading strategy emphasizes the ideological tensions preserved in the anthology's bricolated form: at the same time that this methodology decenters "Life of the Negro Poet" as a privileged focal point within *Poems by a Slave*, it necessarily insists on Madden's primacy and influence as bricoleur. To ascribe him this power, however, is not to suggest he succeeded fully in doing so. This essay lays bare how the volume's form necessarily refuses synthesis and unity, mapping how the turbulence among the assembled texts betrays the power relations that contour their individual compositions and their collective compilation.

El asunto

The story begins in Matanzas, where in the spring of 1835, renowned Cuban literary critic Domingo Del Monte commissioned Juan Francisco Manzano to pen a prose account of his experience in slavery. Although it remains unclear exactly how the two men were introduced, by the time of this particular solicitation, Del Monte had already helped Manzano publish a number of poems in Cuban periodicals—as it was illegal for slaves to publish themselves—including *La Moda, Diario de la Habana,* and *El Pasatiempo.*[14] Manzano expressed some generic (he was primarily a poet) and practical (he was still a slave) uneasiness about the project, but he ultimately agreed and began drafting his memoir later that year. As he wrote, Manzano attended Del Monte's *tertulias* in Matanzas— reading groups comprising Cuba's elite literary men—where his poetry performances inspired his audience to take up a subscription in order to buy his freedom.[15] After a short time, the effort succeeded, and in 1836 Manzano was emancipated. By 1839, *el asunto* ("the matter"), as Manzano obliquely referred to the project in his letters to Del Monte, was completed in two parts; unfortunately, the second half was misplaced and never recovered.[16] Anselmo Suárez y Romero, *criollo* (Cuban-born) writer and *tertulia* attendee, then "corrected" a number of grammatical or orthographical errors in Manzano's narrative before returning the revised manuscript to Del Monte.[17] The finished text, however, was considered unpublishable in Cuba in light of colonial regulations on printing and the simple fact that many of the people whom Manzano describes in his account were influential members of Cuban society. Accordingly, Del Monte tried to take advantage of one of his many foreign connections to find an external outlet for publication.

Meanwhile, British antislavery societies were spearheading early efforts to abolish slavery throughout the Atlantic world (the Slavery Abolition Act had already emancipated the British West Indies in 1833) and to end the resilient illegal slave trade. As the "Gateway to the Gulf of Mexico" and to the major U.S. shipping ports of Mobile and New Orleans, Cuba was a pivotal hub in the slave and sugar trades in the Americas, and it quickly became the British abolitionists' central target. Although Spain had finally folded to international pressures at the 1815 Congress of Vienna—which formally proscribed the importation of Africans to Cuba in 1820—Spanish officials barely enforced the restrictions. Just two years earlier in 1818, Spain opened the island to international trade, effectively increasing planters' dependence on slave labor in order to meet the rising global demands for coffee, tobacco, and sugar. As a result, the appetites of the Atlantic marketplace and the attendant boost to the Spanish imperial economy incentivized lax policing of the illegal slave trade; Cuba quickly became a hub for the trafficking of Africans to the Americas and, therefore, the bane of British efforts to end the slave trade altogether.[18]

In response, Great Britain began stationing an array of whistle-blowers throughout the Caribbean (but particularly in Cuba) in the 1820s and 1830s. One such assignment was given to the Irish-born British diplomat Richard Robert Madden, who, on the heels of his service as a special magistrate in Jamaica, was appointed Cuba's first superintendent of liberated Africans on the Mixed Court of Arbitration in 1836.[19] Though he was new to Havana, Madden's reputation as an abolitionist instigator and an inflexible enforcer of labor regulations preceded him. Captain-General Miguel Tacón y Rosique, authoritarian leader of the Spanish colony (1834–1838), immediately recognized the threat that the British government's endorsement of the abolitionist would pose to the institution of slavery on the island: "Dr Madden is a dangerous man from whatever point of view he is considered, and living in this Island he will have far too many opportunities to disseminate seditious ideas directly or indirectly, which not even my constant vigilance can prevent."[20] Madden's three-year tenure in Cuba vindicated Tacón's concerns. The superintendent became notorious among the Cuban planters for unannounced inspections of *ingenios* (sugar plantations) and for his avid petitioning to shorten the workday for slaves during the cane harvest.[21]

It was from this colonial post that Madden would meet both Manzano and Del Monte in 1837. Although Del Monte and Madden immediately found common cause over their shared desires to end the illegal slave trade through Cuba, their politics and motives in pursuing this end were decidedly different. This contrast offers insight into the eventual publication of Manzano's narrative. Unlike Madden, Del Monte and other white *criollo* intellectuals were not abolitionists but rather were reformists who, according to Ivan A. Schulman, "hoped that by working within the existing sociopolitical and economic structures [they] would be able to bring about gradual but significant changes" to the corrupt Spanish colonial government on the island.[22] Beneath this veneer of colonial reform and Cuban protonationalism, however, runs an insidious undercurrent of plantocratic politics and racial ideology. Jerome Branche has been particularly critical of scholars "glossing over" these biographical details in their depictions of Del Monte as the benevolent sponsor and liberator of Manzano. "Delmontine opposition to slavery as an altruistic vindication of the rights of the enslaved," he persuasively argues, "is a highly questionable proposition. So too is the suggestion that he and his literary group *in toto* espoused the vision of a democratic inclusion of Black ex-slaves in a future Cuban polity."[23] While it is possible Del Monte's reformist vision may have eventually included a plan for gradual, indemnified emancipation on the island, as the owner of more than a hundred slaves and a nine-hundred-acre sugar plantation, he had clear personal and financial investments in finding an alternative to the sudden manumission of Cuban slaves.

In addition to questions of compensation for "lost property," the logistics of immediate emancipation also unnerved the Cuban planting class because of the island's majority African and Afro-descended population, compounded by the continued import of slaves.[24] On the one hand, these demographics exacerbated the ubiquitous anxiety of a large-scale slave rebellion on the island; Cuban planters remembered Saint Domingue well.[25] On the other hand, many white *criollos* in Cuba saw the majority Afro-descended population as an obstacle barring their transformation from colony to an economically and culturally viable nation-state recognized as a peer by the United States and Europe. For Del Monte and his peers, closing the illegal slave trade and reforming Cuban slavery were indispensible steps toward a protonational consciousness on the island that envisioned a future Cuban republic as a white, European-descended nation, more aligned with Anglo progressivism (exemplified by the British and the United States) than retrograde Spanish politics.[26] The progressive narrative of this protonationalist project, however, attempts to mask its encoded, eugenic racial politics. That is, closing the island's borders to the illegal slave trade (and thus an accretion in the island's African population) was only the first step in the "modernization" of Cuba; the next step was a radical plan to sponsor European immigration programs to the island in order to "whiten" the Cuban population.[27]

Strange political bedfellow that Del Monte may have been, Madden looked to exploit their mutual dedication to ending the illegal slave trade. Through Del Monte and his *tertulias,* Madden found "authentic" source materials on Cuban slavery to carry back to London as evidence to intensify British pressure on Spain.[28] Del Monte was only too happy to oblige. To the extent that Madden was (in)famous for his conflict with Nicholas Trist around the same time (1839), he presented a formidable ally for restructuring the island's political composition and an opportunity to disseminate that message to a European public unconstrained by Cuban censorship. Consequently, when Madden prepared to leave Cuba in 1839, Del Monte agreed to an interview about the slave trade and the "state of religion" on the island; Del Monte, in turn, supplied him with a portfolio of "Unpublished Samples" of Cuban writing on the subject of slavery for Madden to take with him back to Great Britain.[29] Among these texts was the Suárez y Romero edition of Manzano's manuscript.

The peculiarities of Del Monte's slavery politics, the protonationalist dimensions of his reform project, and his particular interest in circulating Manzano's *Autobiografía* beyond the island's borders are brought into relief in his letter to Madden accompanying the literary notebook:

> Acompaño á usted las adjuntas "Muestras inéditas" de un nuestra naciente y desmedrada literatura provincial, para que cuando esté usted de vuelta en su dichosa patria, se acuerde, al leerlas, de esta pobre tierra y de los sinceros amigos que supo usted grangearse en ella. Notará usted que excepto las de Manzano, no llevan el nombre de sus autores las demás composiciones de la coleccion. Como casi todas ellas hacen alusiones á asuntos prohibidos por nuestro Gobierno, no he querido que, si por cualquier evento, fuese á parar á otras manos que las de usted ese cuaderno, peligrasen por mi culpa aquellos inofensivos poetas, que en todo han pensado ménos en trastornar la tranquilidad de su país. [. . .]
>
> Como al escoger las composiciones para estas *muestras* me he querido ceñir á asuntos que tuviesen alguna relación con la esclavitud de los negros, por considerarlos más interesantes para usted, no he insertado produccion ninguna de otros jóvenes muy aventajados de los que hoy componen nuestra pequeña república literaria. (original emphasis)

> (I am sending you the attached "Unpublished Samples" of our growing and weak provincial literature so that when you return to your lucky homeland you will remember, as you read them, this poor land and the sincere friends you knew how to win there. You will notice that, excepting Manzano's, the other compositions in the collection do not bear the authors' names. Since nearly all of them allude to subjects forbidden by our Government, I did not wish that, if by chance the album ended up in other hands than yours, those inoffensive writers would be endangered through my fault, because the last thing they intended was to disturb the peace of their country. [. . .]
>
> Since in choosing the composition for this sample I wished to stick with topics that had something to do with black enslavement because I thought those would be of the greatest interest to you, I have not included any works by other very outstanding young men who today constitute our small literary republic.)[30]

Del Monte's allusions to "subjects forbidden by our Government" and "your lucky homeland" reflect his antipathy toward Spain's suppression of the "growing and weak provincial literature" in Cuba and the island's arrested cultural development as a "small literary republic." But why would Del Monte single out Manzano's narrative as the most "exceptional" evidence of the literary potential of the *tertulia,* and why was his the only text on Cuban slavery not rendered anonymous to Madden? On one level, Del Monte took pride in Manzano's writing, which he himself had been editing and publishing for several years; a positive review would tacitly praise Del Monte's discernment and vindicate his endorsement of Manzano. On another level, the decision was pragmatic: not only was Madden's "greatest interest" in Cuban writing on "black enslavement," but he knew Manzano personally.

At the crossroads of these practical concerns, however, Lorna V. Williams convincingly suggests that Del Monte took advantage of Madden's abolitionist and personal predisposition toward Manzano's text to advance a broader political project: framing slavery as the representative Cuban experience by analogizing the power dynamics between slave and master to the colony-metropole relationship between Cuba and Spain.[31] Ironically enough, this political and rhetorical project enabled Del Monte and other white *criollo* intellectuals, many of whom were slaveholders, to conceive of themselves as virtually "enslaved" by the Spanish colonial government. Furthermore, Del Monte remained acutely aware that Manzano's narration of the brutalities of slavery on the island would signify the "backwardness" of the colonial government, encouraging the purportedly benign imperial interventions from Great Britain or the United States.[32] In so far as they framed the slave experience as the representative Cuban colonial experience and piqued the interest of a European publisher (i.e., Madden), Manzano and his narrative provided indispensible contributions to Del Monte's molding of a national literature.

The Bricoleur

After a brief trip to the United States as a special counsel in the *Amistad* trial, Madden sailed to London with Del Monte's literary parcel for the first British and Foreign Anti-Slavery Convention in 1840, where he addressed the meeting on Cuban slavery and the slave trade.[33] Madden's efforts to expose the illegal trafficking of Africans through Cuba to an international audience were enormously successful: in addition to publishing *Minutes of the Proceedings of the General Anti-Slavery Convention*

(1840), the printers Johnson and Barrett published Madden's speech at the convention separately as *Address on Slavery in Cuba: Presented to the General Anti-Slavery Convention* (1840). The conference itself was also quite taken with Madden's presentation and expressed optimism about the potential for his work to influence Spain's colonial control over the island. The delegation resolved that the committee should obtain "a translation of Dr. Madden's statement on the subject of slavery in Cuba for circulation in Spain."[34]

Following the convention, Madden translated and published Manzano's writings as *Poems by a Slave in the Island of Cuba, Recently Liberated; Translated from the Spanish, by R.R. Madden, M.D. With the History of the Early Life of the Negro Poet, Written by Himself; to Which Are Prefixed Two Pieces Descriptive of Cuban Slavery and the Slave-Traffic, by R.R.M.* It merits reproducing the full title again here in order to underscore three significant aspects of Madden's framing. First, the title identifies Manzano as a poet and privileges his verses over his slave narrative, which becomes ancillary to his poetry: the *"History of the Early Life of the Negro Poet, Written by Himself"* of Madden's title appears *"With"* the *"Poems by a Slave."* Second, Manzano's writings are tightly interwoven with Madden's, ultimately comprising only about one quarter of the entire publication. Finally, although Madden appends the iconic slave narrative announcement "Written by Himself" to "Life of the Negro Poet," Manzano's name was completely erased from the compilation.

In light of the nascent single-author slave narrative genre that was emerging from the British West Indies and circulating in the Atlantic world in the decades prior to the 1840 publication of *Poems by a Slave,* Madden's censorship of the author's name requires close examination.[35] He cites the "obvious reasons" for this decision in the preface: "The author of the Poems I have attempted to translate, is now living at the Havana, and gains his livelihood by hiring himself out as an occasional servant."[36] Madden ostensibly demonstrates benevolent discretion here, since publishing the name of the author could potentially endanger his "livelihood" or even his life. Exactly how "obvious" his intentions are, however, remains a point of contention among scholars. For Gera C. Burton, Madden's extensive résumé as an international abolitionist and a personal letter in which he laments Manzano's alleged death speak volumes in defense of his genuine concern for the author's security. Conversely, Sylvia Molloy remains skeptical: "Madden's claims that this was done to protect Manzano, while most probably sincere, are not completely convincing."[37] After all, an attentive Cuban reader or Spanish colonial official would have been able to identify Manzano as the author of the text without difficulty, if not from the singular biographical details (including the names of his masters and the particulars of his manumission), then from the initials "J.F.M." that appear in a quote from Del Monte at the end of Madden's preface or another servant's reference to the narrator as "Juan F" in "Life of the Negro Poet."[38] Following William Luis's careful charting of Madden's translation's effacement of minutia in Manzano's narrative (family names, dates, geographical markers, etc.), Molloy concludes that the abolitionist aimed to craft a representative, "generic account" of Cuban slavery.[39]

As productive as the rigorous debate over Madden's censorship has been, this discussion relies on an understanding of *Poems by a Slave* as a single-author slave narrative in which Manzano's prose testimony is the primary focal point. In actuality, Manzano is one of at least four different authors whose works are assembled in the text, all of whom, with the exception of Madden, are published anonymously: Del Monte appears as "A gentleman of Havana," and the poem "To Cuba"—often attributed to Manzano, but actually set apart from his writings under a separate heading—is also published without its author's name.[40] So what then was Madden's purpose in identifying only himself as a contributor to *Poems by a Slave*? Although it would be tempting to gloss this self-privileging as an attempt to assume sole authorship of the collection, neither the title (which foregrounds the "Slave's" literary contributions) nor the content (carefully balkanized according to author and genre) supports such a reading. More accurately, Madden functions as an anthologizer or as a *bricoleur,* assembling the testimonies available to him on diverse aspects of Cuban slavery in order to provide a fuller picture of the island's entrenchment in that system: "the very abundance of materials," Madden notes, "was an obstacle to the undertaking."[41] More than simply transforming Manzano's life story into a "general account" as Molloy suggests, Madden offers a collage of anonymous Cuban texts, which collectively offer a cross-section of slavery on the island. In censoring the identity of his informants so ostentatiously in his preface, he underscores the Spanish colonial government's totalitarian management of public discourse in Cuba to his abolitionist audience; mentioning that the pieces were "unpublishable" locally "under the ban of the censors of the press" repeatedly in his preface lends urgency to his publication and their intervention.

To some extent though, the rarity of Manzano's perspective still foregrounds his writings within *Poems by a Slave,* provoking Madden to laud

"Life of the Negro Poet" as "the most perfect picture of Cuban slavery that ever has been given to the world, and so full and faithful in its details, that it is difficult to imagine, that the portion which has been suppressed, can throw any greater light on the evils of this system than the first part has done."[42] Although the purported "perfection" of Manzano's account situates his narrative as a representative Cuban slave experience, Manzano's early life in slavery was far from typical. His memoir recalls his preferential treatment by his mistress as "the child of her old age" after his own mother married "one of the head slaves of the house": "I was more at home in his [sic] arms than in those of my mother," he recalls, adding that he "was accustomed to call [his mistress] 'my mother.'"[43] His favored position in his first and second masters' homes gained him access to education, literacy, and mobility; these advantages, the author repeatedly emphasizes to his reader, distinguished him from other slaves.[44] Indeed, whereas Manzano obtained a privileged status within the island's racialized hierarchy, the vast majority of slaves in Cuba labored at a breakneck pace in the tropical heat on sugar plantations, where the cane required constant attention from the field to the refinery, resulting in work days as long as twenty hours during the harvest season.[45]

Madden's claims about the perfect nature of Manzano's narrative, then, are at best misleading, and after three years of inspecting plantations on the island, he would have been painfully aware that Manzano's experience was distinct. Though "full and faithful," "Life of the Negro Poet" offers only a single (if singular) perspective on Cuban slavery, and its "perfection" is mitigated by its necessarily restricted scope. Madden admits as much in one of his included essays: "These domestic slaves, especially those of the opulent proprietors, comparing their condition with that of prædial slaves, may be said to be fortunately circumstanced."[46] Rather than verifying Manzano's testimony or expounding on his character, Madden's writings emphasize the quotidian operations of the sugar plantation and the torturous toiling of the "prædial" slave so as to sketch the more common experience of Cuban slavery that Manzano's account elides.

Madden's texts, therefore, set out to contextualize Manzano's. "To form any just opinion of the merit of these [Manzano's] pieces," his preface instructs, "it is necessary to consider the circumstances under which they were written, and how are these circumstances to be estimated by one ignorant of the nature of Cuban slavery?"[47] Accordingly, Madden adds his own deeply affective experience of witnessing the "general horrors of slavery" to Poems by a Slave. His lengthy poem "The Sugar

Estate," for example, catalogues the moral declivity of the plantation owner and recounts an estate tour during which the *mayoral* (overseer) proudly describes the dehumanized condition of the field slaves to the appalled narrator. He remarks on the cramped boarding ("We stall our negroes as we pen our sheep"), the management of the slaves' "slender" diet, and their meager sleep schedule ("They sleep too much, and have no need for four/Or five hours' rest, his neighbors all agree/That slaves in crop can do right well with three"); the mayoral even comments nonchalantly on the regimentation of violence: "by the way,/Tuesday in common is our flogging day."[48] These impoverished conditions and the psychic violence of perpetual deprivation emerge in stark contrast with Manzano's more comfortable rearing. Whereas "Life of the Negro Poet" depicts violence only in its punitive form, "The Sugar Estate" limns the quotidian cruelties and all-encompassing management of the black body entailed in the labors of the ingenio.

By offering complementary angles on Cuban slavery, *Poems by a Slave* has the curious effect of presenting Madden's testimonies on the institution as parallels to Manzano's. "As portraits, however rudely sketched, of the characters I have attempted to describe," he writes, "the vivid impression which the originals have made on my mind, were too strong to leave these pictures without a resemblance, which an abler artist might have better, though not perhaps more faithfully delineated."[49] By highlighting the exceptional realism of his own writings, he establishes a rhetorical link between his first-person observations of slavery and Manzano's "full and faithful" first-person narrative, introducing the texts as mutually enriching perspectives. Not accidentally, the volume's preface—conventionally supplied to validate the slave's testimony—actually introduces Madden's poetry, rather than Manzano's narrative, thereby vouching for the "faithfulness" of both perspectives. Although it would be inappropriate to term one of Madden's poems a *slave narrative*, each certainly presents a *narrative of slavery* rooted in personal experience and routed through the printed venue of the slave narrative form (*Poems by a Slave*).

Apart from addressing the different experiences of slavery within the island, the interplay between the two authors' writings also adjusts the scale on which the reader comes to confront Cuban slavery. That is, "Life of the Negro Poet" and Manzano's poems offer a highly local (even to the point of interiority) sketch of the traumas of slavery, while Madden's more widely scoped compositions locate Manzano's perspective within the Atlantic trade networks that invisibly contour his experience. Madden therefore renders the foreign milieu of Cuban slavery legible for his decidedly non-Cuban audience at that same time that he holds international powers accountable for their tacit participation in localized violence—the British and U.S. Americans, for Madden, are just as complicit as Manzano's actual tormentors in his suffering. His poems "The Sugar Estate" and "The Slave Trade Merchant," for instance, indict the United States for its passive facilitation of the Atlantic slave trade. As Anna Brickhouse astutely observes, these poems borrow some of their lines directly from Madden's famous 1839 letter to William Ellery Channing in which he exposed the frequent practice of slave ships passing through Cuba flying the U.S. flag in order to avoid inspections of their cargo.[50] With the *Amistad* trial still fresh in his mind, Madden no doubt recycled these verses in order to stress the need for increased pressure on the illegal slave trade from both sides of the Atlantic and to reiterate how the United States' proactive endorsement of the Slave Trade Act of 1794 and the Act Prohibiting Importation of Slaves in 1807 contradict the nation's actual policies in practice. Furthermore, by reappropriating his own scathing critique of the United States' tacit (or in certain circles explicit) support of Cuban slavery, these poems come to chart the culpability of the United States in the illegal slave trade and, by extension, the violence exacted against Manzano.

The second internationally scoped issue that Madden's writings unravel is the purportedly less severe nature of slavery in the Spanish colonies. Made famous in academic circles by Frank Tannenbaum's groundbreaking comparative work *Slave and Citizen: The Negro in the Americas* (1946), this assumption is undergirded by the perception of more legal agency among slaves in colonies like Cuba. The practice of *coartación*, for instance, allowed any slave to purchase his or her freedom for market value; other statutes afforded any slave the option to petition a judge for transfer to a different master if he or she could prove gratuitous mistreatment. While most scholars have since distanced themselves from problematic attempts to measure comparatively human suffering, this opinion was pervasive in the mid-nineteenth century. Madden engages with this assumption explicitly in his essay "Condition of the Slaves in Cuba." He opens:

> If it be true that negro slaves have always been treated with peculiar mildness in the Spanish colonies, it follows, that the slaves of the island of Cuba, for example, are a contented race, that they are not over-worked, nor underfed, nor ill-clad; that the sexes are equalized, that the mortality is small, and the increase by births considerable; that the amount of produce obtained by the

labour of a given number of slaves is less than it has been in former years in the British colonies—that there is a considerable number of aged slaves on the estates—that the pregnant women are allowed exemption from hard field-labour in the last six or eight weeks of their pregnancy—that the females are not usually flogged—that the children are instructed in the elements of the christian [sic] faith—that the negroes on the estates are married by the ministers of religion—that they are suffered to attend a place of worship on the Sabbath-day—that it is not lawful to hunt them down by dogs when they are fugitives from the estates—that when they are scourged to death or killed by violence, the white man, who is their murderer, may be brought to justice, and punished with the utmost rigour of the law—but not one of these measures of justice, or means of protection for the prædial slaves are known to exist in Cuba—not a single one of these I have pointed out is to be looked for, to the law, and yet the law allows these things, and solemnly condemns every withdrawal of them.[51]

This thickly ironic passage speaks directly to a North American audience that perhaps dismissed the urgency of Madden's proposed intervention into Cuba because of slavery's supposed "mildness" there. Furthermore, Madden's examples of suffering from which Cuban slaves were purport-edly spared would have been particularly effective, and affective, for a U.S. readership, resonating with accounts of slavery in the U.S. South. The descriptions of women being flogged or forced to work long hours late into their pregnancies, for instance, are deeply reminiscent of the beating of a pregnant slave named Sarah documented in the first official slave narrative of the American Anti-Slavery Society, *Narrative of James Williams, an American Slave, Who Was for Several Years a Driver on a Cotton Plantation in Alabama* (1838).[52] Alongside the introductory poems' denunciations of U.S. passivity regarding the continued traffick-ing of Africans through Cuba, "Conditions of the Slaves in Cuba" under-scores the economic and practical connections between U.S. and Cuban slavery. From an ethical standpoint, the United States could not outlaw the slave trade on its own shores while accepting African slaves routed through Cuba; nor could U.S. American abolitionists condemn the cru-elty of slavery in the South, while importing sugar, coffee, and tobacco produced in a comparably inhumane Cuban slave labor system that kept these prices low.

Reading Bricolage in Britain

The formal complexities of *Poems by a Slave* were largely lost on most mid-nineteenth-century reviewers, many of whom simply disregarded

Madden's texts and their richly intratextual relationship to Manzano's in their attempts to read the anthology as a single-author slave narrative; others were more confounded in their attempts to read in this way. By cataloging the tensions between *Poems by a Slave*'s bricolated form and the expectations of an abolitionist audience, these reviews reveal the ideological machinery shaping the antislavery print networks of the Atlantic world.

In a number of reviews, Madden's writings often become an afterthought, essentially recentering the slave testimony and relegating the other contributions to the function of peripheral paratexts. In December 1840, the *British and Foreign Anti-Slavery Reporter,* for example, cites passages from "Life of the Negro Poet" and Manzano's "Ode to Religion," dedicating only a passing mention to Madden's "vigorous and effective" poems and "valuable and important" appendixes.[53] The next month the *Christian Observer* published a much longer review of *Poems by a Slave,* which bespeaks the same formalist analysis: it reproduces extensive excerpts from "Life of the Negro Poet" and select stanzas from a number of Manzano's poems, "which are but few, the bulk of the book being taken up with other matter," adding "we must pass over [Madden's verses] in favour of his hero, and also of his own prose illustrations of the atrocities of the slave-trade and slavery in Cuba."[54] Like the *British and Foreign Anti-Slavery Reporter,* the *Christian Observer* still centers Manzano as the "hero" of the publication, but it also seems to grasp the limited scope of his perspective, as Madden aimed to emphasize. "Such is domestic slavery in Cuba," the review reflects after excerpting a fragment of Manzano's memoir, "as depicted in the autobiography of one of its victims."[55] Not only does the review acknowledge that "Life of a Negro Poet" accounts for only "domestic slavery" as opposed to the ingenios, but the author also recognizes that an "autobiography" presents only a single mode of representing slavery, and that Manzano represents only "*one* of its victims" (my emphasis).

Curiously, however, despite its apparent figuration of Madden's writings' as paratextual framing ("other matter") in *Poems by a Slave,* the *Christian Observer* sets out to authenticate his testimonies in the same way that it assumes he has authenticated Manzano's. In introducing selected segments from "Life of the Negro Poet," the review begins: "The authenticity of the work is the first point to ascertain. For this Dr. Madden, who has spent several years in Cuba, and is well known for his zealous labours for the abolition of slavery, vouches."[56] Yet Madden's credentials alone are apparently insufficient. Instead of buttressing its re-production of Manzano's testimony with Madden's "prose illustrations" from *Poems by a Slave*—to which it had already directed our attention—the *Christian Observer* complements "Life of the Negro Poet" with a lengthy excerpt from Madden's recent speech before the Hibernian Anti-Slavery Society. "But to return to Cuba," the review segues, "Let us hear how the 'old tale' still tells in the most recent and authentic statements; for Sir T. Buxton, while arguing that Dr. Madden has understated the im-portations into Cuba, says, 'he is a gentleman whom I have long known and very highly respect,' so that his averments are well endorsed."[57] Thomas Buxton's remarks "vouch" for Madden's observations on the slave trade, but Madden's own "most recent and authentic statements" from the more recent antislavery meeting confirm the "old tale" that he published in *Poems by a Slave*. Whether because of the temporal dis-tance (1840 to 1841) or the geographical distance (Havana to Dublin), Madden's writings are subjected to the same standards of verification as Manzano's. The *Christian Observer* thereby recognizes, if tacitly, the corporate authorship of *Poems by a Slave* through its mapping of generic expectations of the slave narrative (text/paratext, black author/white edi-tor, testimony/authentification) onto the book.

Other reviews were much less subtle in their attempts to read *Poems by a Slave* as a single-author slave narrative. An April 1841 article in the *Eclectic Review* quotes extensively from Manzano's writings and quickly dismisses "Dr. Madden's own productions," which "would af-ford matter for interesting extract if the claims of his protegé were not paramount."[58] This subjunctive construction renders Madden's com-positions as negligible beyond their conditional contextualization of Manzano's. While it would be tempting to argue that this review priv-ileges the slave's testimony over the abolitionist's, the *Eclectic Review* ultimately reinstantiates the seemingly inescapable double bind of the white-authenticated slave narrative. For Beth A. McCoy, benevolent in-tentions hardly ameliorate the disenfranchisement enacted by recasting the authorial economy of black text and white paratext: "Serving neither the text nor its author, the paratext serves something else: an indirect white supremacy, different from the brutality against which white abo-litionists fought but one that interferes with the fugitive writer's autho-rial primacy nonetheless."[59] Through its peculiar casting of Manzano as Madden's "protegé," the *Eclectic Review* subordinates the Afro-Cuban's compositions as somehow sophomoric next to the white abolitionist's more mature writings in spite of their purportedly "paramount" position in *Poems by a Slave.*

IN DESCRIBING *Poems by a Slave* as a bricolated slave narrative, we are seduced by a potentially redemptive reading of Madden's manipulation of Manzano's text in which *Poems by a Slave*'s representation of the local (Cuba) for the Atlantic world allows for Manzano's participation (however unwitting or unwilling it may have been) in a more geographically expansive forum. By the same token, however, reading the volume as an anthology necessarily foregrounds the organizational power of the anthologizer and his vision. Whatever liberating conclusions this framework provides, then, it also forces us to confront the simple fact that the arrangement and editing of *Poems by a Slave* for circulation within a transatlantic arena of antislavery discourse comes at a cost. If the enveloping of the slave narrative by a white abolitionist necessarily transacts white power over black authorship, then the extraordinary ratio of Madden's writings in the volume to Manzano's also dramatically asserts and encodes white authority, despite his political sympathies.[60] The framing of *Poems by a Slave,* in particular, becomes doubly disenfranchising, amplifying not only the white text over the black, but also the European over the Cuban.

It is not overstating the case, then, to suggest that Manzano's memoir, as a written account of his life, was never strictly his own; and yet this may not be as disenfranchising for the author as it initially seems. As Houston A. Baker Jr. contends, "the voice of the unwritten self, once it is subjected to the linguistic codes, literary conventions, and audience expectations of a literate population, is perhaps never again the authentic voice of American slavery. It is rather, the voice of a self transformed by an autobiographical act into a sharer in the general public discourse about slavery."[61] While we might perhaps trouble the existence of such an "authentic voice" of American (or Cuban) slavery, the textual history of Manzano's writings testifies to the powerful influences exerted onto the slave narrative in an instance of publication. At the same time, it insists on the distance between "the voice of the unwritten self" and the narrative persona that appears in print. That is to say, regardless of the conditions under which it was written, Manzano seems fully aware that "el asunto" contracted by Del Monte (which I have intentionally referred to as his "memoir" throughout this essay) and his autobiography were not one and the same—or in Robert B. Stepto's famous formulation, "a slave narrative is not necessarily an autobiography."[62] The disparity between

Manzano's autobiography and his *Autobiografía* crystallizes in one of his early letters to his sponsor:

> Me he preparado para aseros una parte de la istoria de mi vida, reservando los mas interesantes suesos de mi ella para si algún día me alle sentado en un rincón de mi patria, tranquilo, asegurada mi suerte y susistensia, escrivir una nobela propiamente cubana: combiene para ahora no dar a este asunto toda la estension marabillosas de los diversos lanses y exenas por que se necesitaria un tomo, pero a pesar de esto no le faltará a sum. material bastante mañana empesaré a urtar a la noche algunas oras para el efecto.

> (I have prepared myself to draw up for Your Grace a part of the history of my life, reserving the most interesting events of it for myself, [so that] if one day I find myself seated in some corner of my homeland, at peace, assured of my fate and of my livelihood, I may write a properly Cuban novel: for the moment it is best not to give this matter [*Autobiografía*] the spectacular expansion of its diverse occurrences and scenes because it would require a whole volume, but in spite of this Your Grace will not lack sufficient material, tomorrow I shall begin to steal hours from my sleep for that purpose.)[63]

The admission of preserving for himself "the most interesting events" of his life in order to produce his own Cuban novel one day, combined with an earlier missive in which he consents to Del Monte's revisions of his poetry, suggests that Manzano was well aware that any of his writings would be subject to editorial probing prior to print.[64] This necessarily included his prose testimony of slavery. His oft-cited declaration of withholding in this passage assumes a more subversive tone, however, when read alongside a letter from several months earlier in which Manzano assures his sponsor, "espero concluir pronto siñendome unicamente a los suesos mas interesantes" ("I hope to finish soon restricting myself to the most interesting events").[65]

Manzano's slippery phrase—"the most interesting events"—shifts meaning across letters, indicating the withheld content in one context and the provided content in the other. In doing so, he illustrates his understanding that the story he is interested in narrating differs from what Del Monte expected, desired, or required. Rather than events that might more overtly support the Delmontine reformist agenda, the incidents around which Manzano eventually structures his memoir are, in large part, direct responses to his masters' accusations of peccadilloes that led to his unjust or excessive punishment. Thus, *Autobiografía* functions as an intensely personal text aimed at self-exoneration at the same time that it resists ideological incorporation into a political project to which he did not subscribe, namely Del Monte's dubious racial politics masquerading as protonationalism. The Spanish syntax in the letters enacts just this gap: Manzano emphasizes the adjective in regards to what he reserves for his novel ("los mas interesantes suesos"), whereas he deploys the more neutral, more common construction ("los suesos mas interesantes") to describe the content he provides Del Monte. Furthermore, his stated intent of penning "una nobela propiamente cubana," where *propiamente* might be translated as "truly," "correctly," or, as I have rendered it, "properly," suggests subtly that Manzano may have even conceived his novel as a corrective to Del Monte's well-orchestrated portrait of Cuba for foreign audiences. For the author, withholding his most compelling experiences until a time when can he narrate them "at peace, assured of my fate and of my livelihood," certainly meant after his manumission, but it would also require the ability to write and publish without the censorial restrictions of the Spanish colonial government or the editorial caprices of Del Monte, Suárez y Romero, or even Madden.

Poems by a Slave ultimately demonstrates that a slave narrative is not necessarily just a "slave narrative" as outlined by the "linguistic codes, literary conventions, and audience expectations" of the genre; its bricolated assembly and circulation, as well as its fraught reception, necessarily recalibrate our understanding of the form. Beyond simply rendering visible the early coalescence of generic conventions in the Atlantic abolitionist public sphere, *Poems by a Slave* reveals the problematic manifestation of these same audience expectations in our contemporary critical discourse. From Susan Willis's claim that "the slave narrative as a genre had no real presence in Cuba" and was therefore not an influential force in *Autobiografía*'s composition, to Fionnghuala Sweeney's more recent contention that "Manzano's narrative, though a self-authored text by a black man, produced and authorized by a prominent abolitionist, is laden with signifiers that contradict, or at best frustrate the expectations of the slave-narrative form," scholars have anachronistically imposed modern critical standards of what constitutes a slave narrative onto this 1840 text.[66] Although Manzano's memoir does indeed "frustrate" modern generic expectations, the textual history of its composition, translation, and publication emphasizes the incredible malleability of a slave's testimony when projected into the transatlantic networks of antislavery literature and the ways in which the same text could be radically and strategically reappropriated in a plurality of cultural settings.

As part of a collage of texts in Madden's compendium, "Life of the Negro Poet" comes to participate in a multiauthor project testifying to the myriad horrors of slavery in Cuba. Taken as a whole, *Poems by a Slave* is as much a narrative of slavery as is Manzano's "Life of the Negro Poet" on its own; only the totality of Cuban slavery—including the illegal slave trade and international sugar trade that sustain the institution—has displaced Manzano's personal suffering as the purview of its study. As this essay demonstrates, this is not as disenfranchising a structure as it might have initially seemed, especially since the textual metaphor of bricolage insists on our recognizing the uneven incorporation of Manzano's writings (rather than his voice) into *Poems by a Slave*'s abolitionist mission; and as Manzano's letters remind us, Del Monte and Madden could only co-opt his writings to the extent that he allowed for them to do so.

Notes

This essay draws from a number of sources found in the holdings of the Cuban Heritage Collection at the University of Miami, where my research was made possible through generous funding from the Goizueta Foundation and the Amigos of the Cuban Heritage Collection, as well as the library's passionate, dedicated staff. Unless otherwise indicated, I have preserved the original (occasionally incorrect or outdated) spelling and mechanics, and all translations are mine. A longer version of this essay has appeared in *Atlantic Studies* 10.4 (2013): 528–49.

1. See Benítez-Rojo, "¿Cómo narrar la nación?"; Bottiglieri, "La escritura de la piel"; and Luis, *Literary Bondage*. Although Manzano's is the only Spanish American slave narrative written and conceived as such, this is not to say that it is the only intact testimony from an enslaved perspective from Spanish America. For an example of the diversity of resources on slave testimonies available to scholars of Cuba, see García Rodríguez, *Voices of the Enslaved*.

2. Throughout this text, I refer to the Spanish-language version of the text as *Autobiografía*, and unless otherwise noted, all citations to this text refer to Luis's critical edition of the text. Mentions of "Life of the Negro Poet" and *Poems by a Slave* refer to Madden's translation of Manzano's slave narrative and his entire publication, respectively. All citations of the English translation refer to Edward J. Mullen's critical edition of Madden's complete text, *Life and Poems of a Cuban Slave*.

3. Raphael Dalleo ambitiously attempts to periodize the literary historiography of the Caribbean from the early nineteenth century to the present, beginning with the abolitionist movements. For Dalleo, the plantocratic monopoly on published discourse required Caribbean abolitionists to address European audiences and seek European venues for publication; see Dalleo, *Caribbean Literature*.

4. Luis documents at least two different manuscripts of *Autobiografía*, and his 2007 critical edition of Manzano's writings rigorously attends to the discrepancies

between them. For detailed comparisons of the Spanish language text(s) and Madden's translation, see Molloy, "From Serf to Self"; Luis, *Literary Bondage* 82–100; and Schulman, introduction to *Autobiography of a Slave*.

5. Fernanda Macchi also examines Manzano's narrative in its English language translation in the context of British abolitionism and Madden's other antislavery writings; see Macchi, "Juan Francisco Manzano."

6. Fionnghuala Sweeney has also recently reconsidered the form of *Poems by a Slave* and proposes several different analytics for understanding it, including transnational Catholicism; see Sweeney, "Atlantic Countercultures."

7. For a detailed sketch of recent scholarly engagements with the Romantic author-as-genius paradigm and an exploration of the ways in which this ideal remains encoded in both culture and criticism, see Haynes, "Reassessing 'Genius.'"

8. Aljoe, *Creole Testimonies*, 60.

9. Ibid., 90.

10. Prince, *History of Mary Prince*, 55; Aljoe, *Creole Testimonies*, 69–71.

11. For more on authentification, see Blassingame, *Slave Testimony;* Stepto, *From behind the Veil;* Sekora, "Black Message/White Envelope"; McCoy, "Race and the (Para)Textual Condition."

12. Madden, in Manzano, *Life and Poems*, 37.

13. Bakhtin, *Problems of Dostoyevky's Poetics*, 6.

14. Fina García Marruz suggests that Del Monte was most likely introduced to Manzano through the Marquesa del Prado Ameno's second son, Don Nicolás de Cárdenas y Manzano, who, along with Del Monte, was a member of the Sociedad Patriótica; see García Marruz, *Estudios Delmontinos*, 160.

15. For a concise history of the Del Monte tertulias, see Luis, *Literary Bondage*, 29–36; for an extended study, see Martínez Carmenate, *Domingo Del Monte*.

16. In a letter to Del Monte, Súarez y Romero alludes to the lost second half of the manuscript and pleads with him to ask Manzano to recompose the missing segments; see Súarez y Romero to Domingo del Monte, 20 August 1839, in Del Monte, *Centón epistolario*, 2:391–92.

17. See Susan Willis's analysis of the stylistic "flaws" in Manzano's prose in "Crushed Geraniums," 204–5. I enclose "corrected" in quotation marks here to signal Lorna V. Williams's suggestion that Súarez y Romero was probably of little help in editing Manzano's mechanical miscues, owing to his own "grammatical deficiencies"; see L. Williams, *Representation of Slavery*, 24–31.

18. David R. Murray cites annual reports from the British Havana commissioners indicating that from 1820 to 1829, a total of 152 slave expeditions landed 47,272 Africans on Cuba, as well as reports from the British Consul David Tolmé (1833–1840) that estimate that the numbers from 1830 to 1838 more than doubled those of the previous decade, jumping to 353 expeditions and 107,438 Africans; see Murray, "Statistics of the Slave Trade," 141–43.

19. For more on Madden's work as a special magistrate in Jamaica, see Murray, "Richard Robert Madden," 42–48.

20. Tacón to Minister of Foreign Affairs, no. 4, reservado, 31 Aug. 1836, Pérez de la Riva, *Correspondencia*, 252–55, translated and quoted in Murray, *Odious Commerce*, 122.

21. Burton, *Ambivalence and the Postcolonial Subject,* 30.

22. Schulman, introduction to Manzano, *Autobiography,* 17.

23. Branche, "'Mulato Entre Negros,'" 72.

24. According to official census data, Cuba's population in 1827 comprised 311,051 whites, 286,942 slaves, and 106,494 "free colored" persons; by 1841, there were 418,291 whites, 436,495 slaves, and 152,838 "free colored" people on the island; see Murray, "Statistics of the Slave Trade," 136.

25. Matt D. Childs describes the influence of the Haitian Revolution on the culture of slavery in Cuba, locating it as a catalyst for the large-scale slave rebellion planned by José Antonio Aponte in 1812; see Childs, *1812 Aponte Rebellion.*

26. The most vocal and prolific representative of this position was held by José Antonio Saco, who was exiled from Cuba in 1834 because of his political views; see Saco, *La supresión del tráfico* and *Mi primera pregunta.* The racism undergirding not only Saco's patriotism but also that of other *delmontinos* has inspired a reevaluation of their statuses as the "founding fathers" of independent Cuba; see Soto Paz, *La falsa cubanidad.*

27. For more on Del Monte's racial ideologies, see Branche, "'Mulato entre negros,'" 72–75; for more on European immigration programs in Cuba, see Murray, *Odious Commerce,* 149–51.

28. Murray notes that Madden's attempt to take advantage of his relationship with Del Monte was hardly uncommon; see Murray, *Odious Commerce,* 131.

29. This interview appears as "In RE, Slave-Trade, Questions Addressed to Senor — of Havana, by R. R. Madden, and Answers Thereunto of Senor —" and "Questions Respecting the State of Religion in Cuba, Addressed to Senor *** of the Havana, by R.R.M. and the Answers Given to Them" in *Poems by a Slave.* For the contents of the antislavery portfolio that Del Monte sent to England with Madden, see Luis, introduction to Manzano, *Autobiografía,* 18n13.

30. Del Monte to Madden, October 1839, *Revista Cubana* 10 (1889): 323–24, 326, quoted in L. Williams, *Representation of Slavery,* 20.

31. L. Williams, *Representation of Slavery,* 19.

32. Pérez, *On Becoming Cuban,* 83–95.

33. For a full account of the trial, including Madden's pivotal participation, see Barber, *History of the Amistad Captives;* for a more recent scholarly study, see Rediker, *Amistad Rebellion.*

34. *Minutes of the proceedings of the General Anti-slavery Convention,* 31. As suggested, a Spanish translation of Madden's address was published as Alexander, *Observaciones sobre la esclavitud* (1841).

35. In addition to *The History of Mary Prince,* Susannah Strickland also transcribed the oral testimony of Ashton Warner, which was published as *Negro Slavery Described by a Negro: Being the Narrative of Ashton Warner, a Native of St. Vincent* (1831). Relatedly, James Williams's narrative of the transition from slave labor to free labor was published in London as *A Narrative of Events Since the First of August, 1834, by James Williams, an Apprenticed Labourer in Jamaica* (1836). Perhaps evidencing Madden's attempt to distance his text formally from these single-author slave narratives, his publication's title aligns itself more immediately with George Moses Horton's *Poems by a Slave* (1837) and *Memoir and*

Poems of Phillis Wheatley, a Native African and a Slave; Also, Poems by a Slave (1838) than with any of these contemporaneous slave narratives.

36. Madden, in Manzano, *Life and Poems*, 38.

37. Molloy, "From Serf to Self," 405.

38. Madden, in Manzano, *Life and Poems*, 39; Manzano, *Life and Poems*, 105.

39. Molloy, "From Surf to Self," 405–8; Luis, *Literary Bondage*, 82–100.

40. Manzano's poems appear under the heading "Poems, Written in Slavery, by Juan—and Translated from the Spanish by R.R.M.," while "To Cuba" appears immediately following this section under a new heading: "A Specimen of Inedited Cuban Poems, Presented to Dr. Madden on His Departure from Cuba, and Translated by Him from the Spanish." As previously mentioned, we can assume that this author's name was removed by Del Monte, not by Madden.

41. Madden, in Manzano, *Life and Poems*, 38.

42. Ibid., 39.

43. Manzano, *Life and Poems*, 80, 81. Madden mistranslates the gender from the Spanish, which unambiguously refers to Doña Beatriz de Justiz; see Manzano, *Autobiografía*, 84.

44. For more on Manzano's self-differentiation from other slaves, see Branche, "'Mulato Entre Negros.'"

45. In 1827, about 78 percent of slaves in Cuba lived in the *campo*, as opposed to cities; see Aimes, *History of Slavery*, 120. Similarly, about 80 percent of slaves imported to Cuba directly from Africa in the mid-nineteenth century became field workers, while only about 20 percent became urban or domestic slaves; see Knight, *Slave Society in Cuba*, 60.

46. Madden, in Manzano, *Life and Poems*, 182–83.

47. Ibid., 37–38.

48. Ibid., 72, 73, 75.

49. Ibid., 38.

50. Anna Brickhouse, "Manzano, Madden," 234n12; see Madden, *Letter to W. E. Channing*.

51. Madden, in Manzano, *Life and Poems*, 182.

52. J. Williams, *Narrative of James Williams*, 61–64. The use of hounds to hunt fugitives (to which Madden alludes) also plays a prominent role throughout *Narrative* and its authenticating documents. One of the men who helped publish the text was Lewis Tappan, a central figure in the *Amistad* trial who became a friend of Madden. More likely than not, Madden read Williams's *Narrative* while he was in the United States in early 1840.

53. "Slavery in Cuba," *British and Foreign Anti-Slavery Reporter and Aborigine's Friend*, December 1840.

54. *Christian Observer*, 45.

55. Ibid., 56.

56. Ibid., 44.

57. Ibid., 57. The review fails to provide a citation for Madden's speech, introducing the fragment ambiguously enough that it could even be misinterpreted as the work of Buxton. The *Christian Observer* likely reprinted the speech from "Slavery in Cuba," *British and Foreign Anti-Slavery Reporter and Aborigine's*

Friend, February 1841, 21–22; the *Anti-Slavery Reporter* reprinted the speech from the *Dublin Weekly Register*.

58. *Eclectic Review*, 1841 *January–June*, 9:411.

59. McCoy, "Race and the (Para)Textual Condition," 157.

60. Joselyn M. Almeida, for example, has recently expounded on the dangers of such readings. Without attributing insidious intentions to Madden, she argues that the editorial matrix of *Poems by a Slave* recasts an economy of credit and debt, in which Manzano's authorial labor becomes conflated with slave labor as it is translated and appropriated within the British marketplace; see Almeida, *Reimagining the Transatlantic*.

61. Baker, "Autobiographical Acts," 253.

62. Stepto, *From behind the Veil*, 6.

63. Manzano to Del Monte, 29 September 1835 in Manzano, *Autobiografía*, 85.

64. Manzano to Del Monte, 16 October 1834 in Manzano, *Autobiografía*, 79.

65. Manzano to Del Monte, 25 June 1835 in Manzano, *Autobiografía*, 83.

66. Willis, "Crushed Geraniums," 203; Sweeney, "Atlantic Countercultures," 406.

Bibliography

Aimes, Hubert H. S. *A History of Slavery in Cuba, 1511 to 1868.* New York: Knickerbocker Press, 1907.

Alexander, Joseph G. *Observaciones sobre la esclavitud y comercio de esclavos por J.G. Alexander; é informe del Dr. Madden sobre la esclavitud en la isla de Cuba.* Barcelona: A. Bergnes y Cía, 1841.

Aljoe, Nicole N. *Creole Testimonies: Slave Narratives from the British West Indies, 1709–1838.* New York: Palgrave Macmillan, 2012.

Almeida, Joselyn M. *Reimagining the Transatlantic: 1780–1890.* Farnham: Ashgate, 2011.

Baker, Houston A., Jr. "Autobiographical Acts and the Voice of the Southern Slave." In *The Slave's Narrative*, edited by Charles T. Davis and Henry Louis Gates Jr., 242–61. Oxford: Oxford University Press, 1985.

Barber, John Warner. *A History of the Amistad Captives: Being a Circumstantial Account of the Capture of the Spanish Schooner Amistad, by the Africans on Board; Their Voyage, and Capture Near Long Island, New York; with Biographical Sketches of Each of the Surviving Africans; also, an Account of the Trials had on Their Case, Before the District and Circuit Courts of the United States, for the District of Connecticut.* New Haven: E. L. & J. W. Barber, 1840.

Bakhtin, Mikhail. *Problems of Dostoyevky's Poetics*, edited and translated by Caryl Emerson. Minneapolis: University of Minnesota Press, 1984.

Benítez-Rojo, Antonio. "¿Cómo narrar la nación? El círculo de Domingo Delmonte y el surgimiento de la novela cubana." *Cuadernos Americanos* 45, no. 3 (1994): 103–25.

Bottiglieri, Nicola. "La escritura de la piel: La *Autobiografía* de Juan Francisco Manzano." In *Esclavitud y Narrativa En El Siglo XIX Cubano: Enfoques*

Recientes, edited by Salvador Arias, 58–84. Havana: Editorial Academia, 1995.

Branche, Jerome. "'Mulato Entre Negros' (y Blancos): Writing, Race, the Antislavery Question, and Juan Francisco Manzano's *Autobiografía.*" *Bulletin of Latin American Research* 20, no. 1 (2001): 63–87.

Brickhouse, Anna. "Manzano, Madden, 'El Negro Mártir,' and the Revisionist Geographies of Abolitionism." In *American Literary Geographies: Spatial Practice and Cultural Production, 1500–1900,* edited by Martin Brückner and Hsuan L. Hsu, 209–35. Newark: University of Delaware Press, 2007.

Burton, Gera C. *Ambivalence and the Postcolonial Subject: The Strategic Alliance of Juan Francisco Manzano and Richard Robert Madden.* New York: Peter Lang, 2004.

Childs, Matt D. *The 1812 Aponte Rebellion in Cuba and the Struggle against Atlantic Slavery.* Chapel Hill: University of North Carolina Press, 2006.

Christian Observer, conducted by Members of the Established Church for the Year 1841. London: J. Hatchard and Son, Picadilly, 1841.

Dalleo, Raphael. *Caribbean Literature and the Public Sphere: From the Plantation to the Postcolonial.* Charlottesville: University of Virginia Press, 2011.

Davis, Charles T., and Henry Louis Gates Jr., eds. *The Slave's Narrative.* Oxford: Oxford University Press, 1985.

Del Monte, Domingo. *Centón Epistolario.* Edited by Sophie Andioc Torres. 4 vols. La Habana: Imágen Contemporánea, 2002.

Eclectic Review, 1841 January–June. London: Jackson and Walford, 1841.

García Marruz, Fina. *Estudios Delmontinos.* Havana: Ediciones Unión, 2008.

García Rodríguez, Gloria, ed. *Voices of the Enslaved in Nineteenth-Century Cuba: A Documentary History.* Chapel Hill: University of North Carolina Press, 2011.

General Anti-slavery Convention (1st: 1840: London, England). *Minutes of the proceedings of the General Anti-slavery Convention : called by the committee of the British and Foreign Anti-Slavery Society, held in London on the 12th of June, 1840, and continued by adjournments to the 23rd of the same month.* London: Johnson and Barrett, 1840.

Haynes, Christine. "Reassessing 'Genius' in Studies of Authorship: The State of the Discipline." *Book History* 8 (2005): 287–320.

Knight, Franklin W. *Slave Society in Cuba during the Nineteenth Century.* Madison: University of Wisconsin Press, 1970.

Luis, William. *Literary Bondage: Slavery in Cuban Narrative.* Austin: University of Texas Press, 1990.

Macchi, Fernanda. "Juan Francisco Manzano y el discurso abolicionista: Una lectura enmarcada," *Revista Iberoamericana* 78, no. 218 (2007): 179–93.

Madden, Richard Robert. *A letter to W. E. Channing, D.D., on the subject of the abuse of the flag of the United States in the Island of Cuba, and the advantage taken of its protection in promoting the slave trade.* Boston: William D. Ticknor, 1839.

Madden, Richard Robert, and Juan Francisco Manzano. *Poems by a Slave in the Island of Cuba, Recently Liberated; Translated from the Spanish, by R. R. Madden, M.D. With the History of the Early Life of the Negro Poet, Written by Himself; to Which Are Prefixed Two Pieces Descriptive of Cuban Slavery and the Slave-Traffic, by R. R. M.* London: Thomas Ward, 1840.

Manzano, Juan Francisco. *Autobiografía, cartas y versos de Juan Francisco Manzano.* Edited by José Luciano Franco. Havana: Municipio de La Habana, 1937.

———. *Autobiografía del esclavo poeta y otros escritos.* Edited by William Luis. Madrid: Iberoamericana, 2007.

———. *Autobiography of a Slave.* Bilingual ed. Edited by Ivan A. Schulman. Translated by Evelyn Picon Garfield. Detroit: Wayne State University Press, 1996.

———. *The Life and Poems of a Cuban Slave.* Edited by Edward R. Mullen. Translated by Richard Robert Madden. Hamden, CT: Archon Books, 1981.

Martínez Carmenate, Urbano. *Domingo Del Monte y su tiempo.* La Habana: Ediciones Unión, 1997.

McCoy, Beth A. "Race and the (Para)Textual Condition." *PMLA* 121, no. 1 (2006): 156–69.

Molloy, Sylvia. "From Serf to Self: The Autobiography of Juan Francisco Manzano." *MLN* 104, no. 2 (1989): 393–417.

Murray, David R. *Odious Commerce: Britain, Spain, and the Abolition of the Cuban Slave Trade.* Cambridge: Cambridge University Press, 1980.

———. "Richard Robert Madden: His Career as a Slavery Abolitionist." *Studies: An Irish Quarterly Review of Letters, Philosophy & Science* 61, no. 241 (1972): 41–53.

———. "Statistics of the Slave Trade to Cuba, 1790–1867." *Journal of Latin American Studies* 3, no. 2 (1971): 131–49.

Pérez, Louis A., Jr. *On Becoming Cuban: Identity, Nationality, and Culture.* Chapel Hill: University of North Carolina Press, 1999.

Prince, Mary. *The History of Mary Prince, a West Indian Slave, Related by Herself.* Edited by Moira Ferguson. Ann Arbor: University of Michigan Press, 1997.

Rediker, Marcus. *The Amistad Rebellion: An Atlantic Odyssey.* New York: Viking, 2012.

Saco, José Antonio. *La supresión del tráfico de esclavos africanos en la isla de Cuba: Examinada con relación a su agricultura y a su seguridad.* Paris: Panckoucke, 1845.

———. *Mi primera pregunta—¿La abolición del comercio de esclavos africanos arruinará o atrasará la agricultura cubana?* Madrid: Imprenta de Don Marcelo Calero, 1837.

Sekora, John. "Black Message/White Envelope: Genre, Authenticity, and Authority in the Antebellum Slave Narrative." *Callaloo* 32 (Summer 1987): 482–515.

"Slavery in Cuba." *The British and Foreign Anti-Slavery Reporter and Aborigine's Friend.* December 1840.

"Slavery in Cuba." *The British and Foreign Anti-Slavery Reporter and Aborigine's Friend,* February 1841.

Soto Paz, Rafael. *La falsa cubanidad de Saco, Luz, y Del Monte.* La Habana: Editorial Alfa, 1941.

Stepto, Robert B. *From Behind the Veil: A Study of Afro-American Narrative.* Urbana: University of Illinois Press, 1979.

Sweeney, Fionnghuala. "Atlantic Countercultures and the Networked Text: Juan Francisco Manzano, R. R. Madden and the Cuban Slave Narrative." *Forum of Modern Language Studies* 40, no. 4 (2004): 401–14.

Tannenbaum, Frank. *Slave and Citizen: The Negro in the Americas.* New York: A. A. Knopf, 1946.

Williams, James. *Narrative of James Williams, an American Slave, Who Was for Several Years a Driver on a Cotton Plantation in Alabama.* New York: American Anti-Slavery Society, 1838.

Williams, Lorna V. *The Representation of Slavery in Cuban Fiction.* Columbia: University of Missouri Press, 1994.

Willis, Susan. "Crushed Geraniums: Juan Francisco Manzano and the Language of Slavery." In *The Slave's Narrative,* edited by Charles T. Davis and Henry Louis Gates Jr., 199–224. Oxford: Oxford University Press, 1985.

Seeking a Righteous King

A Bahamian Runaway Slave in Cuba

José Guadalupe Ortega

IN 1791, Juan Antonio (*el ingles*), José Rafael, and Juan Francisco left New Providence, Bahamas, for Cuba with the hope of gaining their freedom upon arrival. The onset of the French and Haitian Revolution had spurred rumors of emancipation and abolition from Port-au-Prince and other Caribbean ports to the British West Indies. Convinced that Spanish royal decrees and colonial officials in Cuba were emancipating English slaves of African descent, Juan Antonio and his companions secured a small craft and followed the ocean currents linking the Bahamas to various Atlantic commercial circuits. They arrived at the coast of the province of Puerto Principe and traveled inland. Authorities in Puerto Principe, Cuba, were perplexed by their assertions but found their stories plausible enough to grant Juan Antonio and his companions passage to Havana. Yet, Juan Antonio did not make it to Havana. Instead, various unsavory individuals with questionable moral principles seized Juan Antonio and resold him into slavery in Cuba.[1]

Juan Antonio's narrative of his journey, as told to colonial officials in Cuba, public defenders, and notaries, outlines the existence of a complex of social networks linking peoples of African descent with political and institutional developments during an era of revolution and upheaval. Rumors of liberation reveal the hopes and aspirations of enslaved peoples as they grappled with the heavy weight of economic and institutional frameworks across Atlantic legal slave regimes. Juan Antonio's journey from the Bahamas to Cuba demonstrates the manner in which such structures influence personal and social transformations. Although Juan Antonio struggled to maintain his self-ascribed identity as a free person of color in Cuba, his interactions with public defenders, slave merchants, and masters on the island repeatedly transformed his status.

Yet, Juan Antonio persevered, jealously guarding his identities throughout the many challenges he encountered. His legal dilemmas demonstrate how identity often involves negotiation and contestation. Familiarizing himself with Spanish legal institutions, Juan Antonio struggled to regain the identity of an emancipated slave that he argued Spanish authorities bestowed upon him shortly after arrival. During the turbulent 1790s, Juan Antonio was an English runaway slave, an emancipated slave, a slave once again, and an individual with an ambiguous legal identity. Nevertheless, Juan Antonio's Spanish legal identities enabled him to act as a private contractor with the ability to sell his labor to multiple sugar planters in need of talented laborers. His practical knowledge and agricultural expertise acquired from years of enslavement in the West Indies aided the rise of the Cuban plantation complex. Ironically, by finally securing his freedom in Cuba, Juan Antonio strengthened the very institution that enslaved him upon arrival.

Judicial Testimony, Experience Narratives, and Collaborative Life Narratives

This essay makes use of various judicial records housed in the Cuban National Archives (ANC) in order to evaluate and analyze Juan Antonio's "experience narrative" in Cuba during the last decade of the eighteenth century. As a means of promoting "peace" the Spanish colonial project encouraged individuals from all walks of life to seek legal recourse for private disputes and transgressions that could otherwise derail the social order if left unattended. Thus most members of Cuban society appear in the public record, from patrician landowners to humble and illiterate muleteers of mixed racial descent. Once a petitioner filed a grievance, secular or ecclesiastical notaries duly recorded his or her testimony. Individuals verbally declared specific incidents, circumstances, and related stories regarding their legal action to notaries who functioned as court reporters and transcribed their oral testimonies into written form.

As a genre, depositions present the historian with notable interpretive challenges, but oftentimes their potential yield far outweighs most inherent methodological constraints. For example, from time to time notaries facing time limitations simply summarized oral testimonies, thus excluding the finer points of a personal story or an account. Yet Spanish legal institutions and the very structure of the deposition generated remarkable details about colonial society and daily life. Civil and criminal lawsuits followed a standard format that produced both mundane information and precious minutiae. At the beginning of each lawsuit, the notary recorded the litigant's name, occupation, legal and racial identities, marital status, and country of origin or city of residence. Subsequently, the notary recorded the plaintiff's testimony in the first-person narrative mode. Many times the statements include in-depth descriptions of the developments that brought the supplicant to court. Notaries closely followed their declarations, oftentimes documenting a complainant's verbal uncertainties, hesitations, repetitions, and occasional contradictions. It is not uncommon to discover that notaries reproduced the diction specific to the petitioner, a process that reflected the litigant's gender, social class, and level of acculturation. What's more, other members of the Spanish colonial legal system, principally magistrates and defense attorneys, performed key roles in the production of an individual's testimony or narrative. Magistrates served as inquisitors who asked complainants and witnesses key questions about the case at hand or their "experience." For enslaved litigants, the government appointed a *síndico procurador,* or slave representative, arbitrated conflicts between masters and slaves, and provided the latter with legal consul.[2]

Thus the actors, circumstances, and elements that coalesced to produce Juan Antonio's experience narrative did so through contestation, negotiation, and collaboration. In other words, his story as described in this essay is a hybrid of sorts combining the experience narrative with major components of the collaborative life narrative. Rather than producing a full-length autobiography spanning the life of Juan Antonio, the circumstances and judicial materials amalgamated to construct a portrait of his experience to seek justice during one of the formative decades of his life. Moreover, the story of his experience, focusing primarily on a single defining moment, developed from coercive social and political conditions on the one hand and conflict and collusion with historical actors on the other. It is certainly Juan Antonio's experience narrative, but in some ways it is also a collective biography that includes his English companions, José Rafael and Juan Francisco, formed through multiple collaborations with various other individuals since leaving the Bahamas. All three men passionately held on to their identities as Englishmen and proclaimed so during depositions, even as Spaniards hispanicized or changed their names altogether in order to sell them as newly arrived peoples from the African continent. Though they were not subjects of the British Empire, as former inhabitants of the Bahamas they rightly claimed Englishness. Thus Juan Antonio claimed the identity of *el ingles* during his legal ordeals. Along with Juan Antonio's narrative, José Rafael's and Juan Francisco's testimonies transmitted the concerns, values, history, and worldview of the group during a period characterized by radical developments in the Atlantic world.[3]

Abolition and Emancipation Rumors

In 1791, the Caribbean was teeming with revolutionary upheaval. The French and Haitian Revolutions had unleashed a series of social, political, and economic transformations that led to the abolition of slavery in one of the wealthiest colonies in the world. While establishing fundamental and universal rights for male citizens, the French Declaration of Rights of Man did not immediately address the thorny issue of slavery in Saint-Domingue. The French National Assembly continued deliberations on the matter, but peoples of African descent in Saint Domingue refused to wait for the results of such debates. Instead, slaves on the island claimed the discussion, reinterpreted the declaration, and liberated themselves. Insurgents expanded the meaning and application of the document to "demand liberty by any means" and to include all men regardless of racial background.[4]

Knowledge of the Declaration of the Rights of Man spread throughout Saint Domingue and the Caribbean as slaves, free people of color, and French émigrés traveled or fled the island. Slaves in Saint Domingue fighting against French forces refused to surrender until all slaves gained their freedom. As the revolution expanded, slaves continued layering their demands with language precisely drawn from the document itself. Captured insurgents asserted that "they wanted to enjoy the liberty they were entitled to by the Rights of Man." Others carried copies of the pamphlet of the "Rights of Man" to spread dissension among the population or to utilize them as political amulets while fighting enemy forces. Leaders of the rebellion subsequently translated the declaration into creole, published it, and widely distributed it throughout the island in order disseminate its contents to as many people as possible.[5] As French émigrés fled the island with their slaves and servants to Cuba, the United States, and the British West Indies, including Jamaica and the Bahamas, knowledge of the Republican document broadened to include non-French-speaking people of color.[6]

French émigrés arriving in the Bahamas in 1791 received a cool reception from its English inhabitants and government officials who had been cautiously observing political developments in Saint Domingue since 1789. Fear of contagion and of slave conspiracies led to additional regulations, policing, and deportation of black French émigrés. The Bahamian assembly instituted a number of repressive local decrees, including the demand that all free and enslaved blacks (regardless of nationality), people of mixed ancestry, and Indians register their names, age, color, and address with authorities. In direct response to the Haitian Revolution, Bahamian authorities strengthened police and militia forces and expanded jail and prison facilities. Officials also sought to control the movement of Bahamian slaves and free people of color by restricting their ability to buy and sell goods and to socialize with other blacks. Finally, in an effort to address one of the perceived demographic issues that led to the Haitian Revolution, Bahamian colonial officials passed a deficiency law aimed at establishing a safe population ratio between blacks and whites on the islands.[7]

Seeking Royalist Intervention

The arrival of black French émigrés on the islands led to the development of a hostile political environment in the Bahamas and the zealous persecution of Bahamian slaves. Juan Antonio and his witnesses testified that they encountered an increased level of violence, especially at the hands of their British masters, which compelled them to leave the Bahamas for Cuba. According to their testimony, Juan Antonio, José Rafael, and Juan Francisco left New Providence Island, Bahamas, for Cuba in order to "evade harassment and abuse they were experiencing." Due to its size, proximity, and the direction of ocean currents, Cuba was a popular destination for Bahamian fugitive slaves. Furthermore, non-Spanish-speaking people of color often passed as free blacks on the island. Indeed, Juan Antonio and his companions were part of a steady stream of Bahamian runaway slaves who would serve as crewmen on merchant ships in exchange for passage to Cuba. Typically they would jump ship once they reached a Cuban port. Incredibly, some fugitive slaves used canoes to row their way to the island.[8]

While exact statistics are unavailable, officials in the Bahamas and Cuba initially sought to contain or control the emigration of runaway slaves. The same year Juan Antonio and his companions left for Cuba, another Bahamian runaway slave named Emmanuel stole a boat from the brig *Eliza,* but authorities apprehended the small craft as it drifted near Hyburn Key, one of the Bahamas. Bahamian officials summarily tried, condemned, and executed Emmanuel. In draconian fashion, they publicly displayed his body, still fastened with chains, at the entrance of the harbor in Hog Island, present-day Paradise Island, in order to instill terror among potential runaways. By contrast, officials in Puerto Principe, Cuba, dealt with the immigration of Bahamian runaway slaves by arresting and depositing them in the municipal prison. Known as the prison of the court of appeals district, authorities held them until Spanish judicial officials reviewed their individual testimonies.[9] As the phrase "court of appeals" implies, the Spanish legal process provided slaves with greater latitude to negotiate their fugitive status.

Juan Antonio declared to Spanish colonial officials that he and his companions arrived in Cuba seeking Christianity and the "ability to labor freely as royal vassals of the Spanish King." Juan Antonio reviewed the dire circumstances he experienced in the Bahamas, which, he argued, compelled him to seek refuge in Cuba. His narrative and statements sought to appeal to Spanish moral and legal sensibilities regarding master-slave relations. By demonstrating to officials that his former British master applied corporal punishment beyond humane or normative levels, Juan Antonio argued that his former master lost legal dominion over him and that he should thus be freed.[10]

Juan Antonio and his companions also requested that the Spanish Crown intervene on their behalf. According to their testimony, Juan Antonio, José Rafael, and Juan Francisco came to Cuba after hearing rumors that the king of Spain would grant foreign slaves their freedom if they fled their homeland and surrendered to Spanish officials. Retired colonel Bernardo Ramírez, the governor of Puerto Principe, could not confirm or refute the existence of the royal decree alluded to by the three sojourners. His office detained them briefly until Ramírez released them, instructing them to continue on their travels toward Havana, where they could make their case before the island's General Captaincy.[11]

The rumored emancipation decree was very popular among people of color throughout the duration of the French and Haitian Revolutions, and oftentimes well into the 1810s. It appears that many slaves living in the Caribbean genuinely believed in the existence of such a decree. To many slaves, the advent of the Haitian Revolution signaled the viability of a moral economy based on freedom, fairness, and justice. Others were motivated by the belief that Spain would sell Cuba to the French Republic. For some slaves, demonstrations, work stoppages, marronage, and other peaceful means of resistance seemed like reasonable responses to an unjust and illegitimate economic system. Like Juan Antonio, they imagined the existence of a social order led by a righteous Christian king who would intervene on their behalf against malicious individuals or a corrupt system. Some slaves utilized these rumors as smokescreens or machinations to galvanize popular support for violent rebellions. Much like the contemporary press developed news stories based on mere rumors, these slaves exploited the possibility of the suppression of an authentic emancipation decree by masters in order to justify and organize resistance movements. Certainly, slaves possessed the desire to obtain their individual and collective liberty prior to the French and Haitian Revolutions, but the idea, real or imagined, of a royal emancipation decree motivated them to steadfastly pursue their freedom. Indeed, as Franklin Knight has suggested, these revolutions transformed the "way individuals and groups saw themselves and their place in the world."[12]

Political and Economic Dimensions of Bahamian Immigration

According to Juan Antonio's statements, colonial authorities in Puerto Principe released the group from prison and provided them with legal documents that enabled them to stay in Cuba. Juan Antonio never recovered these documents after slave merchants deceived him and resold him as a slave. Yet, Juan Antonio's public defender introduced a notarized statement corroborating his assertions. An internal government audit confirmed that the *Real Hacienda* or the Royal Estate, reviewed the appeals of two Bahamian slaves, José Antonio Machado and a second unidentified individual, who had "entered the island illegally." According to an official document, the lieutenant governor "set them free on their own account" after reviewing their cases. Furthermore, witnesses speaking on behalf of Juan Antonio reveal the existence of an English expatriate community or "residents" livingly freely in Puerto Principe.[13]

As a result of the political upheaval generated by the Haitian Revolution, provincial authorities throughout Cuba were dealing with a deluge of slaves "from foreign colonies" seeking residency on the island. Officially, the crown restricted the immigration or residency of foreign nationals. Yet the arrival of English slaves on the island presented local colonial officials with administrative, bureaucratic, and logistical challenges that taxed local municipalities. For officials in the landlocked city of Puerto Principe, repatriating English slaves proved to be an impractical if not costly enterprise. It is possible that the Puerto Principe's lieutenant governor may have been unaware of the crown's policy. However, in all likelihood he feigned ignorance to the existence of such a statute. Thus granting English slaves their freedom and releasing them to seek work on the island may have seemed like the only sensible solution to a complex administrative problem.[14]

Furthermore, colonial officials were well aware of the economic benefits that former English slaves like Juan Antonio brought to a burgeoning economy. The Haitian Revolution placed Cuba in a highly advantageous economic position. In the late eighteenth century, Saint Domingue produced nearly half of the sugar consumed in Europe and the Americas. Hailed by contemporaries as the "Pearl of the Antilles," Saint Domingue was once the wealthiest colony in the Caribbean and was fundamentally integrated into the North Atlantic economy. However, between 1791 and 1803 the French colony was transformed by a series of slave revolts that destroyed most colonial institutions, crippled the plantation economy, and ejected large segments of the population from the island. The destruction of Saint Domingue left an economic vacuum Spaniards in Cuba sought to fill and exploit.[15] Aided by the destruction of Saint Domingue, Cuban planters positioned themselves to take full advantage of these transformations and did so by embracing acculturated and skilled English slaves like Juan Antonio.

Juan Antonio and his English companions were part of a rising African population that facilitated the expansion of the sugar mill complex in Cuba. Prior to the mid-eighteenth century the African labor experience on the island was relatively diverse. Slaves and free people of color were occupied in a number of urban and rural sectors of the Cuban economy. However, the Haitian Revolution and the continued European demand for sugar altered the development of African slavery in Cuba, bringing about a relative concentration of slaves in the sugar industry, leading to the increased importation of people of African descent from the continent. No fewer than three hundred thousand slaves were imported into the island between 1790 and 1820.[16]

Yet importing "unseasoned" African slaves from the continent could not fill the demand for acculturated labor on Cuban sugar plantations. The sugar mill, a highly developed social and economic institution, required heavy capital investment, fertile land, the construction of multiple buildings, and a specialized slave work force. Indeed, the sugar mill complex produced a discernable social hierarchy of enslaved and salaried workers that included cane cutters, livestock handlers, muleteers, cartmen, carpenters, boiler room technicians, sugar masters, slave foremen, and assistant foremen.

Free and enslaved labor of African descent, oftentimes sourced from other Caribbean islands, was especially essential at the turn of the nineteenth century, when Cuban planters established additional sugar mills. While the demand for unseasoned slaves was usually met by the Atlantic slave trade, the availability of skilled labor remained an ongoing concern for many planters who needed the expertise of acculturated intermediaries.

At least through the initial years of the nineteenth century, slaves and free people of color imported from the surrounding French and English colonies met some of the demand.[17]

The case of Juan Antonio and his companions demonstrates the existence of multifaceted Caribbean labor circuits traversing Cuba and neighboring regions at the turn of the nineteenth century. Geopolitical conflict or revolutionary upheaval, coupled with the Cuban demand for cheap labor, shifted slaves from one island or region to the next one. And as this essay shows below, island or local labor demands also transferred slaves and their plantation knowledge from one master to another.

An Identity in Transition

Upon their release from the Puerto Principe municipal prison, Juan Antonio and his companions felt a sense of vulnerability in this strange city. Armed with official documents issued by Ramírez's office, Juan Antonio, José Rafael, and Juan Francisco looked for work in Puerto Principe. However, none of them could speak Spanish, a fact that compounded an already difficult situation. Hence they were quite relieved when they encountered a certain George, an Englishman who lived in the city. George assured them that he would find them jobs and a place to stay if they would accompany him. But George had no such intentions. With the assistance of several accomplices he imprisoned the men in a private residence while he forged bills of sale that signified their arrival on the slave ship *Argor* and then sold them as African slaves to unscrupulous Spaniards.[18]

Juan Pitaluga, a Cuban planter, purchased Juan Antonio as an "unseasoned" slave. After being resold into slavery in Cuba, Juan Antonio worked on several sugar plantations. Juan Antonio was well versed in North Atlantic plantation culture, and his talents were soon recognized by managers, who removed him from the fields and transferred him to the plantation boiler room. Since he was one of the slaves responsible for handling bagasse (a byproduct of crushing sugarcane that consists of residue and straw and is used for fuel), maintaining heat at optimum temperature levels, removing residues, and performing other tasks related to one of the final processes in producing sugar, he quickly gained the trust of his master, Juan Pitaluga.[19]

Like many other masters, Pitaluga maximized the value of his slaves by renting them to neighboring planters. On one such occasion, while Juan Antonio was working for Esteban Eligio, his master died. Pitaluga's widow, Rita de Casas y Valdez, saw no reason for Juan Antonio's return and thus continued to honor her husband's rental agreement with Eligio.

Encouraged by Eligio and well aware of the economic and family disarray that usually followed the death of a planter, Juan Antonio took advantage of the situation and sued the estate for his freedom.[20] Eligio provided Juan Antonio with the space, time, and work flexibility to sue his former masters. This conduct was not unusual for planters in Cuba. Planters facing short-term labor market fluctuations lured slaves from their masters with attractive salaries or the promise of liberty. The affected owners complained bitterly that their best and most capable slaves disappeared, "seduced" by assurances of "malignant" individuals. Owners of these transient slaves were often acquainted with the individuals who procured them but were practically powerless once the slaves secured the physical and legal protection of other Spaniards.[21]

It is because Juan Antonio worked in the boiler room that he was in a better position to exploit the Spanish legal process. He achieved a high level of mobility and absence from the sugar mill complex, which allowed him to travel to the city, provide a deposition to a notary detailing his travels from the Bahamas to Cuba, and consult with a public defender. Juan Antonio's narrative outlines the ambiguous nature of informal labor arrangements among planters and between masters and slaves that oftentimes resulted in lengthy legal disputes. With the payment he made to a public notary to initiate legal proceedings, Juan Antonio established a newfound identity as an independent contractor who could freely sell his services. He demanded that his current employer retain the value of his labor prior to the death of Pitaluga, at least until the courts ruled on his petition for emancipation.

His new labor routine called for periods of absenteeism, thereby reducing the practical control masters or employers possessed over him. Juan Antonio thus achieved a certain level of freedom that he jealously guarded, and he resented it when his masters failed to respect his new status. He no longer perceived himself as a slave and demanded that his masters acknowledge his de facto identity as emancipated. Thus the Spanish legal process endowed Juan Antonio with special privileges, which in turn provided him with an economic and social stake in society. In public discourse, he identified himself not as *negro* or a slave but as a *chino* or *moreno*. By identifying with two of the nine different categories that free people of African descent utilized to designate their social status, Juan Antonio demonstrated to Spanish officials his familiarity with the complex racial nomenclature of the island. People in Cuba used the term *chino* to identify a person of black and mixed racial ancestry and the term *moreno* to identify a free person of color. The context for Juan Antonio's use of the term *moreno* signified "ex-slave Creole"—in other words, a person of color born in the Americas. By alternatively using both the *chino* and *moreno* designations he maintained that his racial identity precluded any possibility that he was from the African continent regardless of color, but instead he was born in the Americas to parents, to use his own words, of "diverse nationalities" and mixed racial backgrounds.[22]

According to Juan Antonio's narrative and the testimonies of multiple witnesses, he was born to a Puerto Rican *parda* mother and a "North American" black father in the British West Indies.[23] After the American Revolution, southern loyalists, encouraged by favorable conditions offered by the British crown, left the former colonies for the Bahamas. These refugees transferred their slaves, possessions, and plantation culture to the British West Indies. Like his English companions, before departing for Cuba Juan Antonio worked on one of the many cotton plantations in Nassau that ultimately failed.[24]

Juan Antonio argued that his enslavement in Cuba was instituted through a number of fraudulent actions that rendered him legally free on the island. He referred to the large number of slaves from the British West Indies who had sought refuge in Cuba. Further bolstering his cause was the fact that Spanish officials had deported the Englishman George for committing several other crimes. The most glaring evidence supporting Juan Antonio's case was actually his own racial identity. Pitaluga's heirs largely based their claims over Juan Antonio on the bill of sale that described him as an unseasoned African slave. He repeatedly referred to himself as a *chino* or an individual of "mixed nation," and he pointed to the lighter color of his skin as evidence that he was not born in Africa.[25]

For Juan Antonio, his companions, and other itinerant English slaves on the island, exploiting the inherent contradictions of Spanish colonial legal structures provided the expectation of justice and sometimes a legitimate opportunity to secure their freedom. However, in rural areas the majority of slaves on any given sugar plantation rarely left the plantation to travel to the city. Thus we should be cautious in our interpretation of the Spanish legal process and avoid overemphasizing the resourcefulness of slaves in Cuba. The capriciousness of a master could stall or derail the process of emancipation, necessitating litigation that people of African descent could not immediately afford. In Juan Antonio's case, the Pitaluga's heirs did not respect Juan Antonio's new identity but instead tried to reassert their power and authority by maintaining their "legal property rights" over their runaway slave based on a "purchase made in good faith."[26]

We should avoid as well the temptation to utilize informal labor contracts negotiated between slaves, who were in the process of suing for
their freedom, and other employers, as a gauge for measuring the character of Cuban slavery. The labor arrangements that Juan Antonio negotiated with Eligio certainly offered him the possibility of acquiring his freedom, but this economic relationship was not owing to the benevolence
of his employer. Individuals like Juan Antonio, whose legal identity was
in flux, offered planters the possibility of exploiting the labor of their
subjects without investing in the full price of a slave. For a fraction of
the cost of a regular slave, an employer received access to an acculturated
person of African descent, who was well versed in the Spanish language
and who possessed a number of other practical skills.

Furthermore, Eligio did not pay Juan Antonio the value of his wages
that he generated prior to his suit against the heirs of Pitaluga.[27] Since
Eligio did not own Juan Antonio, he was not legally obligated to provide
for his welfare. Thus Eligio charged his employee for room and board
while working on his plantation. Due to the high costs of court proceedings, Juan Antonio was probably financially indebted to Eligio. For
planters like Eligio, this labor arrangement provided an avenue for the
redistribution of skilled and semi-skilled labor of African descent in an
otherwise costly and fluctuating labor market.

Juan Antonio used the same social and economic networks that had
enslaved him in order to pursue his freedom. For example, Eligio provided
Juan Antonio with a flexible work environment that allowed him to leave
the sugar mill and meet with the defense attorney whom his companions
from the Bahamas had already obtained for their own proceedings. Once
he completed his tenure with Eligio, Juan Antonio refused to return to
Pitaluga's estate. As an independent contractor, he sold his services to
Francisco Martínez, who, like Eligio, benefited from Juan Antonio's newfound freedom. The Cuban economy benefited from multiple migration
flows in the Caribbean basin that brought knowledge and talent to the
island. By serving multiple planters, providing them with the value of his
labor, Juan Antonio strengthened the institution of slavery. At the same
time, Pitaluga, Eligio, and Martínez demanded a type of skilled labor that
was in short supply in the 1790s and thus provided Juan Antonio with a
spatial environment that eventually advanced the cause of his freedom.[28]

THE HAITIAN Revolution and the political and economic upheaval of the
turbulent 1790s transformed the lives of thousands of plantation workers of African descent who labored under the sweltering and tropical

heat of the Caribbean sun. The Haitians who liberated themselves and destroyed the social, economic, and political underpinnings of a colony largely responsible for maintaining France's Bourbon monarchs proposed an alternative societal model based on the revolutionary concept that all citizens, regardless of race or color, were equal. For people of African descent who were unwilling or unable to take up arms against their oppressors, the revolution offered a beacon of hope on an otherwise bleak reality by providing them with the opportunity to fundamentally change their own world. The revolution generated social and political unrest in the Caribbean, especially with runaway slave communities in the British West Indies. It also sent massive waves of French refugees to multiple Caribbean islands, New Orleans, and cities along the Eastern Seaboard who knowingly or unwittingly carried and disseminated the message of freedom.[29]

Abolition and antislavery movements grew stronger as people in the Atlantic world questioned the morality and sustainability of a socio-economic institution based on the vast exploitation of people of African descent. Rumors of liberation and emancipation traversed the Caribbean commercial circuits that transferred labor, goods, and information to island communities. These are the same circuits that Juan Antonio and his English companions tapped into to escape their oppressive conditions in the Bahamas and seek their freedom in Cuba. Juan Antonio was part of a larger English runaway community who in some ways helped revitalize agricultural production in Cuba during the period of Saint Domingue's decline and the rise of the Haitian Republic. Imported, recruited, or migrating to Cuba on their own, workers of African descent from the British West Indies transferred sophisticated agricultural and cultivation expertise to an expanding Cuban economy. As intermediaries, Africans occupied in lower management positions communicated between administrators and unseasoned slaves, while others, like Juan Antonio, operated complex sugar mill machinery. In essence the local and trans-Caribbean social networks that English runaway slaves constructed brought them closer to freedom, but they also bolstered Cuba's economy.

Notes

1. Throughout this essay I have retained the original Spanish translations for the names of English slaves as found in their respective documents. All other translations are mine. Archivo Nacional de Cuba (hereafter cited as ANC), Havanna, Escribanías, Daumy, leg. 721, no. 14, fol. 1. Documents are cited by *legajo* (folder) number, document number, and folio or leaf number.

2. For a gendered approach to the experience narrative see Komisaruk, "Rape Narratives, Rape Silences," 369–72. On the effectiveness of slave representatives in colonial Cuba see Paquette, *Sugar Is Made with Blood,* 63; Scott, *Slave Emancipation in Cuba,* 75; de la Fuente, "Slaves and the Creation," 659–92; Varella, "El canal administrativo," 109–36.

3. McHugh and Komisaruk, "Something Other than Autobiography vii–xii.

4. Dubois, *Avengers of the New World,* 105.

5. Ibid., 105, 162–64.

6. For the impact of abolition and royal emancipation rumors on slave societies see Childs, *1812 Aponte Rebellion in Cuba,* 122, 155–58, 181; Klooster, *Revolutions in the Atlantic World,* 164–65; Gaspar and Geggus, *Turbulent Time,* 8–12; Dubois, *Colony of Citizens,* 85, 90–92.

7. Shepherd, *Working Slavery, Pricing Freedom,* 59.

8. Craton and Saunders, *Islanders in the Stream,* 1:375–76. Jamaican slaves also arrived in Cuba during the same period; see Childs, *1812 Aponte Rebellion in Cuba,* 43.

9. *Bahama Gazette,* 19 Apr. 1791; ANC, Escribanías, Daumy, leg. 721, no. 14, fol. 1.

10. ANC, Escribanías, Daumy, leg. 721, no. 14, fol. 1.

11. Ibid.; Lasqueti, *Colección de datos históricos-geográficos,* 102, 160.

12. Dubois, *Avengers of the New World,* 136–37; Knight, "Haitian Revolution," 104.

13. ANC, Escribanías, Daumy, leg. 721, no. 14, fol. 121.

14. ANC, Escribanías, Daumy, leg. 721, no. 14, fol. 149.

15. Geggus, *Haitian Revolutionary Studies,* 5.

16. Knight, *Slave Society in Cuba,* 23; Eltis, *Economic Growth,* 245; Tomich, "World Slavery," 304; Childs, *1812 Aponte Rebellion in Cuba,* 49–50.

17. ANC, Asuntos Políticos, leg. 4, no. 35 A, 20 May 1792; ANC, Asuntos Políticos, leg. 7, no. 30, 25 July 1798; ANC Asuntos Políticos, leg. 125, no. 32, "Concerns over the introduction of slaves implicated in the Jamaican revolution."

18. ANC, Escribanías, Daumy, leg. 721, no. 14, fols. 2–3, 11, 168.

19. For a vivid description of work duties in the boiler room, see Lowell, *New Year in Cuba,* 78.

20. ANC, Escribanías, Daumy, leg. 721, no. 14, fols. 3, 6.

21. ANC, Escribanías, Guerra, leg. 1124, no. 15570, 9 July 1831; ANC, Tribunal de Comercio, leg. 244, no. 9, "Regarding certain suspicious incidents in the sugar mill, Jesús Nazareno."

22. A *pardo* was a mulatto person with black and white or two mulatto parents. A *chino* was a person with mulatto and black parents. A *moreno* was a person with black parents. In her seminal work on Cuba, Verena Alier-Martínez lists nine social status designations among free people of African descent: 1) free-born *pardo,* white on one side, 2) ex-slave *pardo,* white on one side, 3) free-born *pardo,* on both sides, 4) ex-slave *pardo* on both sides, 5) free-born *chino,* 6) ex-slave *chino,* 7) free-born Creole *moreno,* 8) ex-slave Creole *moreno,* 9) ex-slave *moreno de nación* or born on the African continent. See Martínez-Alier, *Marriage, Class, and Colour,* 98.

23. See note 22.

24. José Rafael, one of Juan Antonio's "English" companions, was originally from Philadelphia. ANC, Escribanías, Daumy, leg. 721, no. 14, fols. 111–21, 216. For a brief history of southern slaves in the Bahamas, see Wright, *History of the Bahama Islands*, 424–25. Some planters were ignorant of soil conditions in the Bahamas and the latest methods available for soil conservation. After initial crop failures these planters returned to North America; see Whittington Bernard Johnson, *Race Relations in the Bahamas*, 12.

25. ANC, Escribanías, Daumy, leg. 721, no. 14, fols. 149, 168–72.

26. Humboldt, *Ensayo político sobre*, 265; Manzano, *Autobiography of a Slave*, 90.

27. Juan Antonio calculated the wages he had lost as Pitaluga's slave and presented his widow with a demand for payment.

28. ANC, Escribanías, Daumy, leg. 721, no. 14, fols. 4–5, 72.

29. Knight, "Haitian Revolution," 104, 113–14; Geggus, *Impact of the Haitian Revolution*, 49, 79, 137.

Bibliography

Blackburn, Robin. "Haiti, Slavery, and the Age of the Democratic Revolution." *William and Mary Quarterly*, 3rd ser., 63, no. 4 (2006): 643–74.

Childs, Matt D. *The 1812 Aponte Rebellion in Cuba and the Struggle against Atlantic Slavery.* Chapel Hill: University of North Carolina Press, 2006.

Craton, Michael, and Gail Saunders. *Islanders in the Stream: A History of the Bahamian People.* Vol. 1: *From Aboriginal Times to the End of Slavery.* Athens: University of Georgia Press, 1999.

Dubois, Laurent. *Avengers of the New World: The Story of the Haitian Revolution.* Cambridge: Harvard University Press, 2005.

———. *A Colony of Citizens: Revolution and Slave Emancipation in the French Caribbean, 1787–1804.* Chapel Hill: University of North Carolina Press, 2004.

Eltis, David. *Economic Growth and the Ending of the Transatlantic Slave Trade.* New York: Oxford University Press, 1987.

de la Fuente, Alejandro. "Slaves and the Creation of Legal Rights in Cuba: Coartación and Papel." *Hispanic American Historical Review* 87, no. 4 (2007): 659–92.

Gaspar, David Barry, and David Patrick Geggus. *A Turbulent Time: The French Revolution and the Greater Caribbean.* Bloomington: Indiana University Press, 1997.

Geggus, David Patrick. *Haitian Revolutionary Studies.* Bloomington: Indiana University Press, 2002.

———, ed. *The Impact of the Haitian Revolution in the Atlantic World.* Columbia: University of South Carolina Press, 2001.

Higman, B. W. *Slave Population and Economy in Jamaica, 1807–1834.* Kingston, Jamaica: University of West Indies Press, 1995.

———. "The Sugar Revolution." *Economic History Review* 53, no. 2 (2000): 213–36.

Humboldt, Alexander von. *Ensayo político sobre la isla de Cuba.* Paris: J. Renouard, 1827.

Johnson, Whittington Bernard. *Race Relations in the Bahamas, 1784–1834: The Nonviolent Transformation from a Slave to a Free Society.* Fayetteville: University of Arkansas, 2000.

Klooster, Wim. *Revolutions in the Atlantic World: A Comparative History.* New York: New York University Press, 2009.

Knight, Franklin W. "The Haitian Revolution." *American Historical Review* 105, no. 1 (2000): 103–15.

———. *Slave Society in Cuba During the Nineteenth Century.* Madison: University of Wisconsin Press, 1970.

Komisaruk, Catherine. "Rape Narratives, Rape Silences: Sexual Violence and Judicial Testimony in Colonial Guatemala." *Biography* 31, no. 3 (2008): 369–96.

Lasqueti, Juan Torres. *Coleccion de datos historicos-geograficos y estadisticos de Puerto del Príncipe y su jurisdicion.* Havana: Impr. El Retiro, 1888.

Lowell, Mary Gardner. *New Year in Cuba: Mary Gardner Lowell's Travel Diary, 1831–1832.* Edited by Karen Robert. Boston: Massachusetts Historical Society and Northeastern University Press, 2003.

Manzano, Juan Francisco. *The Autobiography of a Slave/Autobiografía de un Esclavo.* Bilingual ed. Detroit: Wayne State University Press, 1996.

Martínez-Alier, Verena. *Marriage, Class, and Colour in Nineteenth-Century Cuba: A Study of Racial Attitudes and Sexual Values in a Slave Society.* Ann Arbor: University of Michigan Press, 1989.

McHugh, Kathleen, and Catherine Komisaruk. "Something Other Than Autobiography: Collaborative Life-Narratives in the Americas—An Introduction." *Biography* 31, no. 3 (2008): vii–xii.

Paquette, R. L. *Sugar Is Made with Blood: The Conspiracy of La Escalera and the Conflict between Empires over Slavery in Cuba.* Middleton: Wesleyan University Press, 1988.

Rios, Theodore, and Kathleen M. Sands. *Telling a Good One: The Process of a Native American Collaborative Biography.* Lincoln: University of Nebraska Press, 2000.

Scott, Rebecca Jarvis. *Slave Emancipation in Cuba: The Transition to Free Labor, 1860–1899.* Princeton: Princeton University Press, 1985.

Shepherd, Verene A. *Working Slavery, Pricing Freedom: Perspectives from the Caribbean, Africa, and the African Diaspora.* New York: Palgrave Macmillan, 2002.

Tomich, D. "World Slavery and Caribbean Capitalism." *Theory and Society* 20, no. 3 (1991): 297–319.

Varella, Claudia. "El canal administrativo de los conflictos entre esclavos y amos: Causas de manumisión decididas ante síndicos en Cuba." *Revista de Indias* 71, no. 251 (2011): 109–36.

Wright, James Martin. *History of the Bahama Islands, with a Special Study of the Abolition of Slavery in the Colony.* Baltimore: Friedenwald, 1905.

Literary Form and Islamic Identity in *The Life of Omar Ibn Said*

Basima Kamel Shaheen

In 1995, the original manuscript of *The Life of Omar Ibn Said, Written by Himself,* the most complete American slave narrative in the Arabic language, was rediscovered in an old trunk in Virginia. This was the first time Ibn Said's autobiographical text was seen since its disappearance in the early years of the twentieth century, and in 2011 Ala Alryyes published an authoritative English translation of the narrative, providing scholars with the only edition of Ibn Said's text that preserves the meaning of the original manuscript. This edition of Ibn Said's *Life* brought one of the earliest and most important Arabic texts in American literature back into print, giving scholars their first opportunity to evaluate Ibn Said on his own terms, but the narrative's significance, unfortunately, has yet to receive the full attention of academia or the public.

Given its linguistic and religious separateness from the mainstream tradition of the American slave narrative, *The Life of Omar Ibn Said* calls for a rather different angle of approach. Ibn Said's work stands alone as a literary anomaly that requires scholars to sift through the small amount of extant information available on the man and his work—because the loose-leaf manuscript Ibn Said left represents almost all we know of him—and to disperse the fog of Orientalism that has long enveloped the text.[1] It also demands a familiarity with the cultural and religious dimensions of the narrative, without which it is difficult to understand how Ibn Said's words speak for his inner consciousness while he was enslaved and unable to speak aloud. Here I focus on Ibn Said's use of Arabic literary conventions—the first time they have received sustained critical analysis—to suggest that his work represents a unique development in American literature. The *Life* is a slave narrative that challenges dominant assumptions about abolitionists, slave owners, and even the concept of the American slave narrative, written by a man who lived a remarkable life largely outside the plantation system and composed in a language entirely foreign to the American experience it describes.

Ibn Said was born in about 1770 in Futa Toro, in West Africa, between the Senegal and Gambia Rivers. The son of a non-Arab, wealthy, Muslim family, he received two and a half decades of education in the Arabic language and Islamic theology, as well as in business and other intellectual pursuits.[2] Ibn Said then worked as a teacher for six years, but in 1807 he was captured during a military conflict, the details of which he does not provide, including the identities of the warring parties.[3] Sold into slavery, he was transported to the United States and worked for about two years on a rice plantation in South Carolina before escaping to Fayetteville, North Carolina, in 1810. Soon recaptured (while reportedly praying in a church), Ibn Said became the property of General James Owen, with whose family he lived, in relatively easy circumstances, until his death in 1864. During his enslavement, Ibn Said learned English and in 1820 joined the Presbyterian church; he also wrote a variety of unpublished manuscripts in Arabic, including *The Life of Omar Ibn Said*, which dates to 1831.

Ibn Said's identity and public image were more complex than this simple biographical frame suggests, not least because he was an African slave elevated to a position of public curiosity due to his Arabic literacy. Indeed, for most of his life in America, during which he was mentioned in a variety of newspaper and magazine articles and in abolitionist propaganda, his personal character was more fascinating to the public than anything he wrote. Yet records of how the public perceived Ibn Said are piecemeal and confused, and many accounts are difficult to substantiate, existing only in second-hand reference and quotation. To the extent that we can reconstruct Ibn Said's public image, it appears to have been that of a protected slave, an immigrant attempting to become naturalized, or even something of an oddity on par with carnival performers: a man who appeared to be African, but who wrote and spoke in Arabic. Ibn Said's reputed conversion to Christianity surely helped to validate his identity for the public, which was fascinated by this "Arabian Prince" whose story of being captured by barbaric Africans, sold into slavery, and then rescued by a "kind master" made for an appealing Orientalist variation on the already popular genre of the Indian captivity narrative.

Thus a high degree of ambiguity surrounds not only Ibn Said's blackness but also his religion, the truth of his life story, his literary work, and the public's impressions of him. Yet I contend that Ibn Said may have preserved a degree of his mental and spiritual independence precisely by taking advantage of the ambiguity surrounding him in his own lifetime. With all extant information about him being fraught with misapprehension and misunderstanding, it is easy to see how Ibn Said could take this as an opportunity to conceal his mind and inner life from the dehumanizing forces of enslavement. Indeed, his navigation of the Southern sociopolitical environment during the antebellum period as an intelligent man living the life of a carnival attraction would require the creativity, spontaneity, and cunning of the best stage actors. Moreover, it seems likely that an enslaved man who felt compelled to write in his native language, knowing that none around him could read it, would endeavor to preserve the integrity of his meanings, should the text ever find a sympathetic audience. What I suggest here is that there are two aspects to Ibn Said's Arabic writing: a performative side meant for an audience unfamiliar with either Arabic or Islamic culture, and what Ibn Said wrote for those who could understand him at deeper levels of experience.

Scholars who pursue the challenge of understanding Ibn Said's work will discover a brief but very rich account of antebellum American bondage written partially in the Qur'anic Arabic idiom.[4] Ibn Said's characteristic mode of expression is terse but unconstrained, and it demonstrates familiarity with a variety of Arabic literary conventions, which are discussed at length later in this essay. He gives an account of his life, education, and captivity in South Carolina but diverges from most slave narratives in his marked isolation from the slave community. Ibn Said had little contact with other slaves, wrote about none of them, mentioned no present friends or family, and focused on revealing his own experience and his private and spiritual thoughts. The Arabic language insulated him from the danger of his text being fully comprehended by his masters and their society, and he therefore had an opportunity to indict slavery from an Islamic perspective, undetected. By the same token, however, much of the subtlety of Ibn Said's writing is largely inaccessible to readers or scholars who lack the cultural knowledge to be able to identify when he is "writing between the lines" or otherwise encouraging his reader to infer information based on what is absent from his text.

Few Americans in the nineteenth century, certainly, had the cultural, religious, and linguistic experience needed to understand Arabic literature, and those who did still approached the subject from an Anglo-European, Christian point of view. Abdulhafeth Ali Khrisat has suggested that the pervasive ignorance of and prejudice toward Islam in the nineteenth-century United States led writers such as Harriet Beecher Stowe to suppress or misinterpret the Islamic background of their African or African

American characters—and thus to overlook one of the fundamental sources of a Muslim slave's literacy and cultural identity.[5] In the early translations of Arabic texts, accordingly, the native Islamic perspective tends to fade away—to the point of rendering the texts almost unrecognizable, each translated problematically if not poorly, and often on behalf of editors with their own political agendas. While all translated texts suffer some degree of deterioration of meaning, the problem is particularly acute in the case of Arabic texts translated into English, given the generally scanty or distorted knowledge of Islam in the West.

A solid grasp of Islamic literature—knowledge that must be gained through long study, regardless of one's native language—is necessary before one can properly appreciate or sensitively interpret many texts originally written in Arabic. More broadly, reading these texts from a modern perspective informed by a deep knowledge of Islamic cultural and literary traditions can dramatically illuminate our understanding of antebellum African American slave narratives, challenging some prevalent assumptions regarding the problems of authenticity, authorship, identity, literacy, religion, and the quest for freedom. Since Ibn Said's work in particular offers the clearest possible glimpse into the minds of Muslim African slaves, any approach to the text that is not sensitive to Ibn Said's Muslim identity and his use of Arabic, Qur'anic Arabic, and Islamic literary conventions will necessarily be an impoverished one. Indeed, a fluent or native speaker of Arabic can see that most treatments of the *Life* lack sufficient awareness of Islamic and Arabic literary conventions, and that providing such insight to scholars is the necessary next step in securing a position for Ibn Said as a notable figure in American history and literature. In that spirit, this essay approaches Ibn Said's text with an eye for how both Arabic and Islamic literary genres informed his self-representation and his relationship to Western culture. Specifically, I claim that *The Life of Omar Ibn Said, Written by Himself* contains traces of two important genres of Arabic autobiography, *Tabaqat* (biographical dictionaries) and *Tarjamat* (biographical notices), which allow Ibn Said to speak, subtextually, not only to an Arabic-literate readership but also to an implied Islamic audience and to posterity.

IBN SAID'S autobiographical narrative, like his very image in the culture, has a complex provenance. Although Ibn Said wrote other works prior to his enslavement, the *Life* and a few of his letters are all that survive, and they fortunately remain available due to the original manuscript's good condition.[6] It is unknown for how long he worked on his autobiography, or under what exact circumstances he wrote it, but he was famous in his own day for his ability to write and was likely encouraged to do so. There is little hard evidence regarding Ibn Said's immediate reasons for writing the *Life*, other than his reply to a letter (no longer extant) from a member of the American Colonization Society (ACS), Sheik Hunter, who requested the autobiography (Alryyes, "Introduction" 6). More broadly, however, Ibn Said's primary motive for writing, apart from those reflecting the will of his owners, seems to have been a desire to express his Islamic faith and to resume his former way of life.

The manuscript resided with Ibn Said and the Owenses from 1831 to 1836, when a man named Lahmen Kebby, also called "Old Paul," is recorded as having presented it to Theodore Dwight, who had it translated into English by 1848. Ibn Said's first translator was Alexander I. Cotheal, treasurer of the Ethnological Society and a collector of Arabic manuscripts. Some extracts of Ibn Said's life, taken from this translation, appeared in the *Methodist Review* in 1864. Later, the reverend Isaac Bird, who learned Arabic while on a Christian mission in Syria, translated the text with the assistance of Dr. F. M. Moussa, the secretary of the Egyptian Legation in Washington, D.C. (*The Life*'s provenance is carefully traced in both John Franklin Jameson's annotated version of Bird's translation and in Alryyes's translation.) Prior to its rediscovery, the last confirmed owner of the manuscript text was the curator of the American Numismatic Society in New York (Alryyes, "Introduction" 5). Bird's translation appeared in the July 1925 edition of the *American Historical Review*, and thereafter the manuscript disappeared.

The modern scholarly neglect of Ibn Said's work, therefore, is partly a matter of simple historical circumstance; the extant material on Ibn Said consists largely of Orientalized echoes of obscure sources, so his text probably appeared too insignificant to merit in-depth study.[7] Whatever the case, there is, to date, no volume of his collected letters and the *Life* that has been translated faithfully, that includes explanatory notes expounding upon the Islamic character of the text, and that presents both contemporary and modern accounts of Ibn Said in a manner allowing readers to compare and contrast his evolving portrayal in American culture. Without any authoritative volume of Ibn Said's production, it is extraordinarily challenging for an English-speaking audience to access his text at all. (More research should also be conducted on the Owens family, whose records, if they still exist, could shed much-needed light on Ibn Said's life in captivity.) After his death—the period when the public's memory of someone is most enduringly forged—Ibn Said's reputation was clouded by Orientalist misconceptions, and he eventually faded away, almost entirely, from American culture.

By the time the United States had entered the First World War, the task of locating source material fell to Jameson, who worked without the advantages of our modern archival systems. Whatever sources Jameson missed, we have likely lost. Nevertheless, references to Ibn Said appear in many works regarding slave narratives, the African American experience, and Islam in America. Very few articles or chapters, however, are devoted to Ibn Said alone, and his work is usually referenced as a typical account of enslavement, which, decidedly, it is not. Worse, the text itself is not often the object of critical interest or explanation. As with the Orientalists before them, those who focus on Ibn Said's life, rather than the *Life,* are guilty of ignoring his distinctive voice and strategies of self-representation in favor of dwelling on the unusualness of his personal character.

THE STORY of Ibn Said's misapprehension by American culture begins, of course, in the nineteenth century, and here we should first observe that it took seventeen years for the American Colonization Society to find a person (Cotheal) competent enough to translate the *Life*—a delay suggesting that by the time the text was finally rendered into English, simply getting down a translation was of more importance than finding the best translator. Moreover, the original translation that did appear was shaped by the political aims of the ACS—and in spite of the justness of their ultimate goal, the abolition of slavery, members of the ACS also supported the "return" of ex-slaves to Liberia, where the organization hoped they would serve as missionaries of both Christianity and the Western way of life in Africa. Alryyes argues that the ACS's politics provided motivation not so much to deliberately misuse Ibn Said's text as to frame the text in ways that obscured the original context of its production.

Our first clues to the process of appropriation appear on the title page of the manuscript: "The life of Omar ben Saeed [*sic*], called Morro, a Fulla Slave, in Fayetteville, N.C. Owned by Governor Owen. Written by himself in 1831 & sent to Old Paul, or Lahmen Kebby, in New York, in 1836. Presented to Theodore Dwight by Paul in 1836, Translated by Hon. Cotheal, Esq., 1848" (Ibn Said, *Muslim* 49). This title page is written in a different hand and in English, possibly that of Old Paul, another ex-slave who probably had a close relationship with Theodore Dwight and was likely among the ACS's advocates (Alryyes, "Introduction" 16). Old Paul emigrated to Liberia soon after providing Ibn Said's work to Dwight and vanished to history soon thereafter, and nothing else is known of him.[8]

Thus, the most significant nineteenth-century slave narrative of Muslim authorship came into the possession of a Christian whose personal and political beliefs were steeped in missionary zeal. Theodore Dwight was a prominent member in the ACS as well as the founder of the American Ethnological Society. He was fairly knowledgeable about Islam in Africa and its influence on various African regions and tribes, but from the perspective of a Christian missionary. As a member of the ACS, Dwight advocated the emancipation and emigration to Liberia of American slaves, and he actively sought out Muslim slaves through the ACS, which, according to Lamin Sanneh, "had availed itself of the most sophisticated techniques of mass propaganda, of a web of interlocking local agents fanning out and cohering in one active, coordinating site, with an uncanny ability to pick on the right subject for maximum public effect" (Sanneh, *Abolitionists* 199). That "maximum public effect," Dwight believed, could be achieved by publicizing the cases of slaves who had attained literacy and particularly those who had converted to Christianity, a tried-and-true strategy of abolitionist rhetoric dating to at least the early eighteenth century. As Dwight writes: "it will be surprising to be told that among the victims of the slave-trade among us have been men of learning and pure and exalted characters, who have been treated like beasts of the field by those who claimed a purer religion" (qtd. in Alryyes, "Introduction" 15). Dwight's rhetoric, like that of the ACS generally, emphasized not only the moral and religious responsibilities of white Christians but also the obligations of blacks to convert to what the organization and its members clearly viewed as a superior religion—the only civilized alternative for Africa. It is clear that the ACS, though advocating bodily freedom and "repatriation" for enslaved African Americans, held fast to the goal of spreading Christianity throughout Africa; consequently, their public relations strategy demanded wise, literate slaves who could demonstrate their ability to adapt to and adopt Western culture in order to confirm their humanity to those who denied it. While this strategy was politically expedient in the United States, it worked, of course, to undermine the religious culture of the former slaves whom the ACS intended to resettle and reflected the society's political and philosophical unwillingness to see true value in the native civilizations and religions of Africans.[9]

Given this context, we need to remain alert to ambiguities in the evidence regarding Ibn Said's religious beliefs and his supposed conversion to Christianity.[10] The story of that conversion—commonly remarked upon by his contemporaries—is perhaps the most dramatic example of how religious misunderstanding has tended to overshadow Ibn Said's life and testimony. Some of the "evidence" for his conversion actually reflects editorial interference. For example, a hand that is assuredly not Ibn Said's appears on one of his letters, describing him, in English, as "88 years of age and a devoted Christian" (Jameson, "Autobiography" 787–95). Furthermore, the gloss indicates the writer believes that the last Arabic text that Ibn Said had written was the Lord's Prayer (even though it is actually *Surat* [110], "The Help," which predicts mass conversions to Islam). Clearly, either the Owens family or someone closely associated with them took subtle advantage of contemporary audiences' inability to understand Arabic as well as widespread ignorance of Islamic culture. Moreover, since Ibn Said himself brings a religious sensibility to his work, and since his narrative does employ the rhetoric of Christian belief, it is tempting to take the story of his conversion at face value—particularly if one approaches his writing with only a superficial knowledge of Islam and without ever having read Ibn Said's text with any kind of awareness of Islamic or Arabic literary conventions.

However, the story of Ibn Said's conversion to Christianity is more complicated than merely a politically or religiously motivated misinterpretation of his writing. Since the possibility of remaining vocally and publicly Muslim could not be articulated during his own time, especially not forcefully and not by Ibn Said himself, we must remain open to other ways of interpreting his actions, particularly by considering the content, tone, and style of his writing and the superficial intermingling of Christianity and Islam in his public life. The exigencies of survival in the antebellum American slave system (and the psychological impact of being enslaved) must factor into any analysis of Ibn Said's self-representation as a Christian. It is possible, that is, that he lied about converting and put on a public show in order to preserve his private beliefs, and that the legend of his conversion is the product of his stratagem to survive. The problem of conversion in the text thus stands as a microcosm of its many other challenges to interpretation; Ibn Said's public life was to some degree a performance, and the Islamic subtext of the *Life* is the best evidence for that claim.

Ibn Said frequently addresses his reader directly: "O, people of North Carolina; O, people of South Carolina; O, people of America, all of you" (67). This direct approach suggests, first, that he assumes a position of agency that empowers him to question his readers about their morals and beliefs. Later, he repeats the formulation: "O, people of America; O people of North Carolina: do you have, do you have, do you have, do you have a such good generation that fears Allah so much?" (71). Iterative speech of this sort is a trope of Islamic religious diction and a pattern that Ibn Said sustains throughout his manuscript, both in questioning his readers about their faith and in explaining the rituals of Islamic religion and of his own life before captivity. Compare, for example, Ibn Said's diction to the modes of address in the Qur'anic verse Surah al-'Ahzāb 33:13, which contains the invocation "O people of Yathrib," and in *Surah al-Imran* 3:64 ("O people of the Scripture"). Indeed, throughout many verses in the Holy Qur'an where the children of Israel, believers, and named individuals are addressed, variations on the hortatory phrase "O people" are abundant enough to be conceived of as key elements of classical Islamic composition and rhetoric that, when used in other contexts, would clearly identify the faith of the addressor or addressee.

Through his use of such repetitive invocations, Ibn Said adopts the tone of the Qur'an, leaving no mistake as to whom he intends to overhear his narrative one day—namely, his fellow Muslims. While the exhortation to the people of America and North Carolina to fear God is intended for one audience, the tone and the style of his message is meant for another, one Arabic and Islamic, which will be able to understand the plaintive and mourning tone in this religious gesture: "I am Omar, I love to read the book, the Great Qur'an. General Jim Owen and his wife used to read the Bible, they used to read the Bible to me a lot. Allah is our Lord, our Creator, and our Owner and the restorer of our condition, health, and wealth by grace and not duty. [According] to my ability, open my heart to the Bible, to the path of righteousness. Praise be to Allah, the Lord of the Worlds, many thanks for he grants bounty in abundance" (73). Clearly, although Ibn Said has opened his heart to the Bible, it is only "according to his ability" to do so, a suggestive phrase that subtly implies he cannot fully convert to Christianity. He states that he loves to read the Holy Qur'an, but that Jim Owen and his wife used to read the Bible to him, and he closes the paragraph by praising Allah. His careful use of language, even as translated into English, betrays the fact that he is only accepting Christianity under pressure, and only as much as he finds himself able to do, implying that something is preventing him from opening his heart to the Bible in the fullest sense. He is neither bowing to his master's desire that he convert nor is he confessing intellectual inadequacy. He is asserting—forcefully—his identity, while using veiled language—not simply the term "Allah"—to communicate his condition as a Muslim under oppression.

During his enslavement, Ibn Said lacked for fellow speakers of Arabic and like-minded Muslims, and this is most clearly evidenced in his letter to Sheikh Hunter, as mentioned in the above discussion of the manuscript's provenance. The letter is an apology in which Ibn Said claims that he has "forgotten much of [his] talk as well as the talk of the Maghreb." He ends saying, "O my brothers, do not blame me," as if the letter is not intended for Sheikh Hunter alone, but, rather, Muslims capable and willing to rescue Ibn Said or at least able to send word of his fate to his family (59). Like the *Life,* this short letter suggests two different readerships, the first comprising Sheikh Hunter and his affiliated community and the other comprising the same Muslim audience Ibn Said hopes will read the *Life.* The author seems to know that Hunter does not speak or read Arabic and must transmit the texts to translators among a more advanced and educated audience—and it is among these Arabic speakers that Ibn Said hopes to find one to rescue him. Furthermore, "brothers," in Arabic as in English, is used to designate those with whom the speaker shares social class, profession, or religion.[11] Ibn Said, it appears, is conscious of the fact that his work is destined to go through many hands before it finds an Arabic-speaking translator.

Ibn Said's intimate familiarity with Islamic traditions and beliefs is refracted through language and literary form. For example, he recalls an entire chapter of the Qur'an—the *Surat al-Mulk*—which he reproduces at the beginning of the *Life,* making only one mistake in recording a verse in the thirty-verse sequence (he places the last verse in the middle). Although perhaps rusty (as a Quranic scholar would have been expected to memorize much more), Ibn Said seems to grow more confident as he writes, and he corrects this mistake by rewriting the verse correctly at the end of the chapter. What this illustrates is the depth to which Islamic teaching has penetrated his memory, demonstrating the effort he put into learning about his faith, as well as his ability to maintain his identity without the use of written material and after decades of slavery and isolation from his African Muslim peers. From this perspective, the gestures Ibn Said makes toward Christian belief can be understood in terms other than those of genuine conversion. Indeed, they can be taken as indications that Ibn Said misses a spiritual atmosphere in which to flourish, and that he wishes to be part of the Christian community while remaining a devout Muslim; he has no other choice but to engage in this dialogue between his past and his present and no other means by which he can spiritually comprehend the change he has been forced to endure. It is evident that Ibn Said did nominally convert to Christianity and that he underwent baptism. However, it is my contention that Ibn Said's negotiation of Islamic and Christian texts, routinely taken as statements of conversion prior to 1995, may actually represent his thoughtful consideration of Christian texts in a broader Islamic context, instead of revealing how he held "syncretic" beliefs or actually converted to Christianity.

Such negotiation of two faiths is a form of dialogue that Ibn Said must contain within his mind and in the mysterious Arabic letters that the Owenses are unable to read. In "Surpassing 'Survival': On the Urbanity of 'Traditional Religion' in the Afro-Atlantic World," J. Lorand Matory has argued that enslaved Africans in the Americas did not forsake their ancestral faith or deny that of their enslavers, and neither did they combine the two. Rather, one is balanced against the other just as the future is balanced against the past, and spirituality becomes subject to time. Similarly, Ghada Osman and Camille F. Forbes suggest that although Ibn Said names Moses and Jesus, he does so within an Islamic context and in the order that they are regarded to have succeeded to the station of Prophet in Islam ("Representing" 342). Ibn Said could be involved in "making time" for both Christianity and Islam, but the fact that he dedicated his private writing time to Islam should speak to the value he placed on his Muslim faith and identity above all others that were imposed on him.

Ibn Said's steadfastness is often visible in his language. Discussing Ibn Said's grammar at length, Osman and Forbes maintain that by using the second person plural form of the Arabic word for *lord,* he applies the authority of Islam to his audience by implying that the Prophet Mohammad was God's final messenger and that the message is for all. He is called *lord* in the same manner in which Moses and Isa are also called lords, and it is in no way a recognition of the divinity of Christ, though it would be easy to make this mistake in reading the text. Most likely, I believe, Ibn Said cultivated this ambiguity. Where he was not fully understood, he was free, and others could interpret his words as they wished while only he knew their true meaning. Since his understanding is inherently Islamic and his language indicates an adherence to the faith, it is most likely that the account of Ibn Said's conversion to Christianity is an exaggeration of behaviors that he adopted in order to make his circumstances tolerable while living among Christian slave masters. To an Arabic-fluent reader familiar with Islamic conventions, Ibn Said's rhetoric gives no reason to assume otherwise. The overall style of his prose, his tenor, the hortatory addresses to the people of America and South Carolina, his recitation and memorization of Qur'anic scripture, and his application of the Prophet Mohammad's authority to his audience all speak to his unwavering faith maintained in silence.

IBN SAID's rhetoric and literary style attest to his education and exposure to Arabic literature as well as to his Muslim faith, forming a crucial subtext to the *Life*. His mastery of Arabic is the first thing a native or fluent Arabic speaker will notice in Ibn Said's work, along with a deep familiarity with the conventions of Arabic and Islamic literature. Despite the occasional misspellings and other errors (the result, perhaps, of age, infirmity, or his long disuse of Arabic), Ibn Said's mode of "life writing" shows the influence of distinctive, yet among Western critics little understood, Arabic literary conventions. A brief summary of several of these forms underlies the analysis of Ibn Said's narrative that the rest of this essay pursues in order to reveal the extent to which his life and words have been misunderstood by those unfamiliar with Arabic and Islamic literary traditions, and to allow scholars to proceed with a fuller and more accurate understanding of Ibn Said's life and writing.

The composition of autobiographical text constitutes a long-standing tradition in Arabic and Islamic writing, the earliest development of which can be traced to al-jahiliyya, the pre-Islamic period. During this period, accounts of lives take the form of a "short [oral] narrative called akhbar" in which the narrator recounts his genealogy, including the virtues or recognizable incidents encountered by the narrator or a particular one of his ancestors (Reynolds and Brustad, "Interpreting" 36). When Ibn Said imitates the *akhbar*, he not only gives an account of his ancestry and his journey from Africa to South Carolina, but he also praises the Owenses and gives an account of their progeny. In English, *akhbar* translates literally as "news," but, more accurately, it carries a personal connotation. One delivering the news about an event must have been there to see it and, thus, would involve himself or herself in the story, while other important figures would be mentioned in order for the audience to be able to gauge the accuracy of the narration. Traditionally, if the orator or narrator is telling the truth, he will use other participants in the *akhbar* as authenticating references. Therefore, Ibn Said lists the Owens family as well as his own notable ancestors.

Following *akhbar,* another form of life writing, the *sira,* developed in written form by the ninth century, with the publications of Ibn Ishaq and Ibn Hisham on the Prophet Mohammad. The genre at first consisted of traditional writings that centered on documenting both the personal qualities and sociopolitical life of the Prophet, including his hadith (the Prophet's sayings). These works shed light on what Mohammad approved, his journeys, his spiritual life, the challenges he faced, and the threats and battles he encountered. As the genre developed, the *sira* kept abreast of religious and social developments and came to detail the lives of other influential Muslim figures. Thus, it "document[s] the subject's career from birth to death using eyewitness testimony and list[s] of teachers, students, family members, and works composed" to indicate that these lives were exemplary, worthy of recording and passing down through the generations, and deserving of emulation. (We can see the spirit of *sira* most clearly in Ibn Said's narrative when he digresses from his own narrative in order to expound upon his and the Prophet's beliefs, and when he provides a full account of his education and the institutional pedigrees of his teachers.) *Sira* serves a didactic function and is classified within Islamic literature as a "subgenre of history," which transmits facts about the person(s) concerned (39).

Just as *akhbar* developed into *sira,* at the beginning of the sixteenth century the term *sira* gradually took on a more generic meaning as the life story of an individual. During this time, Arab literature witnessed the birth of the folk epics that glamorize exemplary and legendary lives of poets and warriors. This revolution in the content of the *sira* had important ramifications, particularly the emergence of new forms of autobiography, Tabaqat (biographical dictionaries) and Tarjama (biographical notices), which hereafter became the dominant forms used to designate Arabic autobiographies (40).

Tabaqat was a genre fashionable in the heterogeneous Islamic society of the ninth century, roughly equivalent to "biographical dictionaries" or "biographical compendiums," and "devoted to the generations in a category or class of people" (Reynolds and Brustad, "Interpreting" 40). This form is concerned with the representation of an individual and his affiliation with certain professions such as "Qur'an reciters, physicians, caliphs, scholars of hadith, jurists . . . theologians . . . grammarians" (40). In this kind of autobiography, the author details the information that relates to the "dates, names, book titles, and lists of teachers" that he meets directly or important figures he comes across, as a methodology to provide evidence of his "acquisition, organization, authentication, and transmission of knowledge" (41). Modern scholars have argued that this form of autobiography was mainly concerned with the representation of "classes or (stereo)types" rather than individuals (41). Significantly, the author confirms his assimilation and conformity to Islam by making the required references or, as it were, by meeting the right people and learning correct doctrine from them. As with the *akhbar*, the writer provides references to authenticate his narrative. In this case, they are written.

Interestingly, at this time native Arabs and Arabic speakers did not constitute the majority of Muslim scholars; many influential scholars were non-Arabic and hailed from different regions with different languages, cultures, races, and ethnicities. However, an in-depth knowledge of the Arabic language was still necessary to become an Islamic scholar. Muslim religious authorities, long ago, recognized that translating the Qur'an would corrupt its message; thus, they insisted that Muslims learn Arabic. Therefore, without the legitimacy imparted to him by mastery of the Arabic language, Ibn Said would have had no hope of acquiring Islamic cultural literacy. A convert without sufficient knowledge of Arabic and Islam would not be qualified to be a scholar or to pass knowledge to the next generation. Since Ibn Said was a teacher, it is reasonable to assume that he mastered the Arabic language before learning the Qur'an, or that he learned language and scripture simultaneously.

A third Arabic literary convention that Ibn Said employs is the Tarjama (biographical notice), which is similar to the Tabaqat. However, in "modern Arabic, the term literary means a 'translation' . . . or an interpretation" (Reynolds and Brustad, "Interpreting" 42). During the medieval Arabic period, Tarjama corresponded to the literary genre mainly concerned with "representation of a person" (42). Nevertheless, the conceptual function of representation assumes the physical distance from the original object in which the replica is "an inexact, imperfect copy of a life" that aims to correspond with the external world to explicate the actions "and make them comprehensible to posterity and accessible to the student" (42). Therefore, the actual knowledge of the original person demands proximity either by "reading his [original] work . . . [or] receiving his . . . teaching through oral transmission" (42). Nonetheless, Tarjama provides the most important account of such matter as the person's genealogy, date of birth, teachers, works, travel and pilgrimages, professional affiliation, personal letters, epistles, poetry, visions, dreams, virtues, and minor miracles. In focusing on these key concepts, Tarjama is distinguished by its capacity to represent the person in an intellectual context and to laud his usefulness "as a transmitter and contributor to knowledge and to a shared academic and spiritual heritage" (43).

In its representation of Ibn Said's life and faith, the *Life* adopts the aesthetics of both the Tabaqat and Tarjama genres. The combination of

these two forms provides Ibn Said with a wider scope to employ different strategies not only in telling the story of his life but also in taking the
opportunity to challenge the institution of slavery. The use of these two
forms serves to reveal his religious and cultural identity and to challenge,
from a perspective unfamiliar to most scholars of American literature,
the denial of enslaved people's humanity.

It is notable, yet rarely noted, that Ibn Said's autobiography consists
of two parts: the first contains an entire chapter from the Qur'an; the second part is the life story of Ibn Said. What is significant is that religious
rhetoric is sustained throughout the text. In contrast to the developed
form of Tarjama, Ibn Said chooses to open his autobiography with a
chapter from the Qur'an rather than with his own life story. While this
decision may have been intended to show his humility before God, beginning with the *Surat al-Mulk* (the Sovereignty Chapter) enables Ibn Said
to establish his voice and identity as a Muslim, as well as to reiterate his
allegiance to the principles of his original religion and culture. Simultaneously, this chapter functions as direct commentary on the institution of
slavery, the practice of which it rebuts.

The word *mulk* means "sovereignty" or "control," and, literally, "the
Kingdom." Ibn Said, in placing this chapter as his prologue, emphasizes
his theological training. His inclusion of *Surat al-Mulk* demonstrates, to
an Islamic audience, his belief that God has the ultimate ownership of
this universe. He gives the first verse as follows: "Blessed be He in whose
hand is the mulk and who has power over all things. He created death
and life that He might put you to the proof and find out which of you
had the best work. He is the Mighty, the Forgiving One" (51). Thus for
Ibn Said the verse implicitly challenges the three fundamental claims of
the slave system—ownership, absolute power over life and death, and
superintendence—by emphasizing that it is God who has in his hands the
mulk; the exclusive power and the ownership in the earth and in the seven
heavens. In other words, God is sovereign; the kingdom is his; therefore,
he owns everything. He commands absolute power over life and death,
and, naturally, his superintendence is primary for all humankind. While
a similar theological orientation characterizes many Christian slave narratives, Ibn Said's rhetoric is essentially non-evangelical. It speaks, rather,
to his almost fatalistic sense of powerlessness. These petitions and recitations are not conceived to persuade any of his American readers to turn
against the institution of slavery. Rather, they are private prayers that
sustain him, remind him of his enslaved condition and the injustice of it,
and keep him rooted in his religion and traditions.

The petitions and recitations continue as Ibn Said provides more verses that describe the fate of unbelievers who "deny their Lord" in the sense that they neither believe in him nor keep his laws: "We have adorned the lowest heaven with lamps, missiles to pelt the devils with. We have prepared the scourge of Fire for these, and the scourge of Hell for those who deny their Lord: an evil fate!" (51). Here, he is directly indicting slave owners as unbelievers and violators of God's laws. In describing his previous master, Ibn Said writes that he was "[a] weak, small, evil man called Johnson, an infidel (Kafir) who did not fear Allah at all" (63). Ibn Said symbolically emasculates the man; the physical description deprives him of the physical strength and size associated with masculinity. Additionally, Ibn Said deprives him of the moral strength of religion, rebutting claims of African savagery with his own claims of white Christian savagery. He disabuses his master of his illusions of white supremacy by referring to him as an atheist/pagan who does not fear Allah/God, inverting the rhetoric of slavery apologists who claimed that to enslave the African was to better him by providing him with an opportunity to convert to Christianity.

Significantly, Ibn Said's argument against slavery is not restricted to the American context. He is writing against the Africans who kidnapped him as much as he is writing against the Americans who purchased and enslaved him. For this reason, Ibn Said appears to draw upon yet another Arabic literary genre in his writing, adopting the tone of the Naqd in this section. According to Basil Hatim, Arabic writers during the Abbassid Caliphate (750–1517) developed Naqd (criticism) as an argumentative type of writing that "intended to present proof for settling differences of beliefs among those who engaged in argument. It is used in ideological doctrines, [and] religious debates" ("Model" 49), like the debate over slavery that Ibn Said has entered. Writers of Naqd borrow heavily from and employ Qur'anic verses and quote the hadith "to express elegantly and economically, what goes on in the mind and in the heart" of the writer (49). The Naqd writer's purpose is to express his beliefs and perceptions about what is right and true, as Ibn Said does when he follows the Arabic tradition of quotation to describe the injustice of his enslaved condition. Such echoes and subtexts suggest that Ibn Said's familiarity with Arabic literary traditions prior to enslavement was rich and varied, and that he was not exempting fellow Africans from his argument against slavery.

It is likely that Ibn Said was aware of the context in which his argument appeared. By 1831, two major events had exacerbated hostility toward literate and religious slaves and their writings. The first event was the publication of David Walker's militant *Appeal in Four Articles; Together with a Preamble, to the Coloured Citizens of the World* (1829), which slaveholders in Charleston and New Orleans tried to ban and which led to the imprisonment of blacks who attempted to distribute copies. In addition, slaveholders exercised their power to prevent black ministers from using the *Appeal* in their preaching. The second major event was Nat Turner's sensationalistic rebellion, trial, and execution in 1831, one consequence of which was even stricter controls against the education of slaves. Perhaps to avoid such hostility, Ibn Said uses Qur'anic verses that can only be interpreted and comprehended by highly educated and religious persons; he may have assumed that only the Arabic-speaking translator of his work could truly understand them.

Specifically, the last three pages in the manuscript make important references to the culture of religion he is exposing, both past and present. On the first of these pages, he states that in the past he used to pray, and he recounts the opening chapter in the Qur'an, *Surat al-Fatiha*. This chapter has a unique function in the Islamic tradition, and Muslims recite it each day in prayer, believing that it distinguishes between the three religions (Judaism, Christianity, and Islam). The second verse restates God's sovereignty over the Day of Judgment: "the Merciful, Sovereign (Malik) of the Day of Judgment; it is you we worship" (Ibn Said, "Muslim" 75). Ibn Said emphasizes again not only God's ownership over life and death, as at the beginning of his autobiography, but also his sovereignty on the Day of Judgment, at the end of the human life cycle. At the end of the chapter, there are implicit references to the current condition of the worshippers in the three religions, and I believe that it is in Ibn Said's prayers to God to empower him to keep his faith: "Guide us to the straight path; The path of those [read: Muslims] whom you have favored with grace; Nor of those [read: Jews] who have incurred Your wrath; Nor of those [read: Christians] who have strayed," even though in the Lord's Prayer that follows al-Fatiha, in Ibn Said's autobiography, Ibn Said describes the prevalent faith and belief now practiced in North America as he sees it (75). In quoting these verses, Ibn Said emphasizes his adherence to his original faith, since he knows exactly the chapter's honored position in the Qur'an and in Muslims' beliefs, a knowledge shared among Muslims that emphasizes their distinction from other faiths, but again, he only follows Christianity so far as he is able.[12]

On the second of these final pages, Ibn Said summarizes and repeats the account of his experience with enslavement. He restates the reason behind his residency in North America, writing: "I reside in our country here because of the great harm. The infidels took me unjustly and sold me into the hands of the Christian man (Nasrani) who bought me" (77). He never submits to his current status and keeps the distinction between the two nations according to their faith. He ends this page with a call for help, saying: "I am in a place called Bladen County" as if giving an address for someone to come search for him (78).

On the very last page, Ibn Said praises the kindness of his owner and describes himself as an old, sick man who is unable to do any hard physical work. Ibn Said provides no information about his twenty years' service to the Owenses, but we do learn that he has remained unmarried his entire life. One possibility, as Alryyes suggests, is that Ibn Said knew that slavery would complicate any attempt he might make to rebuild a family in America. Another is that substituting Christian for Islamic ritual may have been going too far for him when marriage was concerned. Or he might simply have seen no need to mention these aspects of his private life. He said the Owenses treated him well, but the full extent of his accommodation is unknown. Also, Arabic life writing does not typically mention familial life as the center of the subject's identity. Accomplishments are more important, so it should not be surprising that Ibn Said only mentions a few relatives—those who had led exemplary lives, or those whose accomplished lives were relevant to his own accomplishments. For example, he does not fail to mention that his brother was one of his teachers. The autobiography also indicates that Ibn Said is isolated from the slave community; it makes no mention of any other slave, male or female. It is very possible that his adherence to his religion and his culture—in which drinking, dancing, wrestling, and premarital sexual relations are forbidden—prevented him from integrating with antebellum slave culture and community.

The Life of Omar Ibn Said, Written by Himself demonstrates that the slave narrative, as a foundational genre of American literature, arose within a transnational network of cultural and religious lines of influence. What I have argued here is that a distinctively Islamic literary tradition, particularly the genres of the Arabic Tabaqat and Tarjama, shaped both the form and the rhetoric of Ibn Said's autobiography in ways that shed light on the complex history of the slave narrative in the United States. In one sense, Ibn Said wrote for himself, preserving his private thoughts in a permanent form, in a language unknown to his oppressors. At the same time, in employing Qur'anic conventions and aesthetics to uphold his faith and identity despite his long captivity, he sought to engage his contemporary audience at a spiritual rather than political level. And he appears to have been writing for the future, hoping his work would find its way to an Arabic-speaking audience. The modern age of information, when Ibn Said's words can reach a global audience through responsible translation and editorial and scholarly analysis, represents such a future. It is also possible that additional information about Ibn Said and his writings will come to light. Indeed, future research may yet reveal that he had intellectual compatriots who also labored in secrecy and in the Arabic language to preserve their culture and heritage.

In the meantime, Ibn Said's autobiography requires more sustained attention from students of slave narratives and of Arabic, Islamic, and nineteenth-century American literature, for it has a role to play in each field and is a point of departure for each. At a personal level, it describes a lonely man, an enslaved celebrity in a gilded cage whose complex characterization has forever made him a mystery to all those who would approach his private text. More broadly, Ibn Said's experience reveals what American life looked like from an Islamic and enslaved African perspective. In fact, his narrative is a valuable relic of a perspective that was systematically and brutally silenced throughout the slaveholding territories—and it could be all that remains of that perspective. Accordingly, *The Life of Omar Ibn Said* has the potential to complicate our notions of African American identity and of the history of the slave narrative. This potential depends, however, on a significant degree of Islamic and Arabic literacy, without which Ibn Said will remain widely unknown and misunderstood.

Notes

1. Edward Said, while noting that England and France possess a deeper history of Orientalist thought than the United States, nonetheless implicates American culture in the workings of Orientalism and writes that the "interchange between the academic and the more or less imaginative meanings of Orientalism is a constant one, and since the late eighteenth century there has been a considerable, quite disciplined—perhaps even regulated—traffic between the two" (E. Said, *Orientalism* 3).

2. At a young age, Ibn Said "lost his father, in one of those bloody wars that are almost constantly raging in Africa. Very soon thereafter he was taken by an uncle to the capital of the tribe. Here he learned and afterward taught Arabic, especially some prayers used by Mahomedans. He also learned some rules of arithmetic, and many of the forms of business. When a young man he became a dealer in the merchandise of the country, chiefly consisting in cotton cloths" (Jameson, "Autobiography" 790). Furthermore, an article in the *Wilmington*

Chronicle in 1847 describes Ibn Said as a Foula or Fulla, a member of an African ethnic group descended from Muslim Arabs who migrated to West Africa in the seventh century. This is the only contemporary reference to Ibn Said that mentions his Arabic and Muslim heritage.

3. Ibn Said later mentions having fought kaffir in jihad, so the only information he provides is that his enemies were pagans and that, perhaps, he had fought them repeatedly before being taken into slavery. Of his capture, Ibn Said's description is reminiscent of Olaudah Equiano's: "there came to our country a big army. It killed many people. It took me, and walked me to the big Sea and sold me into the hand of a Christian man who bought me and walked me to the big Ship in the big Sea" (Ibn Said, *Life* 61).

4. Ibn Said's manuscript consists of twenty-three pages of quarto paper, eight of which are blank. To avoid confusion regarding the use of *Arabic* and *Islamic* or *Muslim* as descriptors of Ibn Said or his text, note that *Arabic* describes the mode of expression—the language and the literary concepts that accompany it, or to Arab culture in particular. *Muslim* and *Islamic* refer specifically to Ibn Said's faith, the religious content or tone of his writing, or to his identity and the broader Islamic context in which it exists. Ibn Said expresses his Islamic identity through the Arabic language, but he is a Muslim, and items of his culture may be referred to as both *Arabic* and *Islamic* simultaneously.

5. "[Stowe] presented a protagonist who was the son of Mandingoes, Muslims, but she did not admit any such religious heritage" (Khrisat, "Authenticity" 74).

6. Sixteen other manuscripts exist, and all are available in Allan D. Austin, *African Muslims in Antebellum America: A Sourcebook.*

7. Very few substantive discussions of Ibn Said's narrative exist. Exceptions include Alryyes; Austin; Osman and Forbes; Turner. Passing references to Ibn Said appear in Harvey; Gardel; Curtis.

8. Here is the only reference to Old Paul in the source documents that Alryyes mentions: "When, more than a year ago, a man by the name of Paul, of the Foulah nation and able like himself to understand Arabic, was preparing to embark at New York for Liberia, Moro corresponded" (Gurley, "Secretary's" 201–6).

9. The complex politics and maneuverings of the ACS are discussed in Burin, *Slavery and the Peculiar Solution.* See also Egerton, "'Its Origin Is Not a Little Curious.'"

10. For example, in his introduction to the Bird edition of Ibn Said's narrative, Jameson writes that Ibn Said was baptized into the Presbyterian Church at Fayetteville by a Rev. Snodgrass, and that he had discontinued observing Ramadan, although he had observed it previously (Jameson, "Life" 86). Jameson places the date of Ibn Said's conversion around 1819–1822, long after the Owenses purchased him (86). Moreover, we are told that Ibn Said visited a church in Fayetteville before he is sent to jail—a fact that seems to indicate he is either praying in the church or seeking refuge there. Yet in Islamic as well as Christian tradition, if a fugitive seeks refuge in place of worship, the civil authorities may not invade that space in order to arrest or harm that person.

11. Alryyes suggests that Ibn Said's apology to Sheikh Hunter "deceptively echoes the rhetorical claim that the author is not up to the task, a de rigueur flourish that accompanies many a literary preface," but he does not recognize the

nod to an Islamic audience the author makes. Ibn Said's use of the word *brothers* combined with his demonstration of his ability to recall the contents of *Surat al-Mulk* all testify to his faithfulness to Islam (6).

12. The appearance of the Lord's Prayer in Ibn Said's work is problematic, indeed, because it lends credence to the argument that he converted, but if one reads the Lord's Prayer carefully, one sees that it is a prayer spoken by Jesus Christ, not a prayer to him. Therefore, Ibn Said could say this prayer and remain true to the beliefs he held in his heart since his words were not, in fact, violating the letter of his belief. This is apparent, especially, in Ibn Said's inclusion of Al Fatiha, the opening chapter of the Holy Qur'an, before the Lord's Prayer. Ibn Said prays to Allah, indeed, using only "the words" of Jesus (Ibn Said, *Life* 75).

Bibliography

Alryyes, Ala. "Introduction: 'Arabic Work,' Islam, and American Literature." Ibn Said 3–46.

Austin, Allan D. *African Muslims in Antebellum America: A Sourcebook.* New York: Garland, 1984.

———. *African Muslims in Antebellum America: Transatlantic Stories and Spiritual Struggles.* New York: Routledge, 1997.

Burin, Eric. *Slavery and the Peculiar Solution: A History of the American Colonization Society.* Gainesville: University Press of Florida, 2008.

Curtis, Edward E. *Muslims in America: A Short History.* Oxford: Oxford University Press, 2009.

Egerton, Douglas R. "'Its Origin Is Not a Little Curious': A New Look at the American Colonization Society." *Journal of the Early Republic* 5.4 (Winter 1985): 463–80.

Gardel, Mattias. *In the Name of Elijah Muhammad: Louis Farrakhan and the Nation of Islam.* Durham, NC: Duke University Press, 1996.

Gurley, Ralph R. "Secretary's Report." *African Repository and Colonial Journal* 13.7 (1837): 201–6.

Harvey, Paul. *Through the Storm, through the Night: A History of African American Christianity.* Lanham, MD: Rowman & Littlefield, 2011.

Hatim, Basil. "A Model of Argumentation from Arabic Rhetoric: Insight for a Theory of Text Types." *British Society for Middle Eastern Studies* 17.1 (1990): 47–54.

Ibn Said, Omar. *A Muslim American Slave: The Life of Omar Ibn Said.* Trans. and ed. Ala Alryyes. Madison: University of Wisconsin Press, 2011.

Jameson, John Franklin, ed. "Autobiography of Omar Ibn Said, Slave in North Carolina, 1831." Translated by Isaac Bird. *American Historical Review* 30.4 (1925): 787–95.

———. "The Life: Autobiography of Omar Ibn Said, Slave in North Carolina, 1831." Ibn Said 81–92.

Khrisat, Abdulhafeth Ali. "Authenticity of Arabic Slave Narratives." *Damascus University Journal* 21.1–2 (2005): 73–92.

Matory, J. Lorand. "Surpassing 'Survival': On the Urbanity of 'Traditional Religion' in the Afro-Atlantic World." *Black Scholar* 30.3–4 (2001): 36–43.

Osman, Ghada, and Camille F. Forbes. "Representing the West in the Arabic Language: The Slave Narrative of Omar Ibn Said." *Journal of Islamic Studies* 15.3 (2004): 331–43.

Reynolds, Dwight F., and Kristen Brustad, eds. *Interpreting the Self: Autobiography in the Arabic Literary Tradition.* Berkeley: University of California Press, 2001.

Said, Edward. *Orientalism.* New York: Vintage Books, 1979.

Sanneh, Lamin. *Abolitionists Abroad: American Blacks and the Making of Modern West Africa.* Cambridge: Harvard University Press, 1999.

Turner, Richard Brent. *Islam in the African American Experience.* 2nd ed. Bloomington: Indiana University Press, 2003.

Coda
Animating Absence

Kristina Bross

HOW DO we gain access to the lives described in the embedded slave narratives of early colonial texts? For a long time, many of us interested in the mission pamphlets, travel stories, exploration narratives, and other writings of the early modern Atlantic world have suffered a degree of analytical paralysis. Those of us earning our critical chops in the 1990s were schooled in theories of discourse and power, convinced by New Historicist and some postcolonial notions that such texts could only be understood as signs and symptoms of European discursive power. This theory and criticism taught us that when we held up a mirror to colonial texts that described or quoted colonized subjects, what we saw was a reflection of the "European imaginary," the Native or African or subaltern figure purportedly at the heart of the text.[1] However helpful in some respects, in terms of opening up the field of literary history to consider the representation of marginalized people, this approach resulted in what was at times an unsatisfying praxis: we read against the grain to gain some purchase on the colonizer-author's mindset, taking the form and content of his text solely as evidence of his biases and ideologies—conscious or unconscious. Hard as we tried, literary historians could do little more than wish we could access the lived experiences of Native peoples, Africans, women, the disenfranchised people of all stripes that could be found only indirectly, mediated by others in the documentary archive.

I take the exchanges between Myra Jehlen and Peter Hulme in the pages of *Critical Inquiry* in fall 1993 to exemplify the ways that the heated debates over theory in that decade—which Hulme describes as more of a U.S. than a British (or, certainly, continental) phenomenon—led to a critical impasse.[2] In it, Jehlen describes Hulme's influential and important work in *Colonial Encounters: Europe and the Native Caribbean,*

1492–1797 (1987) as confirming an untenable critical binary: scholars had read colonial texts as perfectly transparent and dependable (and therefore established a triumphant Western or American tradition) or as completely opaque and unreliable (which therefore had to be fully deconstructed to be understood). Jehlen proposed a nuanced approach in which we were to read certain colonial texts as encoding "history before the fact," that is, as describing events and descriptions whose resistant or subversive meaning was discernible to the modern reader because they escaped the totalizing ideological control of later works, texts written after the facts of colonization, imperialism, or domination were established (the "facts" being understood as constructed, not as existing outside of discourse). Hulme responded by noting, quite rightly, that his arguments and methods did not fall into this neat binary, and questioned why his analyses of the past could not be "both discursive and historical at the same time." Moreover, he argued, "however difficult the task may be, we always end up having to interpret the text."[3] My point is not so much to rehash this debate—as interesting as the Jehlen-Hulme exchange was at the time—but rather to note that however certain Hulme was that his approach did not shut down attempts to understand and to hear Native peoples (and, in fact, his work led many of us to deeper considerations of Native experiences and representation), nevertheless at least one very talented literary historian, Jehlen herself, struggled heroically in her response to his work to propose a method that would lead us out of the perceived stasis. If Jehlen felt stymied by theoretical and critical trends in the mid-nineties, what chance did we mere mortals slogging away in our graduate studies have?[4]

Of course, I exaggerate the effects of critical and theoretical trends—certainly these ways of approaching colonial literature reinvigorated the field, and by directing our attention to colonial texts that contained occluded figures of enslaved, Native, and other marginalized peoples that were so often overlooked, the debate generated new ways of approaching what could have been stale topics and texts. But there's no denying that the life stories of those peoples seemed hard or even impossible to access through literary analysis based on such approaches. Consider the foreword by Paul Eakin to Arnold Krupat's 1985 book on Native American autobiography. In his retrospective account (the foreword was included in the 1989 edition of the book) Eakin argues that "poststructuralism in its various guises did indeed generate feelings of malaise in many students of the [autobiographical] genre."[5] While there certainly were literary scholars dedicated to excavating the life stories of the interesting and unexpected figures we were encountering in colonial literature, skepticism about the degree to which colonial writings could be used to access such figures has dogged our research and publications. It has perhaps even circumscribed our pedagogy as we choose what to include in our syllabi, anthologies, and primary source collections. For example, the editors of a 2002 special issue on interiority for *Early American Literature* noted the striking lack of submissions dealing with the interior life of Native or African-descended peoples in colonial or early U.S. literature.[6] And although in recent years we have seen important publications of early African American literature anthologies, editions, and scholarship, our collective focus continues to be trained on later works produced by individuals whom we can identify as independent authors.

This collection, though many of its chapters focus on such later works, explores what new insights we have to gain if we look obliquely at our established archives or include new genres and figures in in the writings of the African diaspora. The essays encourage speculative analysis alongside archival research, careful historicization, and rigorous close reading. Such methods are promising for—and perhaps even more important to—the study of earlier periods. As a modest example of the possibilities of rethinking our approaches to early modern slave narratives, I turn to the as-told-to narrative of a man we know as Lewis, whose story is embedded in a lengthy work of mid-seventeenth-century propaganda. I offer this essay as a gesture toward what we might gain by suspending critical disbelief and taking seriously the notion that descriptions of colonial encounters encode traces of the experiences, agency, and voices of enslaved peoples and others marginalized in (and by) colonial writings. My essay is not a work of archival excavation per se, because the story has not been lost. In fact, Peter Hulme himself included Lewis's story in his anthology of Carib-European encounters. Rather, Lewis's slave narrative has been overlooked, perhaps because of the critical tensions that I sketched above, which have led us to read this textual moment as wholly concerning the group of Europeans who met him in in the early seventeenth-century rather than giving us some purchase on Lewis himself.[7] Thus, instead of textual recovery, I see my work as an act of critical recovery, much in the vein of Jeffrey Gagnon's essay in this collection, in which he urges us to reorient our understanding of Briton Hammon's narrative as one that details not captivity but a "temporary, cross-cultural social alliance." The reading that such an orientation suggests must be more tentative than we would wish, but it is, even in its provisional nature, a reading that acknowledges the agency of Hammon—and of the Calusa people with whom he lives for a time—as giving shape to the published narrative, even though it is heavily mediated.[8] In what follows, I read anew a text in which there is no claim to authorship on behalf of the enslaved man it represents in order to suggest that we can glean more than we thought possible of the life stories of men and women on the margins of the nascent British empire in the early modern Atlantic world.

The documentary record of Lewis's life is set within the archive of the seventeenth-century debate over the English "right" to the Americas over and opposed to Spanish claims, with some small consideration of indigenous sovereignty thrown in from time to time. Lewis's story—or one version of it—is recorded in a 1648 publication by Thomas Gage, a white Englishman, entitled *The English-American his Travails by Sea and Land: or, A New survey of the West India's*. Gage's work is wide-ranging, but one of its more remarkable elements (remarkable as much for its neglect by critics as for its content) is his inclusion of several "mulattos," "blackamores," "maroons," and African-descended peoples, and in particular the startling anti-Imperial performance of one such figure, the man Gage knows as Lewis.

We don't have any access to this man other than through European writings, a problem matched by the general obscurity of direct documentary evidence of Africans in the Caribbean during this period.[9] In the past, as I suggest above, that archival silence (or the perception of silence) has meant that literary historians thought primarily of representation, of how such figures were constructed by European writers, and what that construction told us about the culture, history, and mindset of those Europeans. Recently, a methodological turn in early American and early Caribbean studies has been met by an archival turn that enables us to think about silences, about gaps in the archives not just as indicators of the mindset or limitations of the "archons" who, in Jacques Derrida's formulation, create and guard the archives, thereby determining what the past will have meant.[10] Rather, as Carolyn Steedman argues in her book *Dust: The Archive and Cultural History*, we must acknowledge "that if we find nothing [in the archives] we will find nothing in a place; and then, that an absence is not *nothing*, but is rather the space left by what has gone: how the emptiness indicates how once it was filled and animated."[11] The man called Lewis once animated a place. Thomas Gage's work, though directed toward his own ends, at least performs Lewis this service: it adumbrates the shape of the absence he once filled.[12]

Gage's text is an account of the twelve years he served as a Dominican friar in New Spain. Born in England to a Catholic family in the 1640s,

Gage returned to England, converted to Protestantism, and began publicizing his experiences, presenting himself as a spy for England in New
Spain. Gage's point is clear and consistent: the Spanish are violent,
ham-fisted, and overconfident colonists who provoke creoles, Indians,
maroons, and others to opposition and violence. By contrast, the English,
represented by Gage, have inherited the best impulses of European expansion in the Americas and oppose the worst.

Chapter 6 of *The English-American* is a presentation in brief of the
work's whole argument. In it, Gage asserts that England has the moral
and even legal right to control the New World. In this chapter, Gage suggests that the legal consequences of Columbus's discovery of the Americas on behalf of Spain are only provisional and that the Spanish hold on
these territories is shaky at best. He argues that England can claim the
Columbian legacy by allying themselves with "New World" inhabitants
who desire to shake off the yoke of Spanish rule. The chapter recounts
the first landfall of Gage's fleet in the Caribbean; in it Gage reenacts
Columbus's voyages, with the promise that the English can gain from
Spanish mismanagement of their colonial holdings, if only authorities in
England have the wisdom to take his advice.

The chapter parallels English publications of Columbus's discovery,
with a few significant changes. For instance, whereas according to Samuel
Purchas in his *Hakluytus Posthumus,* when Caribbean islanders first saw
Columbus's fleet, they thought the ships "were living Creatures," by
contrast these islanders look forward to the arrival of the Spanish fleet:
"Before our Anchors was [*sic*] cast, out came the *Indians* to meet us in
their *Canoa's,* round like *Troughes,* some wereof had beene painted by
our *English,* some by the *Hollanders,* some by the *French,* as might ap-
peare by their severall Armes, it being a common Rode and harbour to
all Nations that saile to *America.*"[13] The detail of the canoes' decoration
is important because, as Gage knew, Columbus had claimed these islands
for the Spanish crown, and Spain subsequently denied entrance to its
national competitors from all its colonial holdings. Nonetheless, as this
international display demonstrates, in practice Native peoples are keeping the West Indies open to "our English," and Gage even goes so far as
to argue that Spanish claims are trumped by Native rights. In his preface,
Gage takes up the thorny issue of Spanish precedence:

> *to me it seems as little reason, that the sailing of a* Spanish *Ship upon the coast
> of* India, *should intitle the King of* Spain *to that Countrey, as the sayling of an*
> Indian *or* English *Ship upon the coast of* Spain, *should intitle either the* Indians

or English *unto the Dominion thereof. No question but the just right or title to those Countries appertains to the Natives themselves; who, if they shall willingly and freely invite the* English *to their protection, what title soever they have in them, no doubt but they may legally transferr it or communicate it to others.*[14]

While the English can look forward to such friendly dealings, the Spanish do not enjoy the support of indigenous peoples, as illustrated by the most striking element of Gage's description of Guadeloupe—an armed uprising that drives the fleet from its shores. A summary of events: Gage and others disembark to wash themselves and their dirty laundry in fresh water, to wander about, meet the islanders, taste new foods; in short, to get their land legs back after weeks at sea. During his rambles, Gage comes across a small group of Jesuits in close conversation with a man dressed like the Caribs, but who turns out to be a man who escaped slavery, a "mulatto" as Gage identifies him: Lewis. The Jesuits urge him to come back to the Spanish fold, promising freedom for him and for his family and reminding him of his eternal damnation should he die a heathen. He agrees to bring his family and meet them the next morning to leave the island with them. However, in the morning, the party found that "the Barbarians were mutinied."[15] They are attacked with a shower of arrows from the trees, several are killed outright, and more are wounded.

What I find especially notable in this anecdote is the response of the Spanish military and religious forces. Although the Jesuits had assured Lewis that they would protect him with their "Souldiers, Guns and Ordnance" (18) and although the "mutiny" was quelled when "our Admirall shot off two or three Peeces of Ordnance and sent a Company of Souldiers to shore to guard it and our people with their Muskets" (and here note that there was no definitive victory for the Europeans; rather, the "Indians soon dispersed"), the Spanish weighed anchor and left the island the next day. Gage makes it clear that the Spanish were routed, despite their seeming military superiority. Just the day before, Gage tells us, most of the friars were charmed by the island and its hospitable inhabitants. Faced with another leg of the tedious journey, they had been pushing to stay and create a mission there. When confronted with the difficulties of establishing a permanent mission on the island, they boasted that they would risk death, "saying that the worst that could happen to them could bee but to be butchered, sacrificed and eaten up; and for such a purpose they had come out of *Spain* to be crowned with the Crowne of

Martyrdome." After the attack, "their zeale was coole, and they desired
no more to stay with such a Barbarous kind of People."[16]

We can better understand the significance to Gage's project of this
defeat of the Spanish fleet by contrasting it with other moments in which
the people he expects will ally with the English against the Spanish
play a significant role. Gage details elsewhere the threat that those who
had escaped slavery pose to the Spanish: "some two or three hundred
Black-mores; Simarrones, who for too much hard usage, have fled away
from *Guatemala* and other parts from their Masters unto these woods
. . . so that all the power of *Guatemala,* nay all the Countrey about
(having often attempted it) is not able to bring them under subjection."[17]
Such allies would make English invasion, Gage suggests, relatively easy.
Although the Spanish cannot conquer them by force, the maroons "have
often said that the chiefe cause of their flying to those mountains is to be
in a readinesse to joyne with the *English* or *Hollanders,* if ever they land
in that Golfe."[18] Given the danger that one such man—Lewis—posed to
the mission fleet in Guadeloupe, the argument that the maroons will be a
potent force on the mainland seems persuasive.

It may be that Gage's grand claims of prospective insurgent support
for the English was also suggested to him by his personal relationship
with a powerful figure, Miguel Dalva, whom Gage describes as a "blackamoor" (even "my blackamoor").[19] Dalva comes on the scene as a personal bodyguard for Gage after he reaches the mainland. In Guatemala
Gage antagonizes Spanish colonists and Indians alike. He provokes the
former by preaching against abuses offered to Indians and the latter by
publicly burning an idol. Throughout, Dalva, "a very stout and lusty
fellow," stands between Gage and the wrath of other colonial actors.[20]
For a time he sleeps in Gage's house, fighting off night-time attackers,
and his very presence is enough to discourage roadside attacks by Spanish enemies. When Gage finally makes the decision to leave New Spain
and return to England, setting in motion the events that will lead up to
the publication of *The English-American,* he turns to Dalva again to aid
him in what was basically an escape from ecclesiastical authority. It is at
this point in Gage's account that the representation wears most thin, or
rather, that we most strongly register the opacity of the text as it stands
between us and the historical figure of Dalva. Despite all the evidence that
Gage gives us of Dalva's skill in negotiating the colonial landscape and
controlling difficult situations, Gage can only understand him as the dupe
of his own machinations. Gage knows "by long experience" that Dalva is

"true and trusty," and moreover Gage believes that they have sentimental ties: "I would not tell him that I intended *England,* lest the good old *Black-more* should grieve thinking never more to see me."[21] Whatever the truth of Gage's suppositions regarding Dalva's motivation and sentiments, the results seem to speak for themselves; he escapes to England with Dalva's help. If Gage does misunderstand Dalva, it is a mistake that ends well for the Englishman. Regardless, we can read the influence of Lewis and Dalva on Gage as evidence of what Wendy Laura Belcher calls "reciprocal enculturation," in which indigenous people shape European identities (and not just vice versa). Here, Lewis and Dalva create Gage's identity as a New World insider who can negotiate allies among enslaved and free black communities and, arguably, shape English foreign policy and national identity by suggesting the viability of the English invasion of New Spain, which will be attempted just a few years after Gage publishes his account.[22]

In Guadeloupe the Jesuits definitely misunderstand, misread, and underestimate Lewis, but without the happy results of Gage's misreading of Dalva's motivations. Moreover, whereas Gage will later recount his intimacy with Miguel Dalva and other African-descended peoples in New Spain, boasting of his ability to befriend and then manipulate them, on Guadeloupe he is as misled by Lewis as any other of the Europeans. Of course, Gage is willing to let himself look foolish in this instance because it serves his larger purpose to show the credulity of the friars, eager to effect a conversion. But also, I would argue, Lewis's manipulation of the Europeans' hopes and expectations is so good that Gage is genuinely left unsure exactly what happened. To my eye, this is a moment that displays rich "texture," a term Kelly Wisecup adapts from anthropologist Neil L. Whitehead. She takes it to indicate "rhetorical signs of encounters" in colonial texts. Wisecup argues that "studying the texture of colonial writing can elucidate how Native and African sociocultural forms and practices are registered in the rhetorical features of colonial texts."[23] The term is useful as well, it seems to me, in identifying moments in which individuals and their choices similarly are registered by European writers.

To return, Gage begins his account of this incident by explaining the presence of Lewis—a man born in Seville—on an island otherwise inhabited entirely by Native people. It is at this point that we can perceive an embedded slave narrative within the confines of Gage's English propaganda. Lewis has twice escaped slavery, running away from two masters because of abuse. Twelve years before he met members of Gage's fleet on a Caribbean island, he had come up with a plan to escape a cruel master, whom he describes as a "rich Merchant." Perhaps Lewis learned about trading and mission voyages, about the logistics of his escape while in service to this master, who was active in one of Europe's busiest trading centers. To escape the merchant's abuse, Lewis put himself in the service of a man bound for America. Upon reaching Guadeloupe, he considered that as long as he was under Spanish control, he could not be safe: "remembering the many stripes which hee had suffered from his first cruell Master, . . . and also jealous of his second Master (whose blowes hee had begun to suffer . . .)."[24] So he jumps ship, hiding in the mountains, and in a move that reminds me of Olaudah Equiano's later entrepreneurship, he takes with him Spanish trade goods to ease his entry into Carib society—perhaps using skills in bartering and negotiating that he had picked up while observing or actively serving his first, "rich merchant" master. Soon, the Indians "liking him, and hee them" (18), he marries within their community and has three children.

Enter the missionaries. For twelve years, Lewis had hid himself when the Spanish made port, but for some reason this time he is spotted. The conversation that follows can be construed a couple of ways; because of Gage's double vision (his desire to reflect the credulity of the missionaries, including himself at the time versus his later, more cynical perspective), we get a tricky little moment in which we witness Lewis's masterful performance to save his life and preserve his freedom. As Gage remembers it, Lewis begins by professing his desire to return to the Christian fold: "Poore Soule, though hee had lived twelve yeares without hearing a word of the true God, worshipping stockes and stones with the other Heathens; yet when he heard again of Christ . . . hee began to weep, assuring us that hee would goe with us." But then Lewis stops himself. There's an impediment: "hee would goe with us, were it not for his Wife and Children."[25]

The missionaries respond by assuring him that they would be delighted, delighted! to welcome his entire family on board. Upon seeing that his expression of patriarchal responsibility has failed to extricate him from the Jesuits' plans, Lewis abruptly changes roles. From a Christian sinner willing to reject his recent, heathen past, he transforms himself into a "poore and timourous *Mulatto*" who fears that the Indians will kill him—and the missionaries—if he tries to leave. Together, Lewis and the missionaries hatch a plan whereby he will trick his family into accompanying him to the beach, where the Jesuits will be waiting for him with a small boat to effect their escape. Lewis specifically asks for the Jesuits to meet him—"whom hee said he should know by their black

Coates"—a request the Jesuits celebrate since it means they will get credit over their rivals the Dominicans for five quick conversions.

In the morning, Gage remembers, "Our *Mulatto Lewis* came not according to his word; but in his stead a suddaine Army of treacherous *Indians.*" Moreover, "most of their Arrowes was directed to the black Markes [that is, the Jesuits' black coats], and so five of them [the Jesuits] in a little above a quarter of an houre slaine and wounded."[26] Despite the evidence of Lewis's betrayal—he had after all, specifically asked the Jesuits to meet him on the beach, knowing that their black clothes would mark them for excellent targets—Gage is still unsure what has happened. In the end it's clear that he understands Lewis as having crossed them, but nevertheless he takes a moment to speculate about his motivation: either Lewis had betrayed them to his fellows or else they "had made him confesse it." It seems Lewis's performance of allegiance to Christianity and his European "rescuers" was persuasive enough at least to open up the possibility that he had betrayed them against his will. Like Gage, we cannot know with certainty anything about his motives in this encounter; Lewis's absence from the archival record is profound. We will never know anything concrete about his experiences in Seville, whether he was seasick on the Atlantic passage, how long it took the Caribs to accept him, the names of his wife and children—or even what he called himself on Guadeloupe. We don't know when he was born or how he died. Nevertheless, this fleeting appearance in Gage's text inscribes the shape of a quick-witted survivalist and sketches the outline of an early Atlantic slave narrative.

What further significance can we give this account of Lewis's successful efforts to rebuff the missionary and military encroachment of Europeans into the island he had made his home? My first conclusion is directed toward the particular time and place of Lewis's story; my second is methodological. First, because of figures such as Lewis, along with his friends and relations among the Carib islanders, Gage—inadvertently to be sure—represents the early Caribbean as a transnational space. In his tract, Gage clearly intends to assert English right and might in the Americas. He affirms the righteousness of English imperial ambition over that of Spain, and Lewis's story is meant to support that claim. Yet it is clear that Gage himself was taken in by Lewis's plot, and the attack on the fleet leaves open the possibility that Native, "mulatto," and other inhabitants will resist English encroachment as well that of Spain. The trading culture created by islanders on Guadeloupe, a culture protected by Lewis's actions, ensures that for a time at least this part of the Americas will not be an outpost of empire, but will continue as a "common Rode and harbor to all Nations." The text gives us an embedded slave narrative in its account of Lewis's upbringing in Seville and escape to Guadeloupe, and also, with its account of this uprising, what we might call, following Gretchen Woertendyke, a "fugitive slave narrative."[27] Through these narratives, the text creates a Caribbean space outside the bounds of the state, a space shaped in significant part by the anti-Imperial performances of its Native and Black inhabitants.

Second, Lewis's influence on Gage's text suggests that we need to understand that American and Caribbean literary history in its earliest moments is shaped by the presence of people who are marginalized by Europeans and in European accounts, including enslaved as well as free peoples of African descent. We need to take the time to investigate—and to speculate—about their position as agents not just subjects in that literary history. The lesson that Lewis can teach us is widely applicable. We will gain a better understanding of Atlantic world texts and of the multiple colonial actors involved in producing them if we take seriously the presence of Native, African, and other marginalized peoples in their pages and if we continue to explore new approaches to even the best-known colonial writings. Consider the analysis of Carolyn Prager in her essay "English Transfer and Invention of the Black," an essay published in 1993, the same year that the Jehlen-Hulme debate appeared. Her careful explication of the ways that English representation of Africans changed with changing international circumstances is focused on the successive intervention of English writers of the figure of "the Black" in early modern through eighteenth-century literature. Her examples make clear that early modern accounts, such as Sir Francis Drake's descriptions of Cimaroons, altered the stereotypical/symbolic representation of Africans as they registered actual encounters. New representations were "invested . . . with human attributes, some historical and some invented."[28] However, her analysis stops short of identifying African-descended peoples as shaping that representational shift.

If we agree that the representation of marginalized peoples in the Caribbean during the early modern period is some combination of the "historical" and the "invented," then we need to ask, from whence come our notions of the historical? Gage's account of Lewis suggests one source: from those who were or had been enslaved, from those who had so much at stake in persuading European observers and writers to accept their self-presentation. The next question is: what avenues of investigation might that influence suggest? In this case, we might look to historical studies of Seville as a slave-trading center. We might investigate archival documents for evidence of limited autonomy among the enslaved, the kinds of autonomy that made it possible for Lewis to meet his second master and conspire with him to escape the first. We might investigate how the conditions of slavery enabled even those who were born to it in early modern Europe, such as Lewis, to be capable of successfully negotiating a huge cultural shift, in his case becoming a valued member of a Carib community.

Further, this line of thought suggests that the performance of identity and the recitation of slave narratives to European amanuenses and other observers become avenues through which "inventions of the Black" by "the Black" entered the documentary record. In our sophisticated attempts to understand tensions, contradictions, and other problems in colonial texts, literary historians have perhaps missed a straightforward explanation. Such texts encode the action and intention of marginalized people who otherwise have no access to the documentary record. In effect I am arguing that the as-told-to narrative of Lewis manipulates the historical record in which it is described. Thomas Gage's account of Lewis reminds me of nothing so much as Amasa Delano's account of the slave ship *St. Dominick* in Herman Melville's masterful critique of nineteenth-century race, *Benito Cereno*. I don't mean to construct Lewis as a manipulative Babo—though perhaps the comparison is not too much of a stretch. But we should consider that Melville himself constructed his novel from the raw materials of nonfiction travel narratives, newspaper accounts, and court records, and that in effect he animated the absence that men such as Lewis have left in the archive.[29] If we do, we may better understand the role that even the most marginalized of early American peoples—and the slave narratives that they constructed—have played in creating our literary history.

Notes

1. Myra Jehlen, "History before the Fact; or, Captain John Smith's Unfinished Symphony." *Critical Inquiry* 19.4 (Summer 1993): 677–92.

2. After Jehlen's "History before the Fact," the debate was continued in Peter Hulme, "Making No Bones: A Response to Myra Jehlen," *Critical Inquiry* 20.1 (Autumn 1993): 179–86 and Myra Jehlen, "Response to Peter Hulme," *Critical Inquiry* 20.1 (Autumn 1993): 187–191.

3. Hulme, "Making No Bones," 182, 185.

4. Ed White considers the critical impasse through a slightly different lens, providing a careful critical history of the scholarly trends of the 1990s. He argues that, ironically, methods intended to recover "muffled voices" (Stephen Greenblatt's

phrase) had the unintended effect of "contributing to their muffling." He argues that "The emergent critical discussions . . . bracketed the apparently irredeemably problematic questions of historical accuracy, focusing instead on the construction of knowledge in a purportedly systematizing field of anthropology." He sees the result for scholars in literary studies as rendering Native (and I would add other marginalized peoples') voices "functionally inaccessible" (phrase also coined by Greenblatt). White sees Jehlen's intervention in such debates as a signal voice of dissent. White, "Invisible Tagkanysough," *PMLA* 120.3 (2005): 753.

5. Paul John Eakin, foreword to Arnold Krupat, *For Those Who Come After: A Study of Native American Autobiography* (Berkeley: University of California Press, 1985; 2nd ed., 1989), xii.

6. Christopher Castiglia and Julia A. Stern, introduction to special issue, "Interiority in Early America," *Early American Literature* 37.1 (2002): 7. While I am focusing here on mediated figures and stories, this critical distrust of the documentary record's ability to encode the authentic emotions and experiences of marginalized peoples can extend even to those subjects who wrote their own stories. I've written elsewhere of just such a critical treatment of Mary Rowlandson's 1682 captivity narrative. Scholars have found in her narrative evidence of "two voices," that of a pious, orthodox Christian believer and that of a radical, restless, independent survivor, with the latter voice often presumed to be more authentically hers. Such an assessment implies that print technology can be effectively wielded only by white male colonists, and that it always stands between the contemporary reader and relatively powerless people from the early modern period. See Kristina Bross, "A Wilderness Condition: The Captivity Narrative as Christian Literature," in *American Christianities: A History of Dominance and Diversity,* ed. Catherine A. Brekus and W. Clark Gilpin (Chapel Hill: University of North Carolina Press, 2011), 313–16.

7. Peter Hulme presents Lewis's story through an excerpt of Thomas Gage's *The English-American* (1648). See Peter Hulme and Neil L. Whitehead, eds., *Wild Majesty: Encounters with Caribs from Columbus to the Present Day: An Anthology* (Oxford: Oxford University Press, 1992), 83–88. Criticism of Gage's tract otherwise concerns New World products or debates the historical accuracy of Gage's accounts of New Spain. See, for instance, Edmund Valentine Campos, "Thomas Gage and the English Encounter with Chocolate," *Journal of Medieval and Early Modern Studies* 39.1 (Winter 2009): 183–200.

8. Judging from more informal critical conversations at recent conferences, many of us take the claims I've made here as a given, but we still struggle with putting our beliefs into practice. Wendy Laura Belcher, in her excellent essay reviewing theories of agency in Africanist scholarship, argues for a "reciprocal enculturation model" for analyzing colonial encounter, in which we can see that "mutual cultural exchange . . . does not elide the agency of the other" (221). She admits that "for many scholars, this point will seem obvious," but points out that despite our widespread acceptance of the truth of mutual exchange and reciprocal acculturation, "very little research is undergirded by this model of agency" (221). Wendy Laura Belcher, "Consuming Subjects: Theorizing New Models of Agency for Literary Criticism in African Studies," *Comparative Literature Studies* 46.2 (2009): 213–32.

9. There are exceptions, of course, and the state of the field is rapidly chang-ing. New scholarship by veteran researchers as well as new scholars is expanding both our critical toolkit and our archival access. For one important collection, see "Ecclesiastical and Secular Sources for Slave Societies," a digital resource directed by Jane Landers and hosted by Vanderbilt University: http://www.vanderbilt.edu/esss/index.php.

10. Jacques Derrida, *Archive Fever: A Freudian Impression* (Chicago: Uni-versity of Chicago Press, 1996): "the question of the archive is not, we repeat, a question of the past. It is not the question of a concept dealing with the past that might *already* be at our disposal or not at our disposal, *an archivable concept of the archive*. It is a question of the future, the question of the future itself, the question of a response, of a promise and of a responsibility for tomorrow. The archive: if we want to know what that will have meant, we will only know in times to come" (36, emphasis in original). New approaches to mediation strive to hear the voices of African, Native, and other disenfranchised people in the Ameri-cas from the early modern era through the nineteenth century, though my focus is on the earliest materials. For instance, see Nicole N. Aljoe, "'Going to Law': Legal Discourse and Testimony in Early West Indian Slave Narratives," *Early American Literature* 46.2 (June 2011): 351–81, and Aljoe, "Creole Testimony," paper presented as part of the "President's Plenary Session: Keywords in Early American Studies of the West Indies," Society of Early Americanists biennial con-ference, Bermuda, 2009; Kristen Block, *Ordinary Lives in the Early Caribbean: Religion, Colonial Competition, and the Politics of Profit* (Athens: University of George Press, 2012); Cassander Smith, "Beyond the Mediation: Esteban, Cabeza de Vaca's *Relación*, and a Narrative Negotiation," *Early American Literature* 47.2 (2012): 267–91; and Kelly Wisecup, *Medical Encounters: Knowledge and Identity in Early American Literatures* (Amherst: University of Massachusetts Press, 2014). Wendy Anne Warren's essay, "'The Cause of Her Grief': The Rape of a Slave in Early New England," *Journal of American History* 93.4 (March 2007): 1031–49, has been influential in my approach to uncovering the experi-ences of enslaved people using spare archival documents. See also Mary Elizabeth Perry, "Finding Fatima, a Slave Woman of Early Spain," *Journal of Women's History* 20.1 (2008) 151–67; and Betty Joseph, *Reading the East India Com-pany Archives, 1720–1840: Colonial Currencies of Gender* (Chicago: University of Chicago Press, 2004). And although Marcus Rediker does not as explicitly address the mediation issue in his *The Slave Ship: A Human History* (New York: Penguin Books, 2007), his approach reads the documentary evidence for clues of human agency, even of those who are most marginalized in the accounts.

11. Carolyn Steedman, *Dust: The Archive and Cultural History* (Manchester: Manchester University Press, 2001; Rutgers: Rutgers University Press, 2002), 11, original emphasis. Susan Scott Parrish brings the archival turn to bear specifically on early American and Atlantic world materials in her essay "Rummaging/In and Out of Holds," *Early American Literature* 45.2 (2010): 261–74.

12. Gretchen J. Woertendyke takes up the issue of archival silence in her essay in this volume. She argues that the silencing of the subjects of "fugitive slave narratives" such as that of Denmark Vesey seems to make room for "the counternarrative of the white community," but if we take seriously the idea

that Vesey may also have chosen silence as "a willful performance of resistance to—and rejection of—the court's theatrical display of state power," we can position Vesey's narrative as a precursor to those slave narratives that assert agency through voice rather than through silence (56, 58). My approach to silence is related to hers, but I focus here on a narrative in which the subject quite obviously asserted his voice, but whose story was only partially and obliquely recorded in the print archive.

13. *Hakluytus Posthumus; or, Purchas his Pilgrimes* (London, 1625), vol. 2 (Glasgow: J. MacLehose and Sons, 1905), 26; Thomas Gage, *The English-American his Travails by Sea and Land* (London, 1648), *Early English Books Online*, 17.

14. Gage, *English-American*, A4r.

15. Ibid., 19.

16. Ibid.

17. Ibid., 130.

18. Ibid.

19. Sir Francis Drake was an obvious influence on Gage's arguments; he began publicizing the potential gains from an English-Maroon alliance decades before Gage, and Gage knew of his efforts. Yet, as Cassander Smith argues, Drake's work was itself structured by his encounters with real historical actors. See Smith, "Washing the Ethiop Red: Sir Francis Drake and the Cimarrons of Panama," in *Race and Displacement: Nation, Migration, and Identity in the Twenty-First Century*, ed. Maha Marouan and Merinda Simmons (Tuscaloosa: University of Alabama Press, 2013). My point is not to reject other influences, but to suggest the significance of Gage's own experiences with enslaved peoples and others we might take to be on the margins, particularly African-descended peoples.

20. Gage, *English-American*, 167.

21. Ibid., 181.

22. Belcher, "Consuming Subjects," 220–23.

23. Wisecup, *Medical Encounters*, 11.

24. Gage, *English-American*, 18.

25. Ibid., 18.

26. Ibid., 19.

27. Woertendyke, this volume.

28. "As the unseen gave way to the seen, however, Britain's earliest encounter with Spanish America foretold the end of the symbolically crafted black." Carolyn Prager, "English Transfer and Invention of the Black," in *Early Images of the Americas: Transfer and Invention*, ed. Jerry M. Williams and Robert E. Lewis (Tucson: University of Arizona Press, 1993), 99, 95.

29. Other literary scholars are pursuing analyses along these lines, including ways that the works of canonical writers such as Melville are shaped by African thought. See Belcher's review of such criticism, "Consuming Subjects" (223–28).

Contributors

NICOLE N. ALJOE is Assistant Professor of English at Northeastern University. Her research and teaching focus on eighteenth- and nineteenth-century Black Atlantic literatures with a particular specialization on the Caribbean. She has published articles and chapters in *Early American Literature, African American Review, Anthurium, The Oxford Handbook of the African American Slave Narrative,* and *Teaching Anglophone Caribbean Literature.* She is the author of *So Much Things to Say: The Creole Testimony of British West Indian Slaves.* Currently, she is at work on a new project that examines the transformation of the neo-slave narrative genre within contemporary Caribbean cultural production.

R.J. BOUTELLE is a PhD Candidate in the Department of English at Vanderbilt University. His work has appeared in *Atlantic Studies, Southern Studies,* and the "Year in Conferences" project for *ESQ.* He is the recipient of a Fulbright Fellowship in Argentina and a short-term research fellowship from the Cuban Heritage Collection at the University of Miami. His dissertation theorizes the circulation of abolitionist print as a transformative and accumulative process through which U.S. American and Caribbean writers could imagine local emancipation movements as part of a transnational struggle for freedom.

KRISTINA BROSS is Associate Professor of English at Purdue University. Her research and teaching interests include early American studies, especially European–Native relations, early modern transatlantic studies, and violence in early America. Her work has appeared in *Early American Literature* and *Common-place,* an online journal of early American culture. Her books include *Dry Bones and Indian Sermons: Praying Indians in Colonial America* and *Early Native Literacies in New England:*

A Documentary and Critical Anthology (coedited with Hilary Wyss). Her current work is a book-length project on the relationship of New England to Cromwell's Western Design.

IAN FINSETH is Associate Professor of English at the University of North Texas. He specializes in American and African American literature of the long nineteenth century, with particular research interests in the slave narrative, Civil War studies, and the environmental humanities. He is the author of *Shades of Green: Visions of Nature in the Literature of American Slavery, 1770-1860* and has edited several books, including *The American Civil War: A Literary and Historical Anthology*. His articles have appeared in *American Literary History, American Literature, Arizona Quarterly, Early American Literature*, and other journals. Currently he is at work on a new study that explores the entanglements of mortality, visuality, historical experience, and realism in the development of postbellum U.S. culture.

JEFFREY GAGNON is the Assistant Director of the Dimensions of Culture writing program at the University of California at San Diego. His teaching and research concerns the intersections of race, gender, and empire in the eighteenth- and nineteenth-century Atlantic world. His current work examines the significance of Black Atlantic social networking in the long eighteenth century.

KEITH MICHAEL GREEN is Assistant Professor of English at Rutgers University at Camden. His main research and teaching interests lie in African American literature, with more specific investments in the study of the antebellum era, self-referential writing, African–Native American literature, and disability. His current book project explores the various kinds of bondage and confinement—specifically Indian slavery, Barbary captivity, and state imprisonment—that African Americans experienced and recounted in the nineteenth century.

LYNN R. JOHNSON is Associate Professor of Africana Studies at Dickinson College. Her research interests are in African American literature, Middle Passage studies, and food studies. She has published articles in the *Encyclopedia of American Studies, Journal of Pan-African Studies*, and *Southern Literary Journal*. Currently, she is completing a manuscript that examines the relationship between food and psychological wellness as portrayed in African American fiction and film.

José Guadelupe Ortega is Associate Professor of History at Whittier College. His scholarly interests include examining the circuits of knowledge and industrial technology between Havana and other Atlantic communities as well as investigating the labor and commercial circuits that contributed to the expansion of the Cuban economy in the early nineteenth century. He is also exploring the complex personal and local social networks that women of African descent constructed in Havana and its hinterlands during the same time period.

Basima Kamel Shaheen is a PhD Candidate and Teaching Fellow in English at the University of North Texas. Her teaching and research interests include postcolonial theory and literature, twentieth-century literature, Palestinian diasporic literature, and questions of identity and space in a global era.

Gretchen J. Woertendyke is Assistant Professor of English at the University of South Carolina. Her research and teaching focus on eighteenth- and nineteenth-century American literature, hemispheric American studies, and theories of the novel. She has published essays in *Early American Literature, Narrative,* and *Atlantic Studies,* and her book, *Hemispheric Regionalism: Romance and the Geography of Genre,* is forthcoming. Her current project looks at the history of secrecy across the Americas in the long nineteenth century.

Index